The Myth of
Nathan Bedford Forrest

The American Crisis Series

Books on the Civil War Era

Steven E. Woodworth, *Associate Professor of History, Texas Christian University*
SERIES EDITOR

The Myth of
Nathan Bedford Forrest

Paul Ashdown
and
Edward Caudill

ROWMAN & LITTLEFIELD PUBLISHERS, INC.
Lanham • Boulder • New York • Toronto • Oxford

ROWMAN & LITTLEFIELD PUBLISHERS, INC.

Published in the United States of America
by Rowman & Littlefield Publishers, Inc.
A wholly owned subsidiary of
The Rowman & Littlefield Publishing Group, Inc.
4501 Forbes Boulevard, Suite 200, Lanham, Maryland 20706
www.rowmanlittlefield.com

PO Box 317
Oxford
OX2 9RU, UK

Distributed by National Book Network

British Library Cataloguing in Publication Information Available

Library of Congress Cataloging-in-Publication Data

Ashdown, Paul, 1944–
    The myth of Nathan Bedford Forrest / Paul Ashdown and Edward
Caudill.
        p. cm. — (American crisis series ; no. 16)
    Includes bibliographical references (p.   ) and index.
    ISBN 0-7425-4300-5 (cloth : alk. paper)
    1. Forrest, Nathan Bedford, 1821–1877. 2. Forrest, Nathan Bedford,
1821–1877—Legends. 3. Forrest, Nathan Bedford, 1821–1877—Public
opinion. 4. Generals—Confederate States of America—Biography. 5.
Confederate States of America. Army—Biography. 6. United States—
History—Civil War, 1861–1865—Cavalry operations. 7. Public opinion—
United States. I. Caudill, Edward. II. Title. III. Series.
E467.1.F72A84   2005
973.7'3'092—dc22
                                                                    2003021590
Printed in the United States of America

♾ ™ The paper used in this publication meets the minimum requirements
of American National Standard for Information Sciences—Permanence of
Paper for Printed Library Materials, ANSI/NISO Z39.48-1992.

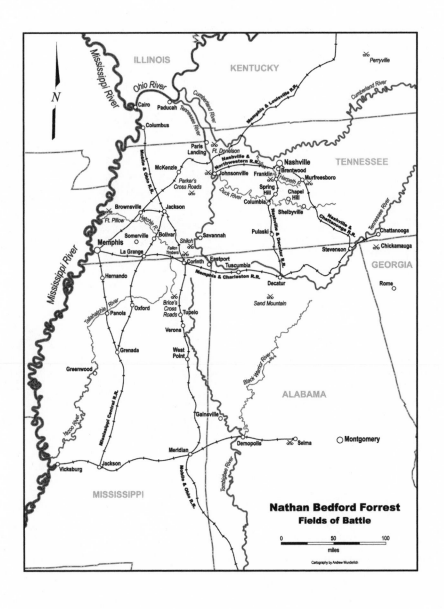

Nathan Bedford Forrest
Fields of Battle

0   50   100
miles

Cartography by Andrew Wunderlich

For Barbara and Lance

For my mother and stepfather,

Reba and Mitch Todoroff

ACKNOWLEDGMENTS

Jennifer Allen
Larissa Caudill
Paul Conkin
Christopher Craig
Larry Daughtrey
Will Fontanez
Tim Hartmann
Anne Hensley
Matthew Hershey
Marcie Hinton
Jennifer Johnston
Diana King

Jean Matthews
Linda Musumeci
James Ogden III
Andrew Plant
David Sachsman
Randall Scott
David Smith
Pat Sterling
Dwight Teeter
Chloe White
Steven Woodworth
Andrew Wunderlich

ABOUT THE AUTHORS

Paul Ashdown (Ph.D., Bowling Green State University) and Edward Caudill (Ph.D., University of North Carolina at Chapel Hill) are professors of journalism and electronic media at the University of Tennnessee. Ashdown is the editor of *James Agee: Selected Journalism* (1985, 2004) and the author of *A Cold Mountain Companion* (2004) and has written and lectured extensively about the media, popular culture, and the Civil War. He is the University of Tennessee Macebearer and won the Robert Foster Cherry Award for Great Teachers, a national competition sponsored by Baylor University. Caudill is the author of *Darwinism in the Press: The Evolution of an Idea* (1989) and *Darwinian Myths: The Legends and Misuses of a Theory* (1997) and co-author of *The Scopes Trial: A Photographic History* (2000). He is associate dean of the College of Communication and Information at the University of Tennessee. Ashdown and Caudill are co-authors of *The Mosby Myth: A Confederate Hero in Life and Legend* (2002).

CONTENTS

INTRODUCTION

No one ever doubted Nathan Bedford Forrest's courage. To have done so would have led to trouble. By the end of the Civil War, the Confederate general claimed to have killed thirty men, a few of whom were on his own side. What more can be said about Forrest, asked John E. Stanchack, the editor of *Civil War Times Illustrated* in 1993, beyond the fact that he was a tough customer, the greatest horse soldier of his era, and arguably a military genius? "Everything else we know about this man is bent to fit some political or intellectual agenda," Stanchack wrote in introducing a magazine series devoted to Forrest. Forrest has what Stanchack described as an image problem in American history and contemporary culture. For example, William S. Fitzgerald, writing in the same series, observed that Forrest's name is anathema to many black Americans and cited three reasons: he was a slave trader; his troops allegedly massacred black Union soldiers at Fort Pillow; and he was allegedly the first Grand Wizard of the Ku Klux Klan. "Any one of these acts or activities would have tarnished the man in the eyes of modern black Americans; all three of them make him insufferable."[1]

"Psychologists and social scientists don't like getting near him," Stanchack said. If they cower at the mention of Forrest's name, however, it is because examining an "image" is problematic and controversial. Let it be said, however, that historians are neither unaware of nor indifferent to the challenges inherent in understanding historical perceptions and how they are created, change, and endure. Nor has Forrest been neglected by talented scholars who have looked beyond the disputed facts of his life and times and probed the mysteries of public memory.[2]

Our understanding of this process is shaped by the study of how stories are told and remembered, first in the form of journalistic accounts and then in folklore, legend, biography, memoir, literature, film, iconography, popular culture, public opinion, and memory, the sum of which we choose to call myth. Myth embraces what Henry Nash Smith defined as "an intellectual construction that fuses concept and emotion into an image." Myths and symbols "have the characteristic of being collective representations rather than the work of a single mind." Examining any culture in terms of its myths is an imperfect method. Laurence R. Veysey pointed out that myth can become "a shield, cloaking crucial distinctions between men and decades behind a bland façade of sameness. When all happenings in American history have been rechristened in mythological terminology, the end result is apt to be . . . more elusive and synthetic than clarifying." Keeping this caveat in mind, we will examine the Forrest Myth not as a shield but as a window, a frame through which to observe the larger political or intellectual agendas that Stanchack saw as barriers to understanding one of the most controversial figures in American history.[3]

THE "GREAT IF"

One version of the Forrest Myth is the "Great If" or "The Great Might Have Been." Those who view Forrest as an incomparable military genius insist that the South *might have been* victorious *if* only the Richmond government had recognized the real importance of the West in the Civil War, that it would take a man like Forrest to defeat the Yankees—not as a raider, not as a mere cavalry general, but as the Heracles of the Hinterlands. You could not win it with the intellectual Jefferson Davis or the aristocratic Robert E. Lee or the vacillating Braxton Bragg. You could not win it with West Pointers. You needed a man like Forrest who would "charge both ways," the "Wizard of the Saddle," the Warlord of the West.

Emory Thomas emphasized the virtue of contrasting Lee and Forrest as two essentially opposite commanders. Lee represented a "conventional" approach to war that marginalized Forrest and his ilk. But, Thomas noted, Lee and other "conventional" generals lost the war, and he asked—could Forrest have won?

> He was a primitive in the mid-nineteenth century, when warfare was evolving toward struggles between whole peoples, fought by massive armies in which relatively small bands of armed horsemen would seem unimportant. But no circumstance is inevitable simply because it happened; people choose, and in this case, Jefferson Davis chose Lee's way of warfare.
>
> When "total war" continued to evolve, primitive behavior again became successful. Bedford Forrest may have seemed slightly out of step in the American Civil War; but he seems ideally suited for combat in Vietnam, Afghanistan, or Croatia. Our "modern" world appreciates the primitive. So, again the question—could Forrest have won? [4]

Jay Winik asked an even more important question in his perceptive book *April 1865: The Month That Saved America*. Although Davis did eventually call for a Forrest-style guerrilla war, Winik thought that Forrest, by ending that war, helped preserve the nation. How long, Winik asked, would it take before the North would "deem the agonies and cruelties of a full-scale guerrilla war, which would inevitably pervert its identity as a republic, to be no longer worth it?" Guerrilla warfare has a long pedigree dating from the Scythians to the Mujahadeen. "Every American, of course, in the final quarter century of the twentieth century saw just how effective guerrilla warfare is. They watched it be turned against them in Vietnam." Winik said Forrest emerged as one of the heroes of the Civil War not so much because of his showy battlefield achievements as because of his decision *not* to continue the conflict as a guerrilla.[5]

Forrest may briefly have contemplated taking his ragged troops to the Far West or to Mexico to fight on indefinitely but eventually came to his senses and said fighting on would be a form of insanity. He told his men they had been good soldiers and could be good citizens of a reunited country that would be magnanimous in victory. His own magnanimity, according to Winik, helped save the nation by preventing a protracted and ultimately disastrous guerrilla war. Forrest, he contended, was in the best position to perpetuate the conflict, especially if Lee and other commanders had fought on, but chose instead to end it. Lee, while besieged at Petersburg, supposedly had told Davis, "With my army in the mountains of Virginia I could carry on this war for twenty years longer." That possibility ended at Appomattox.[6]

Taking exception to Winik's scenario, Martin Gordon asked a different question: What if Forrest and other commanders surrendered only because they expected a "magnanimous" government to look the other way while things returned to the prewar status? By suspending its pursuit of sovereignty and accepting abolition, perhaps the South thought it could put its leaders back in power to resubjugate the freedmen under a new set of rules. When Reconstruction came to mean empowerment of blacks and rule by carpetbaggers, the South responded by fighting a guerrilla war as white-robed Klansmen. That violence essentially reversed the Union victory. When Reconstruction ended in 1877, the South became a country unto itself until President Dwight Eisenhower sent troops to Little Rock, Arkansas, to enforce school desegregation in 1957. A

New Yorker magazine writer, Nicholas Lemann, even drew a specu-
lative analogy in 2002 between the occupied South at the end of
the Civil War and the occupied "West Bank" in the Palestinian conflict. The Klan had launched its own *intifada*, a wave of terrorist
attacks, which was followed by a military crackdown. David W.
Bright, in *Race and Reunion: The Civil War in American Memory*, emphasized that the "failure of racial reconciliation, so crucial to any
ultimate working through of the meaning of the Civil War, took
root in the Klan's reign of terror in 1868–71."[7]

THE TOUGH GUY

Forrest is a familiar sort of masculine American hero: the tough
guy. Rupert Wilkinson identifies three basic sources for the tough-
guy tradition: the frontier, the commoner's disdain for the aristocratic, and the clash within a commercial culture between the
pursuit of mammon and the call to high-minded, moral purpose.
Forrest represented all three strains in conflict. He was a frontiersman who made a fortune in land and chattel and then lost it by
sacrificing himself in defense of a feudal society he both admired
and disdained.[8]

Forrest's mythmakers have looked to the frontier to find the
wellspring for his toughness. His first biographers, Thomas Jordan
and J. P. Pryor, wrote of his boyhood on the frontier, where, "trained
to the hardest manual toil, practiced as a hunter of the game of the
country, and hardened by the manly exercises of the border, Bedford
Forrest grew up to the verge of manhood." For John Bowers, "the
main ingredient in his makeup was that he was a son of the West.
His first home was a log cabin in West Tennessee, his surroundings
a barnyard; small, cleared acreage; and a pack of dogs. . . . He left
the frontier, but the frontier never left him." At the time of Forrest's
death in 1877 the soon-to-be-famous journalist Lafcadio Hearn reported the general's funeral for the *Cincinnati Commercial*. Forrest,
he wrote, "seemed by nature a typical pioneer, one of those fierce
and terrible men, who form in themselves a kind of protecting fringe
to the borders of white civilization."

Ironically, Forrest, although uncivilized, protected the mythic
Southern civilization based on the planter aristocracy to which he
aspired. But he was often in opposition to the aristocrats who led
the Confederacy, even as he sometimes failed to recognize that the

churls and yeomen of the frontier would sustain it. After the war he defended the conquered South through the Klan, ostensibly repented and repudiated its excesses, tried to disband the Klan and called for advancement for blacks, sought to expand the South's industrial muscle by building railroads, and became a Christian. This image of Forrest as a Christian knight-errant holding back the infidels was taken up in the next century by the Nashville Agrarians, most notably Andrew Lytle in his *Bedford Forrest and His Critter Company*, published in 1931.[9]

Forrest was not unusual in an era that produced the likes of Stonewall Jackson, Ulysses S. Grant, and untold others who endured the deprivations of a rough-and-tumble, hardscrabble frontier culture. But Forrest became something extraordinary, a *myth* of manhood, cunning, tenacity, cruelty, untutored genius, and backwater bravery, which resonates today. "Picture the mythological riverboat gambler, and there you have Nathan Bedford Forrest," according to Bowers. "Violence was never far from him at any time. . . . He possessed, in spades, what made civilized folk elsewhere turn in revulsion and horror from the South at that time: a raw naked racism, a dependence on violence, and the inability to restrain himself and do otherwise." He was a hero of the Lost Cause, a symbol of the Civil War's unresolved legacy. And yet, according to historian Gary W. Gallagher, Forrest's wartime contemporaries saw him only as a successful raider; they "scarcely conceived of him as a general whose impact rivaled that of senior officers." Nevertheless, as Winik pointed out, Forrest was "an incongruous amalgam of the proudest and the darkest sides of the Confederacy, walking not in awkward contradiction, but boldly and comfortably hand in hand. . . . To friends and foes alike, even before the war was over, Forrest's reputation had become the stuff of folklore and legend, and he himself had become almost a living myth."[10]

Forrest's primitivism has attracted admirers from the beginning. And so around the Forrest Myth has arisen a series of bumpkin aphorisms and woodsy witticisms that have become part of American folklore. These have been collected and published as *May I Quote You, General Forrest?* Most famously, Forrest is said to have reduced his entire military strategy to the ability to "git thar fustest with the mostest." Most biographers agree that this fractured phrasing was an invention. The fact that an uneducated rube, an American plebeian, could so adroitly, so intuitively, master the art of warfare, indeed make it into an art form, was a reminder to the professional soldier and the aristocrat that much could be learned from a common man.

Just because a man was a slave trader did not mean he could not tell you something useful about military strategy. James D. Porter, governor of Tennessee, told Forrest biographer John Allan Wyeth of his conversation with Jefferson Davis as he accompanied the former Confederate president to Elmwood Cemetery in Memphis after Forrest's funeral. Davis agreed with Porter that Forrest was the greatest cavalry chief of the war and among the half-dozen greatest soldiers of the century. He added that he had underestimated the general during the war because his other generals misled him into thinking that Forrest was merely a raider and not fit for higher command. He might have added that it would have been unseemly to seat a Tennessee bumpkin at the same dinner table with the likes of himself and Lee, gentlemen who might have been reluctant to break bread before the war with Abraham Lincoln or even Grant. Or, as Thomas cleverly put it, "Too often we fail to see the Forrest for the Lees."[11]

Efforts to capture the essential Forrest, the Everyman Hero, got under way immediately after the war when two Memphis journalists and former Confederate officers, Jordan and Pryor, published *The Campaigns of Lieut. Gen. N. B. Forrest and of Forrest's Cavalry* (1868). The work was written with Forrest's approval, and the authors had access to his private papers. Jordan, after the war, was editor of the *Memphis Appeal*. Pryor was in the newspaper business in Memphis before and after the war. Thus, journalists shaped the Forrest Myth from the beginning; in fact, several journalists had served on his staff during the war. Forrest is especially interesting in this respect: as one of those senior officers least capable of constructing their own images through the printed word, he relied on others to write for him, but he learned how to interest journalists and became "a good story" for the press.[12]

FORREST'S MILITARY LEGACY

As a military tactician, Forrest was extravagantly praised by some leading Confederates during the Civil War and grudgingly respected by his opponents. Various sources, none of them highly reliable, quote even Lee as having named Forrest the greatest soldier of the war, and Sherman and Grant knew he was a formidable adversary. Confederate general Richard Taylor wrote admiringly of him and said he doubted that any commander since the days of Richard the Lion-Hearted had killed more enemy soldiers by his own hand—certainly a testimony to Forrest's aggressiveness if not to his prudence and judgment as a field commander.[13]

As a military genius, Forrest found his champion in Field Marshal Joseph Viscount Wolseley, who served as commander in chief of the British army from 1895 to 1900. During the Civil War he had been stationed as a lieutenant colonel in Canada, and in 1862 he visited Virginia, where he met Lee, Jackson, and James Longstreet and first heard of Forrest. In 1892 he produced a long article about Forrest that appeared in the *New Orleans Picayune* and later in British military journals. Wolseley's generous assessment of Forrest's virtues as a soldier emphasized his humble origins and his instinctive military genius. He perhaps saw something of himself in Forrest, according to James A. Rawley. Both were exceptions to Wolseley's own belief that professionally trained soldiers were superior to the citizen-soldier in warfare. Forrest, Wolseley believed, was a natural soldier, a border warlord who fought by instinct rather than training: "If his operations be carefully examined by the most pedantic military critic, they will seem as if designed by a military professor, so thoroughly are the principles of tactics, when broadly interpreted by a liberal understanding, in accordance with common sense and business principles. The *art* of war was an instinct in him." Wolseley also wrote that "if ever England has to fight for her existence . . . may we have at the head of our government as wise and far-seeing a patriot as Mr. Lincoln, and to lead our mounted forces as able a soldier as General Forrest!"[14]

There is irony to that remark. In November 1914, Colonel Granville Sevier, an American officer, struck up a conversation with a British officer in a London bookstore. The officer said he was looking for Wyeth's biography of Forrest, and Sevier led him to a copy of the volume, explaining that he had known both Wyeth and Forrest. After the war, Forrest had come to visit Sevier's father, a former Confederate officer, at Sewanee, Tennessee, where he was teaching at the University of the South, and had shown the then seven-year-old Granville how to bridle, saddle, and mount his father's horse. The British officer was intrigued and went on to discuss so many aspects of Forrest's military career that Sevier said, "You know much more about General Forrest and his campaigns than I, or than most of us in America." The British officer then said that British cavalry officers closely studied Forrest's methods and regarded him "as one of the greatest, if not the greatest, of English-speaking commanders of mounted troops." Sevier later learned that he had been speaking to Douglas Haig, whose First Corps of the British Expeditionary Force had just fought at the first Battle of Ypres. It is a good story, told to Robert Selph Henry by Sevier in 1933. Perhaps Haig had read Wolesley's articles, and it is interesting to speculate about Forrest's impact on the British forces in World War I. But the highly controversial Haig was also the author of the debacles at the Somme and Passchendaele, so it could be argued that he had read all the wrong books and that Forrest's tactics belonged to another era.[15]

A GREAT STORY

The Forrest Myth incorporates all the rude ingredients of the American tales that emerged from the primitive frontier. It embraces violence, race, realism, sectionalism, politics, reconciliation, and repentance. It is a story about the fall and redemption of the darker side of the American dream.

Two historians writing about the Lost Cause cited a 1979 poll in which seventy-five of 100 students at a large Southern university said they had never heard of Forrest. It may be that we have not forgotten Forrest so much as that many may want to forget him. Yet for some Americans, by no means all of them Southerners, he is still the man who would not be slow to answer, whatever the challenge. Forrest represents the fundamental American inclination to protest. If his name often has been abused by all sides in the disputes that roil American society, that would not surprise or even concern him.[16]

NOTES

1. John E. Stanchack, "Behind the Lines," *Civil War Times Illustrated* 32 (September/October 1993): 14; William S. Fitzgerald, "We Will Always Stand by You," *Civil War Times Illustrated* 32 (November/December 1993): 71.

2. Stanchack, "Behind the Lines," 14. See, for example, Merrill D. Peterson, *Lincoln in American Memory* (New York: Oxford University Press, 1994); Paul Christopher Anderson, *Blood Image: Turner Ashby in the Civil War and the Southern Mind* (Baton Rouge: Louisiana State University Press, 2002); Brian Steel Wills, *A Battle from the Start: The Life of Nathan Bedford*

Forrest (New York: HarperCollins, 1992); Jack Hurst, *Nathan Bedford Forrest* (New York: Alfred A. Knopf, 1993).

3. Henry Nash Smith, *Virgin Land: The American West as Symbol and Myth* (1950; reprint ed., Cambridge, MA: Harvard University Press, 1979), xi; Laurence R. Veysey, "Myth and Reality in Approaching American Regionalism," *American Quarterly* 12 (Spring 1960): 37.

4. Emory Thomas, foreword to Wills, *A Battle from the Start*, xvi.

5. Jay Winik, *April 1865: The Month That Saved America* (New York: HarperCollins, 2001), 146–47, 153, 320–22; Dan T. Carter, *When the War Was Over* (Baton Rouge: Louisiana State University Press, 1985), 9.

6. Hudson Strode, *Jefferson Davis, Tragic Hero: The Last Twenty-Five Years, 1864–1889* (New York: Harcourt, Brace, 1964), 370; *Richmond Dispatch*, November 4, 1870.

7. Martin Gordon, "Surrender Temporary for Many in South," *Washington Times*, November 17, 2001; Nicholas Lemann, "The Talk of the Town," *New Yorker* 78 (April 22 and 29, 2002): 55–56; David W. Blight, *Race and Reunion: The Civil War in American Memory* (Cambridge, MA: Harvard University Press, 2001), 122.

8. Rupert Wilkinson, *American Tough: The Tough-Guy Tradition and American Character* (1984; reprint ed., New York: Harper and Row, 1986), 90.

9. Thomas Jordan and J. P. Pryor, *The Campaigns of General Nathan Bedford Forrest and of Forrest's Cavalry* (1868; reprint ed., New York: Da Capo Press, 1996); John Bowers, *Chickamauga and Chattanooga: The Battles That Doomed the Confederacy* (1994; reprint ed., New York: Avon Books, 1995), 60; Lafcadio Hearn, *Occasional Gleanings*, ed. Albert Mordell (New York: Dodd, Mead, 1925), 148 (Hearn's account of Forrest's funeral first appeared in the *Cincinnati Commercial*, November 6, 1877, under the pen name Ozias Midwinter); Andrew Lytle, *Bedford Forrest and His Critter Company* (1931; reprint ed., Nashville, TN: J. S. Sanders and Company, 1992); Winik, *April 1865*, 275.

10. Bowers, *Chickamauga and Chattanooga*, 61; Gary W. Gallagher, "How Familiarity Bred Success: Military Campaigns and Leaders in Ken Burns's *The Civil War*," in *Ken Burns's "The Civil War": Historians Respond*, ed. Robert Brent Toplin (New York: Oxford University Press, 1996), 55; Winik, *April 1865*, 274–76.

11. Randall Bedwell, *May I Quote You, General Forrest?* (Nashville, TN: Cumberland House, 1997); Hurst, *Nathan Bedford Forrest*, 5; John Allan Wyeth, *That Devil Forrest* (1899; reprint ed. of book originally titled *Life of General Nathan Bedford Forrest*, Baton Rouge: Louisiana State University Press, 1989), 560; Thomas, foreword to Wills, *A Battle from the Start*, xiii.

12. Hurst, *Nathan Bedford Forrest*, 389.

13. Robert Selph Henry, *"First with the Most" Forrest* (Indianapolis, IN: Bobbs-Merrill, 1944), 16, 462; Lytle, *Bedford Forrest and His Critter Company*, 357, 383; Richard Taylor, *Destruction and Reconstruction: Personal Experiences of the Late War* (1879; reprint ed., New York: Longmans, Green and Company, 1955), 244.

14. Brian Bond, "Colonial Wars and Punitive Expeditions, 1856–99," in *History of the British Army*, ed. Peter Young and J. P. Lawford (New York: G. P. Putnam's Sons, 1970), 172–89; Robert Selph Henry, *As They Saw Forrest* (Jackson, TN: McCowat-Mercer Press, 1956), 33; Joseph Viscount Wolseley, "General Forrest," *United Service Magazine* (London) 5 (1892): 119; *New*

Orleans Picayune, April 1 and 10, 1892; James A. Rawley, introduction to Joseph Viscount Wolseley, *The American Civil War: An English View*, ed. James A. Rawley (Charlottesville: University Press of Virginia, 1964), xxxiii.

15. Henry, *"First with the Most" Forrest*, 463–64.

16. Thomas L. Connelly and Barbara L. Bellows, *God and General Longstreet* (Baton Rouge: Louisiana State University Press, 1982), 117.

PART ONE

DREAMS OF GLORY

When a man is a Hero, he is a Hero for all of us. . . . [I]t is the Heroes who give us dreams of glory—of vicarious domination—and keep us moving forward. . . . What all men really want, at least once in their life, is to be able to run downhill with a sword, preferably against an outnumbered enemy; but if we have to, if we must, we will run downhill alone toward a battalion of enemies.
—Roger Price, *The Great Roob Revolution* (1970)

The Southerners were outnumbered five or six to one. Forrest charged. . . . He continued to scream, "Charge!" and kept galloping straight at the oncoming masses of Northern infantry. Forrest's men had better sense; they turned back and withdrew to their ridge. So Forrest charged alone. He rode headlong into the ranks of an infantry brigade. He was slashing with his saber, while his enemies surrounded him.
—Emory M. Thomas, *Travels to Hallowed Ground: A Historian's Journey to the American Civil War* (1987)

The best-known portrait of Forrest, this picture captures the piercing gaze, cutting across time and seeming only to deepen the shadows under his brow and through-out his story. *Courtesy of the Library of Congress*

CHAPTER ONE

A FUTURE FORETOLD

To the king and the army Tiresias foretold what the future
held for the boy. What rebellious monsters, on land and by
sea, would Heracles slay.
—Pindar, *Nemean 1*

IN 1918 THE B. F. JOHNSON Publishing Company in Richmond released
Life of Nathan B. Forrest by H. J. Eckenrode.The company had already
produced a series of biographies for young readers of different ages,
including lives of Robert E. Lee, Stonewall Jackson, and Jeb Stuart.
The Forrest biography was written for students in the fifth grade, and
a child, possibly the grandchild of a Civil War veteran, could own a
copy for fifty cents. Eckenrode, a former history professor, said it was
"a fitting time for bringing to the minds of children the life story of
one of the most heroic of Americans," whose exploits were "among
the chief glories of the Confederacy." Reminding readers that Forrest
was both an American and a Confederate was significant in a year
when reunited Americans were fighting in a European war. The
author's didactic purpose was evident on the biography's first page.
The story of Forrest's life "should be known to every boy and girl,"
Eckenrode wrote. *Life of Nathan B. Forrest* begins where a good
American story should begin—in a log cabin in the backwoods. "It
shows us that courage and hard work lead to the highest success in
spite of every hindrance."

The usefulness of Forrest's life as a morality tale was still evident thirty-four years later when the Bobbs-Merrill Company
brought out a new volume in its Childhood of Famous Americans
Series. More than sixty volumes in that series had already been published, including such titles as *Daniel Boone: Boy Hunter*; *Andy
Jackson: Boy Soldier*; *Mark Twain: Boy of Old Missouri*; and *Abe Lincoln:
Frontier Boy*. The 1952 volume, by Aileen Wells Parks, was *Bedford
Forrest: Boy on Horseback*. Children who read these books were
expected to learn that famous men and women had once been boys
and girls like themselves, and the lessons they learned in youth

3

had foreshadowed their mythic greatness later in life. Central to the Forrest Myth was a story of the frontier. Like Boone, Jackson, Twain, Lincoln, and many other heroes in the Childhood series, Forrest came to the mid-twentieth-century reader as a "boy on horseback," a boy of humble origins raised in the wilderness, hardened and tested by hardscrabble land and unforgiving rivers as the children of the 1950s were tested by Cold War communism, racism, and the wilderness of pending nuclear destruction.[1]

RATTLESNAKES AND BLACKBERRY PIE

Bedford Forrest: Boy on Horseback, a novel rather than a biography, begins with 10-year-old Bedford winning a race on a horse owned by the governor of Tennessee. Experiences teach him cunning and self-reliance and foreshadow his later accomplishments. Most of the stories sound like folklore, but some are drawn from early biographies. Wyeth, for example, relates a story he heard about young Bedford killing a rattlesnake to protect a group of children gathering blackberries. In *Bedford Forrest: Boy on Horseback*, the incident is rendered as a boyhood adventure that earns Forrest the admiration of his twin sister. " 'Oh, Bedford,' " cried Fanny, "how big he is! I never saw so many rattles.' " Although perhaps this line is fodder for the Freudians, Parks has Bedford reply: "Well, no snake is going to take a blackberry patch away from me. I like blackberry pie!" Pie notwithstanding, the story suggests a childhood parody of one of the early labors of Heracles, who, as an infant, strangles serpents sent by Hera to kill him. Heracles, a son of Zeus and the greatest of the Greek heroes, like Forrest, has a twin, his half-brother Iphicles. Tiresias, the blind prophet, then foretells a glorious future for the child. Later, Heracles kills another serpent, the many-headed Hydra, one of his Twelve Labors. In another story, Bedford is attacked by wild dogs, which flee before him, much as Heracles scatters the ghosts of Hades and subdues the guard dog Cerberus; Heracles also kills a two-headed dog, Orthus. Bedford battles crows in a cornfield. Heracles fights the Stymphalian birds in Arcadia. Bedford kills a panther that had attacked his mother in Mississippi. Heracles kills a ravaging lion in Nemea.[2]

Barry B. Powell, whose textbook on classical myth is widely used in colleges and universities, says that myths have plot, characters, and setting but differ from other stories in that they are traditional tales "for transmitting one generation's thought to another.

In this way traditional tales maintain contact with the past and pass inherited wisdom on to the future. They explain a society to itself. . . . They describe patterns of behavior that serve as models for members of a society, especially in times of crisis." In that sense, both *Life of Nathan B. Forrest* and *Bedford Forrest: Boy on Horseback* are myths: they have plot, characters, and setting; in the series to which they belong, Americans selected as exemplars of cultural values are part of the national heritage, stories passed on as tradition. In Forrest's case, those values include physical courage, loyalty to family and region, independence, initiative, and citizenship. In shaping a myth, where does fact end and story begin? The Forrest books for children are stories with American themes. Bedford Forrest is a boy who might live in any village. His deeds may have been ordinary for a boy growing up on the frontier, but they are given extraordinary significance because the reader knows in advance that this is a boy who grew up to do something important. "Forrest was like a hero in a story book—he was constantly having adventures," wrote Eckenrode. Like Heracles, he faced challenges and overcame them, as if working out some ultimate destiny. All the ingredients for myth are present. In terms of history, what the story leaves out may be as important as what is put in. In terms of myth, however, the factuality of events recounted hardly matters. A youthful reader in 1918 or 1952 might not see much difference between the Bedford Forrest served up by B. F. Johnson and Bobbs-Merrill and the Heracles found in a children's book of classical mythology.[3]

Developing a myth requires a teller of tales. In the case of a military hero of some significance, the first tellers are usually the military figure himself and his subordinates and opponents, who stand to be aggrandized by shaping the myth. Then come journalists and historians, who write from a point of view and with an eye toward audiences. Then come biographers, novelists, filmmakers, artists, political propagandists, teachers, and other tertiary interpreters of the past. They spawn revisionists who cut the past to fit the needs and values of the present. Scholars may deplore the amateurs who tamper with the documents that seem to tell the true story of events, and they have little patience with the fantasists who create an imaginative past loosely based on what can be gleaned from primary sources. Yet out of all this comes myth, a collection of tales, legends, conflicting interpretations, memory, distortion, and, finally, meaning shaped by the reader and listener.

Ultimately, the boy named for Forrest at the conclusion of *Bedford Forrest: Boy on Horseback*, and Forrest Gump, the dimwitted Everyman of Winston Groom's famous novel, ask the same question: Who was Nathan Bedford Forrest? The question may as well be: Who was Heracles? The inevitable question is, What do the stories mean to us today and how can we use them? But before even asking that question, one should look more closely at a name.

WHAT'S IN A NAME?

In myth and folklore, names often carry special importance and, in some cultures, may even have mystical significance. The English or Scottish name Forrest, or Forest or Forester, is common enough, probably simply designating a dweller on wooded land or a woodsman. Its origin is the Latin word *foris*, meaning out-of-doors. Nathan, from a Hebrew word meaning "gift," was the name of a prophet who was an adviser to King David. Other biblical figures also had the name, as did Forrest's paternal grandfather. Bedford is the county in Tennessee where Forrest was born. The name Nathan Bedford Forrest is thus faintly poetic with its suggestion of prophecy, place, and arboreal sanctuary. Each element contains a pair of syllables, providing euphonious symmetry. Yet, though a good name for a county judge, a sheriff, a cleric, or a sylvan poet, it would be unremarkable except that it has come down to the present as the name of a general known to history for his ferocity, alacrity in battle, and mythic resonance with the Lost Cause.

There is also something deeper in the name, however, something primordial, drawn from the spreading bowers of the wilderness in which both the name and its bearer originate. Longfellow wrote, in the prelude to *Evangeline*, of the forest primeval. Western literature has long known of the Green Man or the outsider who lurks in the woods with the wolves and troubles the dreams of modern man. He is the Wild Huntsman of German folklore chronicled by Sir Walter Scott and others. The legend is that a keeper of a royal forest hunted secretly on the Sabbath. Accursed, he still haunts the forests with his hounds. In medieval epics the woodsman often possesses magical powers, like Merlin, and slouches off to his lair to restore his potency. He is always on the fringes of civilization, always in retreat, doomed by the encroachment he resists. Americans encountered the spectral forest from the beginning. It was the abode of the indigenous Indian, the dwelling place of demons, the kingdom of Evil just beyond the coastal clearing. The whole history of American settlement is the triumph of the ax over the tree, the razing of the forest and the lifting of its darkness. The soldier Forrest came from the forest frontier and symbolized its primal power. He was no more or less a frontiersman than tens of thousands of other Americans who fought in the Civil War, but as his fame grew, his name gilded his legend. Other prominent generals bore good names—Lee, Grant, Beauregard, Pope, Stuart, Jackson, Hood, Chamberlain—and there were two Hills, as well, but only one Forrest.

A monument indicates the site of the pioneer cabin where Forrest was born in Chapel Hill, Tennessee. Photograph by Jennifer Allen. *Courtesy of Jennifer Allen*

GUNFIGHTS AND SILVER BUCKLES

Forrest was born on July 13, 1821, in Chapel Hill, Tennessee, a hamlet near the Duck River. At the age of sixteen the "boy on horseback" was the oldest surviving male in his large family. By the age of thirty he was a Memphis slave trader, and by the beginning of the Civil War he was a prosperous, if not entirely respectable, planter and former city alderman. "Because of his lack of education, his uncouth way of expressing himself, his slang, his poor diction, and his inability to read and write, he could have been viewed as what Southerners called 'white trash,' " according to

Brian C. Pohanka, who adds that Forrest "managed to transcend his upbringing and his lack of education and become a powerful member of the community." If so, this was extraordinary, in Jay Winik's view, because slave traders of the day were pariahs and outcasts, "much like drug dealers today." And yet, according to Eckenrode's biography for children, "by his honesty and his kind treatment of the blacks," Forrest overcame the reprehension of the

A historical marker in Memphis indicates the location of Forrest's antebellum home. Tennessee has not forgotten one of its most famous sons. Photograph by Dwight Teeter. *Courtesy of Dwight Teeter*

community and "won the esteem of his fellow-citizens. He kept the negroes clean, looked after their health, and took care not to part husbands and wives and mothers and children. Many slaves begged him to buy them because of his good name." Forrest's first biographers, Jordan and Pryor, were at pains to explain Forrest's slave trading in the context of the times. Slave traders were disliked, they acknowledged, but some, including Forrest, overcame prejudice to achieve standing in the community. He was a kindly master, and "we are satisfied his slaves were strongly attached to him." That he later rose to prominence in Memphis in spite of his occupation was testimony to his character.

Apologists for Forrest have made a good deal out of such claims. It may be true he was the best of a bad lot, but he was still in a sordid business, as the general opprobrium toward the enterprise attests. Testimony that he was a humane broker of chattel notwithstanding, Forrest's slaves were "attached to him" by shackles as much as by good will. Retrospective morality, however, is not the point. The Forrest Myth had to account for a messy set of facts as it evolved from master of bondage to "boy on horseback."[4]

In any event, beneath the semirespectable exterior, Forrest remained a rough character. His most recent biographer, Jack Hurst, notes how "almost desperately, he assumed the role of gentleman. His civilian dress has been characterized by admirers as bordering on foppish, and his good name he regarded even more seriously than was normal on the

CITY DIRECTORY.

FORREST & MAPLES,
SLAVE DEALERS,
87 Adams Street,
Between Second and Third,
MEMPHIS, TENNESSEE,

Have constantly on hand the best selected assortment of

FIELD HANDS, HOUSE SERVANTS & MECHANICS,

at their Negro Mart, to be found in the city. They are daily receiving from Virginia, Kentucky and Missouri, fresh supplies of likely Young Negroes.

Negroes Sold on Commission,
and the highest market price always paid for good stock. Their Jail is capable of containing Three Hundred, and for comfort, neatness and safety, is the best arranged of any in the Union. Persons wishing to purchase, are invited to examine their stock before purchasing elsewhere.

They have on hand at present, Fifty likely young Negroes, comprising Field hands, Mechanics, House and Body Servants, &c.

An advertisement from the *Memphis City Directory*, 1855.

brawling, chip-on-shoulder frontier along which he grew to manhood." He was, Hurst concludes, two men at once: "a soft-spoken gentleman of marked placidity and an overbearing bully of homicidal wrath."[5] The "boy on horseback" gave no quarter when battling panthers and serpents, but was he really a murderous, white-trash bully, the equivalent of a modern drug dealer masquerading as a Southern gentleman in a tailored white linen suit and broad-brimmed hat?

All Forrest's biographers tell the story of an incident that occurred March 10, 1845, on the public square of Hernando, Mississippi, where Forrest was working in partnership with his uncle, Jonathan Forrest. Details vary, but it seems four men rode into town seeking to settle a grievance with Forrest's uncle, and Bedford was drawn into the quarrel. Guns blazed, and the young Forrest fired back, charged into the melee with a bowie knife in hand, and ran off the bloodied assailants. Jonathan Forrest was mortally wounded,

Before his military career had begun, and at about the age of forty, Forrest appears as the well-dressed businessman. He was noted for his meticulous appearance and attire, in spite of his reputation as anything but a gentleman. Photograph from the *Memphis Appeal*.

and Bedford was injured. In short, it was a Wild West gunfight, with Bedford Forrest still standing and blowing smoke from his pistol when it was over.

In another cinematic twist, Forrest also got the girl. Her name was Mary Ann Montgomery, and she was allegedly descended from the same Irish family as General Richard Montgomery, who had fought with Benedict Arnold at Quebec in 1775. Evidently, the gunfight was not enough to warn her off from her suitor, although her uncle and guardian, a Presbyterian minister, initially had reservations. His niece had attended the Nashville Female Academy and presumably was a cut above the likes of Bedford Forrest. The uncle gave in, however, and married the couple on September 25, 1845. Mary Ann Forrest was, of course "the best of wives, and Forrest's married life lasted with unbroken happiness until the day of his death," according to Eckenrode. If Forrest was indeed a ruffian, he evidently had sufficient charm to transcend his press clippings and be welcome at the manse. And if he was a bully, he was also capable of some *High Noon* heroics in defense of principle when the odds were against him. Nor should his rude background disqualify him from the right to acquire a brocade vest and silver buckles and a modicum of social polish on the borders of civilization.[6]

"WE SHOULD HAVE GAINED A GLORIOUS VICTORY"

Forrest had various business interests in addition to slave trading, including a stage line between Hernando and Memphis, a brick-

Forrest's house in Hernando is shown in a photograh taken about fifty years after the Forrests were married. By then it had fallen into disrepair. It no longer stands. From J. Harvey Mathes, *General Forrest* (New York: D. Appleton and Company, 1902).

yard, and a cattle and horse brokerage. In 1851 the brickyard failed, and he moved to Memphis, where he expanded the slave-trading business and dabbled in real estate. When war came, he was temperamentally as ready for combat as any civilian in North America. He enlisted as a private in the Tennessee Mounted Rifles on June 14, 1861; by July 10 he had been commissioned a lieutenant colonel by Tennessee governor Isham G. Harris and ordered to raise a battalion of mounted rangers. Forrest had political influence in Memphis and used it advantageously. By November he had assembled 650 men and moved into action in western Kentucky. In one of his first engagements he routed a Federal detachment, personally killing several soldiers in hand-to-hand combat. The hunt was on.

Forrest's first major military success occurred on February 16, 1862, when he led some 500 men out of Fort Donelson in Tennessee on a flooded road rather than surrender his command to General Ulysses S. Grant after several Confederate generals had set in motion the surrender of some 13,000 soldiers. As Andrew Lytle tells the story, this incident marked Forrest's "first disillusionment about

Forrest rides at the head of the Confederate cavalry in action near Fort Donelson. Bold action requires bold art, and Forrest's decisiveness is a critical component of his myth. Artists did not typically witness these events and had to imagine them. Even the horse, prancing boldly through the snow, seems poised to respond to the general's orders. From H. J. Eckenrode, *Life of Nathan B. Forrest* (Richmond, VA: B. F. Johnson Publishing Company, 1918).

Forrest confers with Major David C. Kelley during the bombardment of Fort Donelson. From John Allan Wyeth, *Life of General Nathan Bedford Forrest* (New York: Harper and Bros., 1899).

that class of Southern leader he was to term loosely, 'West P'inter.' " His constant friction with professional soldiers—the "West P'inters" —is an essential part of the Forrest Myth. He fought by raw instinct and attitude and grew impatient with academy-trained, by-the-book strategists. He was not the only successful "amateur" soldier of the war, but he was arguably the most successful and therefore a hero to anyone ever underestimated or restricted by lack of organizational credentials, the right degrees, the appropriate training, and the experience to do a job officially sanctioned by the powers-that-be. After the Fort Donelson debacle, Forrest rebuked his superiors, claiming that "two-thirds of our army could have marched out without loss, and . . . had we continued the fight the next day, we should have gained a glorious victory."[7]

SHOWDOWN AT SHILOH

On February 18, 1862, Forrest turned up in Nashville. It was about to be overrun by forces under the command of Union general Don Carlos Buell, and Forrest managed to save valuable supplies from gangs of looters and restore some order to the panicked city before retiring to Murfreesboro on February 23. As soon as he arrived there, General Albert Sidney Johnston ordered him to withdraw to Alabama and rebuild his forces. The aggressive Forrest probably balked at quitting Tennessee but soon pulled together enough troopers to reach regimental strength and earn promotion to full colonel. Johnston summoned him to the railroad town of Corinth, Mississippi, where he was consolidating his forces in order to check Grant, who was moving south from Fort Donelson, and Buell, who was coming from the vicinity of Nashville. With about 42,000 men, Johnston moved north from Corinth toward a bend in the Tennessee River where Grant was disembarking his troops at Pittsburg Landing and awaiting the arrival of Buell.

Early on the morning of April 6, Johnston struck Grant's forward position, beginning the Battle of Shiloh, and almost overran the field before Union resistance stiffened at the fabled "Hornet's Nest." Forrest's cavalry was positioned on the Confederate right flank to protect against a possible Union attack from the southeast. Hearing the sounds of battle in the distance and feeling that the flank was secure, he moved his command to a marshy field near the Hornet's Nest and found the battered forces of General Benjamin Cheatham. Union artillery opened up on the cavalrymen, and Forrest told Cheatham that he must either charge or retreat. Cheatham said, "I cannot give you the order, and if you make the charge, it will be under your own orders." That was enough for Forrest, who stormed ahead. Cheatham, following behind the cavalry, slammed into the Union lines while Forrest hit the retreating infantry and artillery from the flank. Cheatham later gave Forrest no credit for his part in the assault, which was part of a wider encirclement of the Union troops at the Hornet's Nest. The Confederates took 2,200 prisoners, but the Union forces had held for six hours. By the time Forrest's men and other Confederate forces reached the bluffs above Pittsburg Landing, the attack had faltered at dusk. When Union artillery on the bluffs and gunboats on the river below opened up on the Confederates, Forrest was ordered to pull back to the relative safety of a ravine south of Pittsburg Landing, and then to a secondary encampment.[8]

Forrest next turned his attention to scouting the riverbank. Wearing Union overcoats, some of his men sneaked up to Pittsburg Landing and saw Buell's army, after a hard march from Savannah, Tennessee, already crossing the river. Ambrose Bierce, a Union soldier who later became a famous journalist, described the scene: "Before us ran the turbulent river, vexed with plunging shells and obscured in spots by blue sheets of low-lying smoke. The two little steamers were doing their duty well. They came over to us empty and went back crowded, sitting very low in the water, apparently on the point of capsizing. The farther edge of the water could not be seen; the boats came out of the obscurity, took on their passengers and vanished in the darkness."[9]

Forrest, when he learned of this crossing from his scouts, realized that the battle was lost without an immediate attack before the rest of Buell's army could reinforce Grant. He made the rounds to find a general who would raise the alarm, probably looking for Johnston and perhaps not knowing that the commanding general had been killed in the day's battle. He first reached General James Chalmers and then the corps commanders, General John Breckinridge and General William Hardee, but was unable to find General P. G. T. Beauregard, who was then the commanding general on the field. He again sought out Hardee, who told the flustered Forrest to return to his regiment and report any hostile movements of the enemy—which, presumably, was just what he was doing. In the creation of the Forrest Myth, all this nighttime perambulation is significant because it seems to show Colonel Forrest as the only officer who understood the strategic situation on the field. According to Eckenrode, Forrest actually found Beauregard immediately and told him he must attack, yet Beauregard did nothing while "the Southern soldiers slept through the night." Eckenrode's version makes a better story, but it never happened.[10]

While learned generals pored over their maps or slept in their tents, then, the dashing colonel might have saved the battle had they only listened to him. Hurst points out, however, that the commanders had already been told by a captured Union general that Buell was crossing the river, but they chose not to credit that report. Even if they had, organizing a difficult night attack by a bloodied and exhausted army that had just lost its commander would have been daunting. In any event, by midafternoon the next day the Confederate army was in retreat, with Forrest and his cavalry covering the rear after helping to break several Union attempts to smash the Rebel lines and cause a complete rout. The battle had been costly for both sides. More than 100,000 men had been engaged, and about one in five was a casualty. A total of 3,477 men died in what to that point had been the bloodiest battle of the war. Although Lytle seems to have considered Shiloh a draw and even a morale booster for the Confederates, the Southern armies had been driven from the field with more than 24 percent casualties and had lost their commanding general. [11]

On April 8, Forrest clashed with troops under General William Tecumseh Sherman at Fallen Timbers, some four miles south of Shiloh on the road to Corinth. Leading a charge into Sherman's lines, Forrest became separated from his troops and was surrounded by Union soldiers shouting, "Shoot that man! Knock him off his horse!" Forrest was shot above the left hip, the ball lodging against his spine, but his horse, although fatally wounded, managed to leap through the cordon and carry the bleeding colonel to safety. One other detail of that incident speaks to the creation of the Forrest Myth. Most twentieth-century biographies claim that Forrest escaped by hoisting an undersized Union soldier to the rear of his saddle to use as a shield while he extricated himself and then tossing him to the ground when he was out of range. Hurst traces this story to a 1902 biography by J. Harvey Mathes, who said he was assisted in his research by Forrest's son. Hurst concludes that even though such a feat of strength by a wounded man would have been "miraculous," it was "the only plausible explanation" for how Forrest could have escaped with only a single bullet wound. Perhaps. But without further documentation, the miraculous elevation stretches credulity. Forrest was known to be strong, but was he strong enough to collar a struggling soldier and lift him to the back of his horse in the midst of a battle? Movie cowboys have been known to do this sort of thing, but could it have happened at Fallen Timbers? How small was this bantling in blue snatched from the midst of his frenzied comrades, who were evidently the worst

marksmen of the Civil War? Or were Forrest's later admirers simply hoisting history by the scruff of the neck and tossing it aside
when it suited them?[12]

"A HEAP OF FUN"

In any event, Forrest's charge, according to Sherman, delayed the
Federal pursuit and may have allowed the Confederate army to
slip away to Corinth. The irrepressible Forrest himself hastened to
Memphis to mend and soon placed an advertisement in the *Memphis Appeal* asking for 200 able-bodied men to present themselves
at his headquarters in Corinth "if you want a heap of fun and to
kill some Yankees." By July he was riding at the head of a 1,400-
man brigade, and like a riverboat gambler he bluffed 1,200 Federal
soldiers into surrendering at Murfreesboro after a sharp skirmish
on July 13. Taking the town "was one of the finest cavalry feats of
the war," Eckenrode told his young readers. "It made Forrest famous." This was probably true; at any rate, he had helped check
Buell's movement toward Chattanooga.

Eckenrode danced around some of the more unseemly aspects
of that engagement, however. In his account, "A soldier fired at
Forrest from behind a wagon only a few feet away. The bullet missed
its mark and the cavalry leader shot the man with a pistol." But
Jordan and Pryor added another detail. In their version, Forrest
was fired upon by "a negro camp-follower, one of whose balls cut
his hat-band; but just as the negro was about to fire the fifth time,
Forrest killed him with his pistol at the distance of thirty paces."
After the war, a Union general enlarged on the story of Forrest's
conduct during the battle. A Tennessee civilian, the general claimed,
told him Forrest had shot a mulatto who was a servant to one of
the Union officers. Forrest also had apparently admonished a soldier who failed to shoot a captured black. And a diarist noted that
blacks were afraid to become familiar with Northerners because
they heard that Forrest had hanged the blacks he captured at
Murfreesboro and elsewhere.

These stories all show the difficulty of interpreting and documenting the Forrest Myth. Wills says Forrest may have been forced
to confront the issue of race in the context of war for the first time
at Murfreesboro. He points out that Forrest was angry about any
participation by blacks on the Union side—as, undoubtedly were
most of the Confederate army and the political hierarchy. At the

time, blacks were being used officially only as Union noncomba-
tants. Whether Forrest was attempting to make a statement or issue a warning by his actions—if they even occurred—is unclear.
Simply shooting a black man who was shooting at him could hardly
be considered an atrocity. But it is noteworthy that biographers such
as Eckenrode distort the incident. If Forrest was murdering black
prisoners, the problem for his mythmakers multiplies, but as Wills
notes, what is true and what is conjecture simply is not clear. Wills
has Forrest grappling with the issue of race and facing a dilemma
because of it, a dilemma that may have been less a problem for him
than for the mythmakers. His apologists can hardly deny that he
was a racist in a conflict that had much to do with race. Whether he
was a compassionate racist, a brutal racist, an inconsistent racist,
or even a recovering racist—compared with what standard?—is an
entirely different and probably unanswerable question, but a question the mythmakers must attempt to answer.[13]

ITCHING TO FIGHT

Murfreesboro made Forrest's name "demonic in the minds of the
Federals," according to Hurst, and his growing reputation soon led
to a field promotion to brigadier general. For the next few months,
Forrest harassed Union forces in Middle and East Tennessee while
General Braxton Bragg moved into Kentucky. On September 14,
Forrest took command of all the cavalry supporting General
Leonidas Polk on the right wing of Bragg's army. But eleven days
later Bragg ordered Forrest to turn over his command to General
Joseph Wheeler and return to Middle Tennessee to recruit more
troops. After suffering 3,400 casualties at Perryville on October 8,
Bragg pulled out of Kentucky.

Having consolidated his new forces around Murfreesboro,
Forrest received another order from Bragg assigning him to
Breckinridge, who sent him to the gates of Nashville with 3,500
poorly equipped cavalry supported by some infantry units. Little
was accomplished, thanks to Bragg's shifting movements, and
Forrest was ordered to report back to Wheeler again. Ordered by
Bragg on December 10 to move into West Tennessee to annoy Federal troops operating in Mississippi, Forrest fought several impressive engagements and did a great deal of damage to railroads and
supply depots before running into a substantial Union force at
Parker's Crossroads near Lexington, Tennessee. There he found

himself trapped on New Year's Eve between two brigades, and, asked by a subordinate how he proposed to get out of the situation, famously is supposed to have replied: "Charge them both ways." He got out of the pocket bloodied by some 400 casualties and the loss of several artillery pieces, but he gave as good as he got.

By the time Forrest directed his troops across the Tennessee River on New Year's Day, 1863—an incredible logistical feat in itself—he could look back on his December activities with great satisfaction. He had covered more than 300 miles in two weeks. In concert with General Earl Van Dorn's movements in Mississippi, he had broken Grant's supply lines and kept him out of Vicksburg for a while. Grant thereafter relied more heavily on the Mississippi River as a principal supply line. But while Forrest was withdrawing from Parker's Crossroads, Bragg had fought a hard battle at Stone's River against General William Rosecrans and had pulled back to Shelbyville. Joining him there on January 26, Forrest learned that some of his troops were now under Wheeler's command and were heading toward the Cumberland River to attack supply transports and disrupt the important river-route invasion strategy favored by the Union. By the time Forrest caught up with him, Wheeler had decided to attack the depot town of Dover next to Fort Donelson. Forrest opposed the attack, reasoning that Wheeler's force was too small and ill equipped to take the fort or to hold it against Union gunboats if it *were* captured. As Forrest predicted, the attack on February 3 was a fiasco. He had two horses shot out from under him while leading impulsive and poorly timed assaults and later vowed never to serve under Wheeler again. Although Wheeler took responsibility for the failure to capture the fort, part of the blame accrued to Forrest, who showed an inability to coordinate with his commander.[14]

He soon had a new one. Van Dorn had been given command of a cavalry corps on the left wing of Bragg's army, and Forrest's brigade was put in action under him. On March 5 at Thompson's Station, about 10 miles south of Franklin, Tennessee, he managed to get behind some infantry regiments that had been fighting off the larger Confederate force for five hours and bring about a surrender. Out of this fight came another tale that contributed to the Forrest Myth. One of Forrest's casualties during the fight was a favorite horse, Roderick, who had carried the general up a rocky ridge into the Union lines during a critical charge. Seeing that

Roderick had been shot three times, Forrest mounted his son Willie's horse and told the young lieutenant to take Roderick to the rear. Roderick's saddle and bridle were removed in a holding area, and he might have survived his wounds had he not jumped three fences and galloped off to find Forrest when he heard the sound of more gunfire. Just as the horse reached Forrest, it was struck by a fourth bullet and killed. Roderick had been an unusually loyal horse and reportedly had often trotted after Forrest in camp like a hunting dog. Given the twenty-nine mounts that the aggressive general, it is said, had had shot out from under him during the war, it is hard to imagine him as a credible horse whisperer, at least from the viewpoint of the horses, but like a true mythic hero, he seemed to have supernatural powers over man and beast. Roderick's gallant dash and subsequent death at the feet of his master is one of the best horse stories to come out of the war, whether or not Roderick was really trying to find a quiet pasture somewhere or even turn himself in to the Federal quartermasters before he took another bullet.[15]

Forrest's horses did not last long in battle. The general did not usually step gracefully from the saddle when a horse was shot out from under him, however. From John Allan Wyeth, *Life of General Nathan Bedford Forrest* (New York: Harper and Bros., 1899).

Hard fighting continued south of Nashville during the next two months. Forrest captured 800 Federals at Brentwood on March 25 and fought off a flank attack during a reconnaissance at Franklin on April 10. Despite the aggressiveness of the Confederate cavalry wing during this interlude, however, relations between Forrest and Van Dorn had been deteriorating and evolved into a conflict toward the end of April, when Van Dorn rebuked Forrest for some infraction of military rules. Just what initiated the dispute is not clear, but some accounts have it that Van Dorn also accused Forrest of having planted stories in the *Chattanooga Rebel* giving himself more credit for the successes at Thompson's Station than Van Dorn thought he deserved. Forrest testily denied the accusations, and both generals briefly brandished swords before they calmed down and realized the unseemliness of this testosterone-charged display. Whatever bad blood lingered between them did not matter long, because Van Dorn was shot to death by a jealous husband on May 7.[16]

Bragg sent Forrest to Alabama on April 23 to support Colonel P. D. Roddey at Tuscumbia. Roddey was scuffling with Union general Grenville Dodge, who was active in the area. But what neither Roddey nor Forrest knew was that the Federals had launched two raids into the Deep South with the intention of cutting Bragg's supply lines below Chattanooga and supporting Grant's siege of Vicksburg. The raiders who would test Forrest were under the command of Colonel Abel Streight, whose troopers had been brought up the Tennessee River to Eastport, Mississippi. Streight would be crossing rough country to get to the Georgia railroads, so he took a gamble by using mules as well as horses.

On April 26, Forrest and Roddey learned that a Federal force had slipped behind them. Forrest, with about 1,000 men, caught up with Streight, who had almost twice that many soldiers, at Sand Mountain on April 30 and fought a running battle with him all the way across northern Alabama. Streight crossed the Black Warrior River just ahead of Forrest and burned the only bridge in sight. But Forrest solved the problem with the help of a 16-year-old girl, Emma Sansom, who became one of the heroines of the war. When Emma told the general she knew a place where the crooked river could be forded, he swept up the girl onto his horse and galloped off to a spot where they could creep through some underbrush without being seen by the soldiers on the other side of the river. Forrest crossed at the hidden ford and continued his pursuit, but not before asking for a lock of Emma's hair and leaving her a hand-scrawled message of thanks for her gallant conduct. Emma kept the message long after the war, and its contents were classic Forrest: a third of its words, including the girl's name, were misspelled. Eckenrode gushed that "Emma Sansom lives in history as an American heroine." Wyeth obtained Emma's story directly from the heroine herself and dedicated his 1899 biography to her.

Emma Sansom, at age nineteen, three years after she showed Forrest the Black Warrior ford. She became a symbol of Southern womanhood—beauty and daring, faithfulness to the cause. From John Allan Wyeth, *Life of General Nathan Bedford Forrest* (New York: Harper and Bros., 1899).

Forrest eventually ran down Streight on May 3 about 20 miles from Rome, Georgia, and bluffed him into surrendering by using his favorite trick of parading soldiers and guns around so that Streight would think he was outnumbered. Jon Latimer cites this incident in his book, *Deception in War*, as one of history's best examples of military theatrics. At the time of the surrender, Forrest had no more than 600 men, who rounded up almost 1,700 Union raiders and marched them into Rome. The town's name was fitting: like a victorious Roman general, Forrest entered the city to a hero's welcome; his path was strewn with flowers, and he was presented with a laurel wreath and a magnificent horse. Wolseley later wrote that the story of the exploit "reads like an exciting novel," and well it might, because it was a myth in the making.[17]

"NO DAMNED MAN SHALL KILL ME AND LIVE"

After the death of Van Dorn, Forrest was given his command and was reorganizing his forces in Columbia, Tennessee, when he had another confrontation with an officer, this one with fatal consequences. During the fight at Sand Mountain he had hotly reprimanded Lieutenant Andrew Gould for abandoning two fieldpieces during a Federal attack and later sought to have him transferred to another unit. Gould was affronted by what he thought was an unjustified assault on his honor and approached Forrest in his office for an explanation on June 13. Talk became intemperate, the two tussled, bystanders heard a gunshot. In a few moments, Gould staggered out into the street, blood spurting from a knife wound in his right side, and Forrest hobbled after him, a bullet lodged just above his left hip. Other officers intercepted the general and pulled him into a doctor's office. When told he was seriously wounded, he rushed out of the office shouting, "No damned man shall kill me and live." He located two pistols and started stalking Gould, who was being treated in a tailor's shop by two doctors who had found him on the street. As Forrest rushed in, Gould fled into a back alley; Forrest fired at him, but the shot went awry and wounded a soldier. The general found Gould lying in some high weeds, nudged him with his boot, assumed he was dead or soon would be, and returned to the tailor's shop.

A further examination by doctors revealed that Forrest's wound was not mortal, but Gould died a couple of days later. Various accounts, one of which Lytle credits in his biography, claim that the two men had some kind of reconciliation before Gould died—an acceptable conclusion to the sordid incident and congruent with the Forrest Myth. Eckenrode says that Forrest "not only forgave him but showed great grief over his fate. Hot-tempered as Forrest was, he bore no malice for wrongs done him. His nature was generous and forgiving." But he is also supposed to have said that if

Gould had showed as much mettle on the battlefield as he had during the fatal brawl, he would still be alive. Whatever actually occurred, the altercation had resulted in three casualties, including the death of a young officer.[18]

What Forrest really wanted during this third summer of the war was an independent command along the Mississippi River from Vicksburg to Cairo, Illinois, a plan he proposed to Jefferson Davis's adjutant general, Samuel Cooper, on August 9, 1863. Bragg, however, persuaded Davis that as he fell back toward Chattanooga, he could ill afford to lose Forrest. Instead, he gave Forrest command of cavalry north of Chattanooga. When the clash finally came between the Union armies commanded by Rosecrans and Bragg's Army of Tennessee at Chickamauga Creek in northern Georgia on September 18, Forrest was in command of the cavalry on Bragg's right wing. Early that morning, according to John Bowers's dramatic account, "one of the first sights in evidence, ready to impress his will and get things going, was a strange upright figure, theatrically outfitted in a white linen duster, a sword and pistol strapped at his waist. . . . [Forrest] was the first Confederate in the battle that became known as Chickamauga, firing away, itching to fight."[19]

He got all the fight he wanted. He and his men were engaged throughout the battle, struggling to control critical fords, bridges, and roads, repulsing Federal attacks both on foot and on horseback, and slashing at the Federal flank. The Confederates broke through a gap in the Federal lines on September 20 and almost precipitated a rout. Before sunrise the next morning, Forrest and 400 troopers were in pursuit as the Federals scrambled back to Chattanooga, starting a "chain of events that has helped create the Forrest legend," according to Bowers. His horse took a bullet in a neck artery, and Forrest stuck a finger in the bullet hole to stop the spurting blood and galloped forward. When he finally removed the finger, the horse collapsed and died. Forrest then continued his pursuit on another horse, following the Federals to within a few miles of Chattanooga. When Bragg declined to send him the reinforcements he wanted, possibly missing an opportunity to destroy Rosecrans's army, Forrest is said to have shouted, in regard to his commander, "What does he fight battles for?"

Bragg further angered Forrest a few days later when he ordered him to assign some of his cavalry to Wheeler. Enraged, Forrest confronted his commanding general and said he would no longer obey his orders, promising that "if you ever again try to interfere with me or cross my path it will be at the peril of your life." And thus, according to Lytle, the war was lost because of Forrest's pique: he "would make the South pay a great price—for he had done the Southern cause such an injury that all his genius would be powerless to repair it. Bragg's bloodless cheeks did not run white from fear alone. He would be satisfied for this mortal insult. In the end, the man who is ambitious and designing always triumphs over a man like Forrest." Lytle had his villain—Braxton Bragg—in his story of the western battles.

Whether Forrest could have saved the South is the Great If. It is true that because he could not get along with Bragg and was usually in conflict with all his superiors, the Southern cause was compromised. For Lytle, however, Forrest is much more than just a Confederate soldier. He is a universal hero, but in the end "the hero always fails. He either dies as Roland dies; or the cause for which he fought is lost; or he wins the fight and the calculators who take over gamble it away, as with Forrest. Never in the world are the powers of darkness finally overcome, for they inhabit matter; nor, without the conflict of the cooperating opposites of light and dark, good and bad, would life as we know it be." Cast in this Manichaean framework, the South was fighting a cosmic battle against darkness. Lytle was writing theology, not history. In reality, the Confederacy was more like Forrest's horse at the Battle of Chickamauga. The Confederacy, too, was mortally wounded and could be sustained as the Lost Cause after the war only by the hand of myth.[20]

Forrest had an opportunity to present Davis with his list of grievances against Bragg during a meeting in late October in Montgomery, Alabama. Forrest accompanied Davis on a trip to Atlanta, and along the way he must again have urged Davis to approve his request for a transfer to a western command. Davis listened attentively and, after conferring with Bragg, approved the request but did not provide all the forces the general wanted. Just what Davis thought of Forrest at this point is uncertain, but it seems probable that Bragg had persuaded the Confederate president that Forrest was just a raider. Raiders could be useful, but they were unpredictable, and supplying them with already scarce resources was risky. Perhaps Davis, as some have suggested, thought Forrest was a frontier bumpkin and a military amateur. Perhaps, too, Davis was slow to understand the importance of the western theater of the war, especially that part of it that now interested Forrest. And perhaps he had a hunch Forrest might save the Confederacy. In any case, with just 310 men, Forrest departed for Okolona, Mississippi, and reported to his new commander, General Stephen D. Lee, who had previously urged Bragg to send Forrest to him. By the beginning of the new year, Forrest had collected some 5,000 recruits, provisioned them with supplies (some of which he purchased with his own funds), launched several raids into West Tennessee, reorganized his entire command, and been promoted to major general.[21]

His first real test that year would come against Sherman and a young cavalry general, William Sooy Smith. Sherman and Grant had concocted an audacious plan that in some ways anticipated Sherman's bold March to the Sea later in the year. The plan called for Sherman to march 20,000 infantrymen out of Vicksburg (which had been in Federal hands since July 4, 1863), cross into Alabama, destroy the Confederate arsenal at Selma, and then plunge south to the Gulf of Mexico at Mobile. Meanwhile, a diversionary force would march to Greenwood, Mississippi, while Smith led 7,000 cavalry from Memphis to join Sherman at Meridian, Mississippi. Smith did not get started until February 11, however, and never reached Sherman, who had left Vicksburg on February 3 and was in Meridian by February 14. Without Smith's cavalry, Sherman's grand plan could not work, so he set fire to the city and started marching back to Vicksburg on February 21.

Forrest, meanwhile, was keeping his forces spread out between the Union armies, uncertain of their intentions. He stalked Smith carefully as the Union general moved along the Mobile and Ohio Railroad, drawing him deeper into the Mississippi countryside that was home territory to Forrest and many of his soldiers, including his brother, Colonel Jeffrey Forrest. It was Jeffrey's brigade that caught up with Smith at West Point, Mississippi, and tried to draw him through the Sakatonchee Swamp into a trap. At this point, Smith seems to have gotten cold feet. His battle reports made it sound as if he were retreating to a better position so he could stand and fight, but his retreat rolled all the way back into Memphis, with Bedford and Jeffrey Forrest right behind. He soon found it was a lot easier to ride into Mississippi than to ride out.

Bedford Forrest, leading a smaller force, kept hitting the rear of Smith's retreating columns, stopping when necessary to fight pitched battles and then resuming the pursuit. In one of these battles, Jeffrey was shot through the neck while leading a charge and was dead by the time his brother reached him. Forrest then seemed to go mad, according to one of his subordinates, and led a charge right into the Union lines, slashing with his sword and firing his pistol. In hand-to-hand combat, according to one account, he killed three men and had two more horses shot out from under him. By the time Smith reached Memphis on February 26, fifty-four of his men had been killed, 179 were wounded, and 155 were missing. Forrest suffered 144 casualties, including Jeffrey. Grant and Sherman were incensed, and Sherman, blaming Smith, admitted that his attempt to throttle Forrest had "failed utterly." Sherman later claimed that he never intended to go to Mobile and that the plan had been a diversion.[22]

NOTES

1. H. J. Eckenrode, *Life of Nathan B. Forrest* (Richmond, VA: B. F. Johnson Publishing Company, 1918), 5, 9; Aileen Wells Parks, *Bedford Forrest: Boy on Horseback* (Indianapolis, IN: Bobbs-Merrill Company, 1952).

2. Parks, *Bedford Forrest*, 91, 192; Wyeth, *That Devil Forrest*, 11.

3. Barry B. Powell, *Classical Myth*, 2d ed. (Upper Saddle River, NJ: Prentice-Hall, 1998), 2–3; Eckenrode, *Life of Nathan B. Forrest*, 23.

4. Brian C. Pohanka, quoted in *Civil War Journal: The Leaders*, ed. William C. Davis, Brian C. Pohanka, and Don Troiani (Nashville, TN: Rutledge Hill Press, 1997), 379–80; Winik, *April 1865*, 275; Eckenrode, *Life of Nathan B. Forrest*, 23; Jordan and Pryor, *The Campaigns of General Nathan Bedford Forrest*, 25–26.

5. Hurst, *Nathan Bedford Forrest*, 6–7.

6. Jordan and Pryor, *The Campaigns of General Nathan Bedford Forrest*, 22–25; Wills, *A Battle from the Start*, 22–26; Hurst, *Nathan Bedford Forrest*, 16–17; *American Eagle* (Fort Pickering, TN), March 21, 1845; Wyeth, *That Devil Forrest*, 15–16; Eckenrode, *Life of Nathan B. Forrest*, 22.

7. Hurst, *Nathan Bedford Forrest*, 75–82; Lytle, *Bedford Forrest and His Critter Company*, 76; *War of the Rebellion: A Compilation of the Official Records of the Union and Confederate Armies* (hereafter *OR*), 70 vols. (Washington, DC: Government Printing Office, 1890–91), scr. 1:7, 383–87.

8. Hurst, *Nathan Bedford Forrest*, 87–90.

9. Ambrose Bierce, "What I Saw of Shiloh," *Shadows of Blue and Gray: The Civil War Writings of Ambrose Bierce*, ed. Brian M. Thomsen (New York: Forge, 2002), 205.

10. Hurst, *Nathan Bedford Forrest*, 90–91; Eckenrode, *Life of Nathan B. Forrest*, 41.

11. Hurst, *Nathan Bedford Forrest*, 91–92; Lytle, *Bedford Forrest and His Critter Company*, 83.

12. Jordan and Pryor, *The Campaigns of General Nathan Bedford Forrest*, 147–48; Hurst, *Nathan Bedford Forrest*, 3; J. Harvey Mathes, *General Forrest* (New York: D. Appleton and Company, 1902), 60.

13. Hurst, *Nathan Bedford Forrest*, 97; Wyeth, *That Devil Forrest*, 65–67; Jordan and Pryor, *The Campaigns of General Nathan Bedford Forrest*, 170; Wills, *A Battle from the Start*, 71–78; Eckenrode, *Life of Nathan B. Forrest*, 46; D. S. Stanley, "Is Forrest a Butcher?—A Little Bit of History," *New York Times*, September 14, 1868; Tennessee Cavalry, Regiment Fourth, Folder 13, Military Units, Confederate Collection, Civil War Collection, Box 17, Tennessee State Library and Archives, Nashville, quoted in Wills, *A Battle from the Start*, 77; George Richard Browder, *The Heavens Are Weeping: The Diaries of George Richard Browder, 1852–1886*, ed. Richard L. Troutman (Grand Rapids, MI: Zondervan Publishing House, 1987), 125.

14. Hurst, *Nathan Bedford Forrest*, 104–14; Wills, *A Battle from the Start*, 84–104.

15. Henry, *"First with the Most" Forrest*, 128–30.

16. Hurst, *Nathan Bedford Forrest*, 115–17; Henry, *"First with the Most" Forrest*, 143.

17. Hurst, *Nathan Bedford Forrest*, 117–26; Wills, *A Battle from the Start*, 109–19; *Southern Confederacy*, May 8 and 16, 1863; Wyeth, *That Devil Forrest*, 165–99; Eckenrode, *Life of Nathan Bedford Forrest*, 77; Jon Latimer, *Deception in War* (New York: Overlook Press, 2001), 30–31; Joseph Viscount Wolseley, "General Viscount Wolseley on Forrest," in Henry, *As They Saw Forrest*, 41.

18. Wills, *A Battle from the Start*, 122–27; Hurst, *Nathan Bedford Forrest*, 127–30; Lytle, *Bedford Forrest and His Critter Company*, 182; Eckenrode, *Life of Nathan B. Forrest*, 80.

19. Hurst, *Nathan Bedford Forrest*, 131–33; Bowers, *Chickamauga and Chattanooga*, 60.

20. Bowers, *Chickamauga and Chattanooga*, 159–60, 168–69; Lytle, *Bedford Forrest and His Critter Company*, xxvi, 239.

21. Hurst, *Nathan Bedford Forrest*, 140–46.

22. Ibid., 147–55; Wills, *A Battle from the Start*, 158–68; William T. Sherman, *Memoirs of General William T. Sherman*, 2 vols. (1875; reprint ed., Bloomington: Indiana University Press, 1957), 1:387–95.

Chapter Two

A River of Blood

With Smith and Sherman out of the way for a while, Forrest gave his ragged riders a short rest while he conferred with his superiors, General Stephen Lee and General Leonidas Polk, in Demopolis, Alabama. Polk, the fighting Episcopal bishop, seemed to run hot and cold on Forrest, but for the moment he was pleased and awarded him three Kentucky regiments under the command of General Abraham Buford. But the new riders lacked horses, and the place to find horses was Kentucky, and that is where Forrest's command, or part of it, was headed. Leaving behind some troopers and artillery to protect Mississippi, Forrest and Buford, followed later by another new division commander, General James Chalmers, spread out and began moving into West Tennessee around March 16.[1]

Although the internal conflict had been worse in East Tennessee, where the prevailing sentiment had remained Unionist, the bloodletting was spilling over into the middle and western counties, which had become an American Bosnia, crisscrossed by invading armies and ravaged by partisan cutthroats and assorted desperadoes in their wake. After arriving in Jackson, Tennessee, on March 20, Forrest wrote Polk about the depredations committed in the area by Colonel Fielding Hurst, a Tennessee Unionist. Forrest charged Hurst and his "regiment of renegade Tennesseans," the U.S. Sixth Tennessee Cavalry, with crimes ranging from extortion and wanton destruction of property to torture of prisoners and outright murder. Confederate deserters, too, were reportedly mixed up in these alleged crimes, and one purpose of Forrest's raid was to round up these turncoats as well as those who had been avoiding military service.[2]

The first blow from Forrest's invasion force was delivered by Colonel W. L. Duckworth, who bluffed the commander of the Union garrison at Union City into surrendering his 479 troops and about 300 horses to the inferior force on March 24. The next day, Forrest and about 2,000 men from Buford's division struck at Paducah, Kentucky. Although he was able to capture valuable supplies and do some damage in the town, he was repulsed when he attempted to seize the Union earthwork fort near the Ohio River. Significantly, about one-third of the defending force was composed of 274 men of the First Kentucky Heavy Artillery. These soldiers, apparently the first black troops Forrest had engaged, gave a good account of themselves.

This embarrassing encounter might have been on the minds of Forrest and his storied fighters several weeks later at Fort Pillow. Nor were they indifferent to accounts in the Northern press that characterized Forrest's invaders as little more than a drunken mob of horse thieves and pillagers more interested in killing blacks than taking on the fort's gritty defenders. In fact, the papers claimed, the Confederates had made off with horses owned by Southern sympathizers and overlooked 140 government horses hidden in a foundry. While Buford returned to see if he could find the horses, simultaneously creating a diversion, Forrest drifted back toward Jackson, Tennessee. Colonel J. J. Neely of Chalmers's Division, meanwhile, had skirmished with Hurst's regiment between Bolivar and Somerville on March 29 and had driven it off toward Memphis after capturing a wagon train and ammunition. Forrest, with Union commanders trying to figure out his next foray, turned his attention toward Fort Pillow, which was located on a bluff on the eastern bank of Mississippi River some 50 miles north of Memphis. What happened there would become the most important element of the Forrest Myth.[3]

Fort Pillow needs to be understood in the context of the military situation in April 1864. Forrest boasted, in an April 4 letter to Polk, that he effectively held the entire region between the Mississippi and Tennessee Rivers in two states. He was beginning, also, to see what Sherman was up to: building up his supplies in Nashville, which suggested that he was going to drive south, perhaps heading this time for the Atlantic rather than the Gulf of Mexico. The way to stop Sherman, Forrest reasoned, was to get behind him and smash his communications. West Tennessee, therefore, could become a vital theater as the war entered what Forrest had already determined was its final phase. If he could keep himself supplied, he thought, he could draw off Federal troops, slow Sherman's advance, and even relieve some of the pressure on Lee in Virginia. Sherman seems to have credited Forrest with more insight than did

Forrest's commanders, who largely ignored him. To keep him contained, Sherman was counting on General Stephen A. Hurlbut, who was in Memphis, though he was anything but an aggressive commander.

While Forrest pondered the strategic chessboard, he was also concerned with local matters. In Jackson, the stories he heard about the Union garrison at Fort Pillow boiled his Rebel blood. Stationed there was the Thirteenth Tennessee Cavalry, a unit commanded by Major William F. Bradford, a lawyer who, like Forrest, was a native of Bedford Country, Tennessee. Jordan and Pryor, writing their biography of Forrest with the general's assistance, noted that Bradford's command included Confederate deserters and Tennessee Unionists who "had traversed the surrounding country with detachments, robbing the people of their horses, mules, beef cattle, beds, plates, wearing apparel, money, and every possible movable article of value, besides venting upon the wives and daughters of Southern soldiers the most opprobrious and obscene epithets, with more than one extreme outrage upon the persons of these victims of their hate and lust." Thus "grievously wronged, despoiled, and insulted, and in one or two cases fearfully outraged," the families of many of Forrest's soldiers and other Confederate loyalists in the vicinity asked Forrest for protection. (In relating the situation to Jordan and Pryor after the war, Forrest presumably used language considerably less circumspect in expressing his loathing for Bradford, Hurst, and other "homemade Yankees.")[4]

Added to this provocation was the related issue of black soldiers serving in the Union army. Early in the war, some Union commanders had attached escaping slaves to their forces in non-combat roles as "contraband," while others actually returned the slaves to their owners on the grounds that they had no legal authority to keep them. The situation in the border states was especially ambivalent. With the Federals penetrating more deeply into the South, the U.S. Congress had strengthened the president's authority to use blacks in the army in 1862 by passing the Second Confiscation Act and the Militia Act. The Confederate Congress countered the affront by mandating that white officers leading black units could be executed if captured and the slaves returned to their owners. Lincoln, sensitive to political realities, hesitated to take overt action on enlistment of blacks until after he issued the Emancipation Proclamation. The War Department then created the Bureau of Colored Troops in May 1863.

In the South, some free blacks had attempted to serve in Confederate militia units early in the war but were demobilized. In January 1864, Confederate general Patrick Cleburne proposed training slaves for military service, but Davis rejected the plan. Finally, on March 9, 1865, the Confederate Congress gave Davis the authority to enlist blacks, but by then the war was almost over, and no regularly enrolled black soldier ever actually went into battle for the Confederacy. The prospect of either confronting armed blacks or fighting beside them horrified most Southerners, rekindling images of the slave insurrections they had always feared. Forrest seems to have regarded blacks as nothing more than property, not soldiers, regardless of which side they were fighting for. Wills concludes that in Forrest's mind black troops in the Union army "were deluded miscreants, coerced from the fields by their new masters. But their current behavior, as misguided as it might be, could not be tolerated." Some of these black troops were stationed in Memphis under Hurlbut while Forrest lingered in Jackson, contemplating his move against Fort Pillow.[5]

On March 28, Hurlbut sent two black units—a battalion of the Sixth U.S. Heavy Artillery and a company of the Second U.S. Light Artillery—to Fort Pillow under the command of a white officer, 25-year-old Major Lionel Booth, who became the ranking officer at the fort. This addition brought its total troop strength to between 578 and 605 men, including 284 black soldiers. Ironically, the new troops had been sent in violation of Sherman's previous orders; on January 11, trying to consolidate his forces to strike deeper into the South, he had told Hurlbut to abandon Fort Pillow and some other rear-echelon garrisons. But for some reason Hurlbut moved Bradford's unit back into the fort after he had abandoned it and then, with Forrest in West Tennessee, moved Booth to Fort Pillow to support Bradford. He told Booth, however, that he doubted Forrest would be interested in menacing any of the river fortifications after his repulse at Paducah and promised to withdraw him as soon as Forrest crossed the Tennessee River. But Forrest knew that black troops had been moved to the fort, and some historians have speculated that because he had been roughly handled by the black troops defending Paducah, he had a double motivation to settle some scores at Fort Pillow. Whatever the case, he was now ready to move.[6]

On the afternoon of April 11, Forrest sent Chalmers west from Brownsville, some 40 miles from the fort, with two brigades commanded by Colonel Tyree Bell and Colonel Robert "Black Bob" McCulloch. Chalmers arrived early on the morning of April 12, driving in pickets and surprising Booth, who only a week before had told Hurlbut everything near the fort was "very quiet" and "perfectly safe." As Chalmers spread his men out to threaten the fort from several directions and positioned sharpshooters at key vantage points, Booth ordered an artillery barrage. About 9:00 A.M., Booth was killed by a bullet that struck him in the heart, and Bradford assumed command. Forrest arrived about an hour later and examined Chalmers's positions. While reconnoitering the lines he almost suffered Booth's fate, but the victim, as usual, was another of Forrest's short-lived steeds, which bucked its rider to the ground, reared, and fell over backward on top of him. Forrest mounted another horse, which was also shot and killed. Told by an adjutant that he was tempting fate by remaining mounted, Forrest reportedly said he could as easily be shot on foot as on horseback and could see better if mounted. His third horse was then shot but survived. Badly bruised but unbowed, Forrest continued to plan his assault on the fort.[7]

What happened next is one of the most studied and highly contentious episodes of the entire Civil War. The assault was the subject of U.S. Army and congressional investigations, and historians still grapple with the contradictory accounts. When most of the killing finally stopped late that afternoon, the Confederates had won a complete victory at a cost of about 100 casualties, including few more than a dozen dead. The exact number of Union dead is variously estimated at between 277 and 297. A more highly suggestive statistic is that the kill ratio for blacks was about double what it was for whites. Furthermore, in the aftermath of the battle a variety of witnesses—including Confederates—described atrocities: men, some of whom had surrendered or were wounded, nailed to a floor, burned alive, buried alive, bayoneted through the eyes, hacked apart with swords, bludgeoned to death, or shot at close range; women and children in or near the fort killed; Bradford captured and reportedly murdered. Meeting with his cabinet on May 3, Lincoln said it was "now quite certain that a large number of our colored soldiers, with their white officers, were, by the rebel force, massacred after they had surrendered, at the capture of Fort Pillow." Forrest himself later reported that many Union soldiers had jumped into the Mississippi River, where they were shot and drowned. "The river," he said, "was dyed with the blood of the slaughtered for 200 yards." The stain of blood, however, was also a stain on the Forrest Myth that began spreading almost immediately after the battle and would, according to a 2001 article in *Confederate Veteran*, "make Forrest a monster beyond redemption in the eyes of many, even to this day."[8]

"THERE MUST BE SOMETHING IN THESE REPORTS"

When Forrest had looked north that spring morning, he saw a horseshoe-shaped, earth-walled fortification about 70 yards wide situated on a clay bluff that overlooked a bend in the Mississippi River and a creek that flowed into it. The thick walls of the fort were about the height of a standing soldier. To reach the fort, the attackers would have to cross a deep, 12-foot-wide ditch and scale a ragged ledge while its defenders could stand on a bench behind the parapet and shoot at them. Farther outside the breastworks, Forrest's 1,500 Confederates also had to cross two deep ravines, trenches, rifle pits, and other obstacles. Nearer the fort stood a series of buildings that served as barracks, a hospital, supply centers, and the kind of commercial establishments that usually surround an army post. Below the bluff, under the command of Captain James Marshall, a 137-foot-long, wood-burning U.S. gunboat called the *New Era* held steady in the current of the narrow river channel. Marshall could just see the fort, which stood at the top of a steep slope about 100 feet above the river, while three 24-pound howitzers lobbed 5-inch shells and shrapnel toward the Confederate positions. Although he would fire more than 260 rounds that day, Marshall had to sight his guns on the basis of signals relayed to him from the fort, and the inaccurate shelling that resulted caused the Confederates little inconvenience. Their return fire, however, caused him constantly to shift position and realign his guns. Throughout the morning and early afternoon, Forrest methodically worked his troops in closer and captured the exposed outbuildings, exploiting various weaknesses in the fort's defenses and awaiting the arrival of his ammunition wagons. At about 3:30 P.M. he thought he could get the fort to surrender and sent Booth a message offering to treat all its defenders as prisoners of war. Forrest did not know Booth was dead, and Bradford saw no need to tell him when he asked, in Booth's name, for an hour to consider the proposal.[9]

Out on the river, meanwhile, things were happening. Forrest's scouts on the bluff had seen several steamers coming toward the fort, one of which seemed to be carrying troops. Marshall waved two of the steamers past the fort as a third turned back, but Forrest was suspicious and began moving troops to repel any kind of landing along the river; later, he would be charged with taking advantage of the brief truce to further envelop the fort. Perhaps thinking that "Booth" was trying to stall until the gunboats could maneuver into a favorable position, he demanded the fort's surrender in twenty minutes. More messages were exchanged, and then Forrest was handed a final refusal to surrender.

Just what was going on in the fort at the time is disputed. In his history of black troops in the Civil War, Noah Andre Trudeau observes that "there is nothing in the historical record to suggest that the attitudes of the pro-Union whites in the 13th Tennessee Cavalry differed markedly from those held by their neighbors serving under Forrest." At Fort Pillow, the two commands were segregated before the battle; in other words, racism was not peculiar to one side of the ramparts or the other. But the extent to which that racism manifested itself in battle, and in the memory of the battle, is another matter. Wyeth, writing at the end of the nineteenth century, claimed that the soldiers in the fort had been given whiskey. "To those familiar with the two classes, black and white, which composed the private soldiers in the garrison at Fort Pillow, and their fondness for intoxicating drinks, especially so with the Negroes just free from slavery, it will readily be accepted that they did not fail to take advantage of the opportunities here offered to drink to excess," he wrote, which is a polite and long-winded way of saying what he really meant—that blacks and low-class white Tennesseans could not hold their liquor or control themselves. The state of their intoxication, according to Wyeth, was confirmed after the battle by none other than Forrest, Chalmers, and their colonels, putative gentlemen all. Drunken men behave badly, of course, so it was not surprising, according to Lytle, that "some of the negroes had been shooting during the truce. Others had been jeering, making grimaces, and doing insulting things with their hands." According to Wyeth, Union troops, "especially the colored soldiers," shouted at the Confederates, "daring them to try to take the fort, and hurling epithets at them couched in most obscene and abusive terms and accompanied by gestures and actions not to be described."

Mathes, who recounts the "reckless and insane" defense of Fort Pillow, also refers to "ignorant, half-drunken creatures" cavorting on the ramparts. The effect of such provocation on Forrest's troops can easily be imagined.[10]

But Richard L. Fuchs, in a more modern study of the battle, argues than the drunken-garrison theory is a fabrication: "The ad hominem appeal to racial prejudice and a remonstrance that has its basis in the purported impeccable authority of self-serving declarants is hardly anchored in logic and fact." Furthermore, he quotes a surgeon in the fort as stating in an 1879 letter that there was "considerable alcohol outside the fort, which Forrest's men must have got hold of long before the charge was made."[11]

In any case, the charge *was* made: the Confederates swarmed over the walls, and the slaughter commenced. Bradford reportedly panicked and told his troops to run for the bluff. Some kind of fallback plan had been worked out between Booth and Marshall in the event of just such a rout. In theory, at least, retreating soldiers might have been able to get down to the river under the covering fire of the gunboat and then make a last stand before being evacuated from their predicament relatively unmolested. Apparently, though, there was no possibility of the gunboat cannonading the cliffs without further slaughtering Union troops with "friendly fire."

Those investigating the battle have looked for answers to critical questions. Was there a surrender? Did Forrest order a massacre or did he try to stop it? Were black soldiers singled out for slaughter? Some reports had Forrest ordering the massacre. Others had Forrest running between his men and the fleeing Unionists and stopping the slaughter, even killing one of his own soldiers for refusing to give quarter.

The Northern press reaction bordered on the hysterical, and Forrest became the scapegoat not only for the Fort Pillow incident but for the entire Confederate policy toward blacks in the Union army. The Southern press and the Richmond government discounted the reports, and on May 23 the Confederate Congress issued a joint resolution thanking Forrest and his troops for their "brilliant and successful campaign" during the previous month. The subsequent congressional investigation left little doubt that a massacre had occurred or that Forrest and the Confederate government bore the ultimate responsibility. Considering that the investigation took place during 1868, a Federal election year, however, its propaganda value was significant. Lincoln's navy secretary,

Gideon Welles, rendered the opinion that there "must be something in these terrible reports, but I distrust Congressional committees. They exaggerate."[12]

Harper's Weekly's "Fort Pillow Massacre" shows Confederate soldiers executing unarmed blacks and Federal troops. Although exactly what happened at Fort Pillow is open to debate, such renditions helped to fix in the public mind the conviction that an atrocity had taken place. In this drawing, all of the advancing Confederates are armed, while weapons are absent from the hands of the Union troops. From *Harper's Weekly*, April 30, 1864.

SILVER SPURS AND SAVAGE TREACHERY

But did they exaggerate? The Forrest Myth is a collective response to that unanswerable question shaped by the point of view of the mythmakers. A reporter from the *St. Louis Missouri Democrat* who arrived on the scene immediately after the battle wrote, "I have witnessed many revolting results of war, but can assure your readers that the conduct of the rebels, towards our little garrison at Fort Pillow, beggars all description, for fiendish brutality and savage treachery." Yet Jordan and Pryor claimed in 1868 that there was "neither cruel purpose or cruel negligence of duty, neither intention nor inadvertence, on the part of General Forrest, whose course, therefore, stands utterly devoid of the essence of outrage or wrong." Even Sherman was as generous in his memoirs, published in 1875: "No doubt Forrest's men acted like a set of barbarians, shooting down the helpless negro garrison after the fort was in their

possession; but I am told that Forrest personally disclaims any active participation in the assault, and that he stopped the firing as
soon as he could. I also take it for granted that Forrest did not lead
the assault in person, and consequently that he was to the rear, out
of sight if not of hearing at the time, and I was told by hundreds of
our men, who were at various times prisoners in Forrest's possession, that he was usually very kind to them."

Wolseley, in his 1892 articles about Forrest, initially refused to
take sides in the controversy but then dismissed Northern press
accounts like that of the *Missouri Democrat* as a "skillful seasoning
of horrors which only those can equal who are accustomed to prepare these sort of repasts for the public, or who have some party
object to accomplish." Wyeth, writing in 1899, concluded that the
incidents reported by Congress were "greatly exaggerated and cleverly distorted" and that "it must be clear that there was no massacre as charged." Eckenrode, in 1918, could hardly commend Forrest
to his youthful readers without some sort of explanation about Fort
Pillow, so, perhaps relying on Jordan and Pryor and on Wyeth, he
simply denies the findings of the congressional investigation and
says the "killing of the negro troops was chiefly due to their failure
to surrender." Forrest "was not to blame. He was without the fort
when the fighting took place; the moment he entered it the struggle
ended, and he showed great kindness to the prisoners."[13]

Lytle, in 1931, says little about Fort Pillow, claiming that the
charges against Forrest were all propaganda and noting the insig-
nificant detail that he was rewarded later in Brownsville by women
who sent him a pair of silver spurs made from thimbles. Henry,
writing in 1944, gives a fuller account of the battle but frames the
massacre theory as the sort of atrocity story that had been invented
during World War I. Writing in *Civil War History* in 1958, Albert
Castel reviewed the evidence and, though he stopped short of claiming that Forrest had ordered the massacre, concluded that his troops
did kill "a large number of the garrison after they had either ceased
resisting or were incapable of resisting." He included the essay in
an anthology published in 1996 and claimed that before its publication "all biographers of Forrest, and for that matter the majority
of Civil War historians, denied that there was a massacre at Fort
Pillow. I am confident that no competent historian will ever again
make such a denial."

By that time, Fuchs had produced a book-length study of the
battle, and Wills and Hurst had published their biographies of

Forrest, extensively vetting the Fort Pillow controversy. According to Fuchs, "Forrest intended a massacre at Fort Pillow because he was obeying the higher law of a government that encouraged and sanctioned such barbarity." Wills concludes that Fort Pillow became "a collective release of pent-up anger and hatred. It became, in clinical terms, a group catharsis. And as the overall commander of the troops on the scene, some of whom carried out these acts, Nathan Bedford Forrest was responsible." Hurst says that even if Forrest did not actually order a massacre, "he probably didn't have to; there was enough rancor between his men and the armed former slaves, as well as the Tennessee Unionists, that about all he had to do to produce a massacre was issue no order against one."[14]

Although it is doubtful that this logic would convict Forrest at a modern war crimes tribunal, it illustrates the problem faced by the general's apologists. If Forrest cannot be exonerated, he still stands indicted by history. And Hurst adds an important point when he says that the Fort Pillow assault "is notable not only for its intrinsic ugliness but because it can be viewed as a prelude to other horrors. . . . As the [Ku Klux] Klan's first national leader, [Forrest] became the Lost Cause's avenging angel, galvanizing a loose collection of boyish secret social clubs into a reactionary instrument of terror still feared today." James D. Lockett goes further, characterizing Fort Pillow as a crime against humanity, a military lynching, and the South's first shot in a war to maintain white supremacy in a defeated Confederacy.[15]

"WE WILL RIDE RIGHT OVER THEM"

But the Confederacy was not defeated quite yet in that bloody spring of 1864. After Fort Pillow, Forrest returned to Mississippi. He had little time to refresh his ranks before he was facing another adversary. Sherman, still worried about his lines of communication and what Forrest might do to them, had ordered General Samuel Sturgis to march out of Memphis, strike the Mobile and Ohio Railroad below Corinth in northern Mississippi, lay waste to the region's croplands (rich with field corn and grain nourished by spring rains), push the prowling Forrest off his supply lines as he marched through Georgia, and dispatch the "Wizard of the Saddle." On June 1, Sturgis was on his way with 5,000 infantry and artillerists—including 1,200 revanchist black soldiers ready to avenge Fort Pillow—plus 250 wagons and twenty-two artillery pieces. Joining the expedition were 3,300 cavalry under the command of General Benjamin Grierson, who had led a daring raid through Mississippi in 1863, later depicted in the 1959 film *The Horse Soldiers*, starring John Wayne.

This was no movie, however, and Forrest was facing formidable odds. Without knowing where Sturgis was going, he spread his 4,800 troopers across the muddy Mississippi backcountry and looked for an opportunity to strike. Swatting mayflies and mosquitoes in the stifling heat as he rode beside Colonel Edward Rucker toward Brice's Cross Roads, near Tishomingo Creek, he outlined a plan that would use the weather and topography to his advantage: "I know they greatly outnumber the troops I have at hand, but the road along which they will march is narrow and muddy; they will make slow progress. The country is densely wooded and the undergrowth so heavy that when we strike them they will not know how few men we have. Their cavalry will move out ahead of the infantry, and should reach the crossroads three hours in advance. We can whip their cavalry in that time. As soon as the fight opens they will send back to have the infantry hurried up. It is going to be as hot as hell, and coming on a run for five or six miles over such roads, their infantry will be so tired out we will ride right over them."[16]

Early on the morning of June 10, some of Grierson's cavalry scattered Confederate skirmishers at a small wooden bridge over Tishomingo Creek and then ran into Colonel H. B. Lyon's brigade in a tangled thicket of blackjack and scrub oak trees near the crossroads. Forrest arrived and took command while he awaited the arrival of Rucker, Colonel W. A. Johnson, and Colonel Tyree Bell. The outnumbered Confederates held on through hand-to-hand fighting, and at a critical point in the battle, Forrest rallied his retreating troops and ordered a charge that drove the Federals back just as the sweating infantrymen arrived after a four-mile forced march. As Forrest had predicted, they were in no condition to put up much of a fight. With Buford now on the field and commanding Forrest's right wing, and with Bell on the left, Forrest sent his 4,800 troopers forward while Captain John Morton's batteries raked the fraying Union infantry lines with grape and canister. Meanwhile, Colonel Clark Barteau had worked his way into the Union rear and the outflanked Federals began pouring back across Tishomingo Creek.

Colonel Edward Bouton, commanding the Fifty-fifth and Fifty-ninth U.S. Colored Infantry and a two-gun battery of the Second

U.S. Colored Light Artillery, got his men into position on some high ground and covered the retreat, possibly saving Sturgis from total destruction. One of Forrest's troopers, Lieutenant William Witherspoon, later recalled that the Confederates "were feeling pretty well fagged out, but when the cry rang out, 'Here are the damned negroes,' new life, energy and action coursed through our bodies and we bounded forward." Forrest hammered the Union rear, driving Sturgis back across the Hatchie River, where he is said

Forrest's cavalry captures a battery. From H. J. Eckenrode, *Life of Nathan B. Forrest* (Richmond, VA: B. F. Johnson Publishing Company, 1918).

to have told Bouton, "For God's sake, if Mr. Forrest will let me alone I will let him alone. You have done all you could and more than was expected of you, and now all you can do is to save yourselves." Forrest chased the retreating Federals all the way to La Grange, Tennessee, and when it was all over, the Federals reported 223 men killed, 394 wounded, and 1,623 missing. Forrest had ninety-six men killed and 396 wounded. Bouton's brigade reported 110 men killed, 134 wounded, and 168 missing. Casualties among the black soldiers had been heavy, because, according to Wills, "Forrest lost control of the actions of many of the individuals in his command."

If so, it was Forrest who thought himself the aggrieved party. On June 14 he wrote General Cadwallader C. Washburn, the new

Federal commander in Memphis, complaining that the black troops who had marched into Mississippi under Sturgis had reportedly been exhorted to avenge Fort Pillow by giving no quarter to Forrest's soldiers. Accordingly, he said, casualties on both sides had been higher than they needed to be because neither side felt safe in surrendering. When Washburn replied than the Fort Pillow affair fully justified the desperation and determination exhibited by the black soldiers, Forrest countered by denying that he had intentionally slaughtered the Fort Pillow garrison and adding that treatment of captured black soldiers was a matter to be determined by the respective governments, not individual officers. [17]

"IS FORREST SURELY DEAD?"

Forrest's victory at Brice's Cross Roads was his singular masterpiece as a commander. Sherman fumed, writing Secretary of War Edwin Stanton, "I cannot understand how he could defeat Sturgis with 8,000 men." Still determined to knock Forrest out of the war, Sherman sacked Sturgis and promised he would send Generals Andrew Jackson Smith and Joseph Mower to "follow Forrest to the death if it costs 10,000 lives and breaks the Treasury. There will never be peace in Tennessee till Forrest is dead." All this uproar added even more luster to the Forrest Myth: "No more splendid victory was won in the whole war," wrote Eckenrode; Lytle proclaimed that no other Civil War battle had seen such hard fighting or a more crushing victory; and Wolseley, with characteristic understatement, called it "a most remarkable achievement, well worth attention by the military student." Grant, in his memoirs, said Forrest had handled Sturgis "very roughly, gaining a great victory over him. This left Forrest free to go almost where he pleased, and to cut the roads in the rear of Sherman, who was then advancing."[18]

Cut supply lines were, of course, what Sherman feared, and Forrest might have made a difference had Davis and Bragg ordered him into Tennessee to trouble the peace behind Sherman rather than keeping him in Mississippi under his cautious departmental commander, General Stephen D. Lee. This order, Steven Woodworth has argued persuasively, "was sheer folly for the Confederacy, for whom Mississippi had become a backwater and Georgia the scene of life-and-death struggle." Meanwhile, Smith and Grierson moved out of Memphis in late June with 14,000 infantry and cavalry, bumping into Forrest and Lee at the abandoned town of Harrisburg near

Tupelo on July 14, which was not what Forrest wanted or expected; he had wanted to draw Smith into a trap below Pontotoc. But Smith was proving a more wily opponent than Sturgis. He had turned east toward the Mobile and Ohio Railroad and dug in while Lee and Forrest bickered about the best way to get at him. Lee ordered charges into the Union lines throughout the morning of the 14th, followed by a rare night attack, none of which was successful. The next day, Smith pulled back toward Memphis, with Forrest in pursuit. Near Old Town Creek, Forrest was struck by a minié ball that passed through the sole of his right foot, temporarily incapacitating him as Smith slipped away. The engagement had been costly for the Confederates. Smith and Grierson had destroyed large quantities of supplies, torn up the railroad around Tupelo, and inflicted 1,326 casualties, about twice their own losses. Forrest often had been listless and out-of-sorts throughout the campaign and was unable to work effectively under Lee. The real winner was Sherman, who was by then at the gates of Atlanta facing a new Confederate commander, General John Bell Hood.[19]

While Forrest recuperated from a multitude of ailments in a Tupelo hospital, rumors began circulating that he had died of lockjaw. "Is Forrest surely dead?" asked Sherman, who probably believed he would never be rid of his old adversary until he first drove a stake through his heart. Knowing the effect these rumors were having on his own troops, Forrest managed to get up from his bed, mount his horse, and "like El Cid in Spanish lore," according to Wills, gallop splendidly in his shirtsleeves through the ranks among his rejoicing troopers. Dead or alive, to friend and foe alike, Forrest now fully embodied the Forrest Myth. And although for the next month he had to bear the humiliation of being hauled around in a buggy with his crippled foot elevated on a board, he had shown that if he was no longer a Heracles, he was yet an Achilles.[20]

He would need to be an Achilles to meet Smith's next advance into Mississippi, this time coming south with 20,000 men. His columns moved out of Memphis on July 28, following the Mississippi Central Railroad and crossing the Tallahatchie River above Oxford on August 9. Rain slowed the advance for the next week, giving Forrest time to concentrate some forces at Oxford. On August 18, realizing he could not hold off Smith for long with 4,000 men, he divided his forces, leaving Chalmers with orders to bluff Smith into thinking he was facing heavier resistance, while Forrest took a detachment west to Panola and then made a dash north toward

Memphis. In the early morning hours of August 21, a Sunday, Forrest and about 1,500 riders, including two of his brothers, swarmed into the streets of the heavily garrisoned city. Captain Bill Forrest rode his horse right into the lobby of the Gayoso House, the hotel where he expected to find General Hurlbut, who was spending the night elsewhere. Lieutenant Colonel Jesse Forrest, meanwhile, made for Washburn's headquarters, but the West Tennessee district commander had already scurried off in his night-clothes. Other raiders located the quarters of General R. P. Buckland, the garrison commander, but he had rushed to a barracks and fired an alarm. Unfortunately for the Confederates, all three prize blue-birds had flown the coop, and the Rebels had to ride out of town without netting the generals.

The raid resulted in 480 Union casualties, mostly prisoners taken by Forrest, whereas twenty-two Confederates had been killed, about fifteen wounded, and twenty-five captured. What damage Forrest had done in Memphis was primarily psychological. Chalmers had pulled out of Oxford, but not before attacking Smith and convincing him that Forrest had been reinforced. Smith settled for burning much of the city and then retiring to Memphis with Chalmers snapping at his rear columns. Another Mississippi invasion had been turned back, but Sherman would soon be in Atlanta. Meanwhile, in Memphis, the grand jury of the Circuit Court of the United States for the District of West Tennessee, noting that Forrest had appeared in the city on August 21 "with guns, swords, pistols and other war like weapons," as well as causing much mischief on other occasions, indicted him for treason and ordered a U.S. marshal to arrest him.[21]

FROM CORINTH TO CHICAGO AND CAPITULATION

Forrest had more mischief in mind and set about planning yet another raid into Tennessee. On September 16 he left Corinth on a 500-mile sweep through Alabama and Middle Tennessee with 4,500 troopers, an action that resulted, after some hard fighting, in the capture of 2,360 Union soldiers, 800 horses, weapons, and much valuable provender, plus the destruction of parts of the Nashville and Decatur Railroad. Relentlessly pursued and usually badly out-numbered, he returned to Corinth on October 12, physically exhausted. But a week later he was again on his way to Tennessee.[22]

Meanwhile, Atlanta had fallen on September 2, and Hood, who had replaced General Joseph Johnston as commander of the Army of Tennessee on July 17, soon began a westward flanking movement originally intended to cut off Sherman's supply lines between Nashville and Chattanooga. In mid-October, however, Hood concocted a delusional plan to march to Nashville, resupply his army, and then amble through Kentucky to threaten Cincinnati. He envisioned a turn through the Cumberland Gap and on into Virginia, where he could relieve the besieged Lee at Richmond, and then the combined forces could either march on Washington or turn south to defeat Sherman and end the war. On October 19 the Army of Tennessee was on the move, and by November 21 it was across the Tennessee River with Forrest's cavalry at Tuscumbia, Alabama. Sherman, meanwhile, had left Atlanta on November 16 and was on his way to the sea, believing he could detach himself from his base of operations at Nashville and live off the land as he pillaged Georgia.[23]

Before joining Hood at Tuscumbia, however, Forrest had launched one of his boldest raids. On October 24 he headed north from Jackson, Tennessee, with Buford and Chalmers, and by October 29, while Hood was marching through Alabama, he was at the west bank of the Tennessee River between Fort Heiman and Paris Landing, about 10 miles from the Kentucky state line. Deploying some 3,500 cavalry and infantry, Forrest captured a steamboat and several transports in a well-executed artillery ambush. Using the vessels as a diversion while he moved his horsemen south, he secretly positioned ten cannons 1,100 feet across the river from Johnsonville, a heavily fortified supply depot at the terminus of the Nashville and Northwestern Railroad. On November 4, Forrest's gunners opened fire on three gunboats, eleven transports, and eighteen barges from Ohio and Mississippi river ports.

Union forces in this engagement numbered about 2,000 men. Assuming that Forrest was ready to cross the river with more than 13,000 troops, the Union commanders burned the vessels to prevent them from being captured; fanned by a strong wind blowing across the levee, the fire spread to the docks and warehouses. Further, the Federal batteries positioned in fortifications above the depot could not be depressed sufficiently to eliminate the well-entrenched guns across the river. In the resulting confusion the stationmaster headed east with a train loaded with supplies and

400 men, some of whom had looted the stores. The blazing docks and warehouses illuminated the river sufficiently to enable Forrest to evacuate his positions and move most of his forces six miles south. An artillery detachment left behind as a rear guard continued shelling the town the next morning, and by the time Union reinforcements arrived, Forrest's artillery had been removed. It was one of the most extraordinary raids of the war. Forrest's movements caused panic, and rumors had him in disguise in Chicago and Canada, or moving on Chicago with a huge army to sack that city. General Joseph Hooker, who commanded the Northern Department at Cincinnati, took such reports seriously enough to move troops from Indianapolis and St. Louis to defend Chicago.[24]

"QUEER DOINGS" IN THE REBEL LINES

Hooker's fear that Forrest might actually orchestrate some kind of Chancellorsville in Chicago and drive the Union armies into Lake Michigan suggests the potency of the Forrest Myth, even this late in the war. Lytle was convinced that Forrest at that moment was the one man in the South "around whom the people, especially the plain people, and the army would have rallied." But the moment belonged not to Forrest but to Hood, who envisioned the final Götterdämmerung in Virginia as Hood and Lee commanding the combined forces of the Army of Tennessee and the Army of Northern Virginia in the glorious battle that would save the Confederacy. But first Hood had to get to Nashville. With Forrest in command of his cavalry, a force of about 6,000 men, Hood planned to place his 40,000 troops around a 25,000-man Federal army commanded by General John Schofield, which was blocking his way at Pulaski, Tennessee; he intended to cut off Schofield before he could cross the Duck River at Columbia and join General George Thomas, who was trying to concentrate his scattered forces at Nashville. Schofield, however, got to Columbia first, and then started evacuating the town in a snowstorm on November 28. Forrest, meanwhile, was seizing fords across the Duck River east of Columbia, and fighting Union cavalry commanded by General James Wilson.

Once across the Duck, Hood tried to get his army up to Spring Hill ahead of Schofield, but again the Federals managed to get there before him. Just why this happened, or what Hood would have done if he had gotten there first or blocked the Federal advance, is an enigma and much disputed, but historians at least agree that there was a series of confusing orders, and Hood's advance was badly coordinated. Forrest tried to hold the turnpike on which Schofield was advancing and capture the town after a day of hard fighting, but he had insufficient ammunition and wasn't clear as to what Hood wanted him to do. Hood evidently went to bed believing that Forrest did hold the turnpike north of Spring Hill, thus preventing Schofield from advancing to Franklin during the night of November 29. But on the morning of November 30, Hood discovered that Schofield had slipped past his army.

What happened that night has been the subject of rumor

The last military photograph of Forrest. From James Dickins, *Personal Recollections and Experiences in the Confederate Army, 1861–1865* (Cincinnati: Robert Clarke Company, 1897).

and conjecture. One story has it that Hood was drunk or doped up on laudanum; others, that Cheatham, his lead corps commander, and several division commanders were drunk. Rumors allege that Cheatham and Forrest may have dallied with an attractive widow at her home in Spring Hill, and a Union colonel later wrote of "queer doings in the rebel lines among some of the leading officers," including drinking and dancing and revelry at the home of the aforementioned widow. Whatever happened that night, the next day was one of the most tragic of the war for the Confederacy.[25]

Although technically Schofield was retreating, he was actually moving closer to the fortified city of Nashville and the succor of Thomas, the "Rock of Chickamauga." With Forrest still chasing him on the morning of November 30, Schofield determined to make a stand at Franklin on the Harpeth River. In order to storm Schofield's breastworks in front of the town, the Confederates would have to make a charge that looked practically suicidal to Hood's senior commanders. Forrest suggested a flanking movement, but Hood was determined to fight it out at Franklin, reasoning that he had a better chance to dislodge the Union army from a position they had hastily fortified than to fight them at Nashville. Historians have advanced many reasons why Hood ordered such an attack. James Lee McDonough and Thomas L. Connelly suggest that "attack was all that Hood knew. It was, again, the pattern of a life, molded into his personality years before the Civil War. . . . Hood wanted to be a Lee. The irony is that Hood did not realize that the war had changed even Lee's mode of combat."[26]

While Hood's brigades formed for battle at about 2:00 P.M., Forrest crossed the river on the far right of the Confederate lines, sending Chalmers to the far left. Schofield apparently had little confidence that Wilson, his cavalry commander, could handle Forrest, but this time Wilson surprised him, driving Forrest's divided force back across the river while Chalmers was bottled up at the other end of the line. Wilson later claimed Forrest had made a fatal mistake by dividing his forces, giving Wilson the opportunity to put more troopers into action on one wing and preventing Forrest from getting behind Schofield's army. "For once," according to Winston Groom, "Forrest had not lived up to his reputation or, for that matter, to Hood's expectation." But it might not have mattered anyway. Hood's charge was a disaster, costing the Confederates 6,252 casualties, including the lives of five generals; the Federals suffered 2,326 casualties. Schofield's army reached Nashville by noon the next day, skirmishing with the pursuing Forrest, who spent the night within sight of the capital.

Now, Hood faced 60,000 entrenched troops with a battered army half that size. But Forrest would not be in the Nashville fight. Hood sent him off toward Murfreesboro to destroy the Nashville and Chattanooga Railroad while Chalmers stayed behind. Reinforced by infantry under the command of General William B. Bate, Forrest struck Murfreesboro on December 6–7. When a Federal charge routed the infantry, he rode in among the fleeing soldiers and shot a color-bearer who refused to halt. Taking up the colors, Forrest finally rallied the troops, pummeling panicked soldiers with the flagstaff and the back of his saber, and remained near Murfreesboro until learning that Thomas had defeated Hood's army at Nashville. At a crossing over the Duck River, Forrest had an altercation with Cheatham, and it was only the intervention of Stephen Lee that prevented a battle between the two Tennesseans and their respective forces. Forrest then covered the stampede of Hood's army all the way back across the Tennessee River on December 27 after a sharp skirmish with Federal cavalry on Christmas Eve.[27]

"THAT WE ARE BEATEN IS A SELF-EVIDENT FACT"

General Richard Taylor assumed command on January 13, 1865, of what was left of Hood's army. On January 24, Forrest was put in command of all cavalry in Alabama, Mississippi, and eastern Louisiana, a scattered force of about 10,000 men. He established his headquarters at Verona, Mississippi, and on February 28 he was promoted to lieutenant general. He had less than a month to prepare to fight Wilson, who swept into Alabama on March 22 with 15,000 cavalry. With his forces scattered and Wilson advancing, Forrest threw up a defensive line on April 1 at Ebenezer Church near Bolger's Creek in the wooded hills about 20 miles above Selma. He may have had as few as 1,500 men, including some untested militia, in position to stop Wilson's 9,000 troopers, but he was in the thick of the fighting and at one point was surrounded by a half-dozen soldiers intent on killing him. A Union captain, James D. Taylor, charged at Forrest, who was mounted on his favorite horse, King Phillip, and, after a running fight of some 200 yards, slashed him on the arm with a saber before the general managed to shoot him. The Confederates retreated to Selma, one of the South's primary industrial centers, where again Forrest had to improvise, garrisoning the city with militia, civilians, and the remnants of his own battered brigades. By the evening of April 2, Wilson had broken through the city's defenses, and Forrest and his generals barely escaped.

Richmond fell that same day, and Lee, Johnston, and Taylor soon surrendered. "As Wilson rattled around inside its skeleton, the Confederacy fell apart," wrote Hurst. Early in May, the governors of Mississippi and Tennessee urged Forrest to try to fight on with General Edmund Kirby Smith across the Mississippi River. Forrest's response: "Any man who is in favor of a further prosecution of this war is a fit subject for a lunatic asylum, and ought to be sent there immediately." He had often been called a devil, but he was no lunatic. On May 9, at Gainesville, Alabama, he said farewell to his troops. "That we are beaten is a self-evident fact, and any further resistance on our part would be justly regarded as the very height of folly and rashness. . . . I have never on the field of battle sent you where I was unwilling to go myself, nor would I now advise you to a course which I felt myself unwilling to pursue. You have been good soldiers, you can be good citizens. Obey the laws, preserve your honor, and the government to which you have surrendered can afford to be and will be magnanimous."

For Bedford Forrest, the war was over. The Forrest Myth was only just beginning.[28]

NOTES

1. Hurst, *Nathan Bedford Forrest*, 155–57.

2. Digby Gordon Seymour, *Divided Loyalties: Fort Sanders and the Civil War in East Tennessee*, 3d ed. (Knoxville: East Tennessee Historical Society, 2002), 3.

3. Henry, *"First with the Most" Forrest*, 242; Hurst, *Nathan Bedford Forrest*, 160–64.

4. Hurst, *Nathan Bedford Forrest*, 161–63; Jordan and Pryor, *The Campaigns of General Nathan Bedford Forrest*, 422–23.

5. Noah Andre Trudeau, *Like Men of War: Black Troops in the Civil War, 1862–1865* (Boston: Little, Brown and Company, 1998), 8–13, 60–62, 409; Wills, *A Battle from the Start*, 180.

6. Richard L. Fuchs, *An Unerring Fire: The Massacre at Fort Pillow* (Rutherford, NJ: Fairleigh Dickinson University Press, 1994), 43, 48–49, 101; John Cimprich and Robert C. Mainfort Jr., "The Fort Pillow Massacre: A Statistical Note," *Journal of American History* 76 (December 1989): 835–37; Trudeau, *Like Men of War*, 158–62; Hurst, *Nathan Bedford Forrest*, 165.

7. Trudeau, *Like Men of War*, 160; Fuchs, *An Unerring Fire*, 51; Hurst, *Nathan Bedford Forrest*, 168; Henry, *"First with the Most" Forrest*, 252.

8. Fuchs, *An Unerring Fire*, 23, 69, 104–25; Cimprich and Mainfort, "The Fort Pillow Massacre," 835–37; Albert E. Castel, "The Fort Pillow Massacre: A Fresh Examination of the Evidence," in Albert E. Castel, *Winning and Losing in the Civil War: Essays and Stories* (Columbia: University of South Carolina Press, 1996), 35–50; Trudeau, *Like Men of War*, 168; Paul M. Angle and Earl Schneck Meir, *Tragic Years, 1860–1865: A Documentary History of the American Civil War*, 2 vols. (New York: Simon and Schuster, 1960), 2:754; Hurst, *Nathan Bedford Forrest*, 175; John L. Jordan, "Was There a Massacre at Fort Pillow?" *Tennessee Historical Quarterly* 6 (June 1947): 99–133; Bruce Tap, " 'These Devils Are Not Fit to Live on God's Earth': War Crimes and the Committee on the Conduct of the War, 1864–1865," *Civil War History* 17 (1966): 116–32; Eddy W. Davison and Daniel Foxx, "A Journey to the Most Controversial Battlefield in America," *Confederate Veteran* 6 (2001): 33.

9. Fuchs, *An Unerring Fire*, 46–53; Hurst, *Nathan Bedford Forrest*, 173.

10. Hurst, *Nathan Bedford Forrest*, 169–71; Trudeau, *Like Men of War*, 161–63; Wyeth, *That Devil Forrest*, 322–24; Lytle, *Bedford Forrest and His Critter Company*, 278; Henry, *"First with the Most" Forrest*, 264–65; Mathes, *General Forrest*, 227.

11. Fuchs, *An Unerring Fire*, 117–18.

12. Ibid.; Hurst, *Nathan Bedford Forrest*, 171–80; Tap, " 'These Devils Are Not Fit to Live on God's Earth,' " 116–25.

13. *Missouri Democrat*, as reprinted in the *Philadelphia Inquirer*, April 20, 1864, quoted in Trudeau, *Like Men of War*, 157; Jordan and Pryor, *The Campaigns of General Nathan Bedford Forrest*, 453; William T. Sherman, *Memoirs of General William T. Sherman*, 2:12–13; Woseley, "General Forrest" and *New Orleans Picayune*; Henry, *As They Saw Forrest*, 44; Wyeth, *That Devil Forrest*, 337–38; Eckenrode, *Life of Nathan B. Forrest*, 101.

14. Lytle, *Bedford Forrest and His Critter Company*, 280–81; Henry, *"First with the Most" Forrest*, 248–68; Castel, *Winning and Losing in the Civil War*, 35–50; Fuchs, *An Unerring Fire*, 157; Wills, *A Battle from the Start*, 196; Hurst, *Nathan Bedford Forrest*, 177.

15. Hurst, *Nathan Bedford Forrest*, 6; James D. Lockett, "The Lynching Massacre of Black and White Soldiers at Fort Pillow, Tennessee, April 12, 1864," *Western Journal of Black Studies* 22 (Summer 1998): 84–93.

16. Hurst, *Nathan Bedford Forrest*, 182–87; Wyeth, *That Devil Forrest*, 350.

17. Henry, *As They Saw Forrest*, 124; Hurst, *Nathan Bedford Forrest*, 182–95; Wyeth, *That Devil Forrest*, 349–71; Trudeau, *Like Men of War*, 170–81; Henry, *"First with the Most" Forrest*, 286–300; Wills, *A Battle from the Start*, 204–15; *OR*, ser. 1:32, pt. 1, 586–91.

18. *OR*, ser. 1:39, pt. 2, 121; Trudeau, *Like Men of War*, 181; Lytle, *Bedford Forrest and His Critter Company*, 304; Henry, *As They Saw Forrest*, 46; Woseley, "General Forrest" and *New Orleans Picayune*; Ulysses S. Grant, *Personal Memoirs of U. S. Grant*, 2 vols. (New York: Charles L. Webster and Company, 1886), 2:306.

19. Steven Woodworth, *Jefferson Davis and His Generals: The Failure of Confederate Command in the West* (Lawrence: University Press of Kansas, 1990), 278; Michael B. Ballard, "Tension at Tupelo," *America's Civil War* 15 (May 2002): 52–74.

20. *OR*, ser. 1:39, pt. 2, 233; Wills, *A Battle from the Start*, 230.

21. Hurst, *Nathan Bedford Forrest*, 210–15; Wills, *A Battle from the Start*, 237–48; Henry, *"First with the Most" Forrest*, 328–44.

22. Henry, *"First with the Most" Forrest*, 345–65; Wyeth, *That Devil Forrest*, 422–51.

23. Winston Groom, *Shrouds of Glory: Atlanta to Nashville, the Last Great Campaign of the Civil War* (New York: Atlantic Monthly Press, 1995), 80–81, 97–104, 113.

24. Wills, *A Battle from the Start*, 263; Norman R. Denny, "The Devil's Navy," *Civil War Times*, August 1996, 24–30; Philip L. Bolté, "Dismount and Prepare to Fight Gunboats," *Civil War Magazine* 65 (December 1997): 22–31; Jonathan K. T. Smith, *Benton County* (Memphis, TN: Memphis State University Press, 1979), 88–92; Henry, *"First with the Most" Forrest*, 380–81; Paul Ashdown, "The Battle of Johnsonville," *Tennessee Encyclopedia of History and Culture* (Murfreesboro: Tennessee Historical Society, 1998), 489–90.

25. Lytle, *Bedford Forrest and His Critter Company*, 357; Groom, *Shrouds of Glory*, 136–55; James Lee McDonough and Thomas L. Connelly, *Five Tragic Hours: The Battle of Franklin* (Knoxville: University of Tennessee Press, 1983), 22–59; Hurst, *Nathan Bedford Forrest*, 229–33; Wills, *A Battle from the Start*, 278–84.

26. McDonough and Connelly, *Five Tragic Hours*, 63–67.

27. Groom, *Shrouds of Glory*, 175–77; Hurst, *Nathan Bedford Forrest*, 238–47.

28. James Pickett Jones, *Yankee Blitzkrieg: Wilson's Raid through Alabama and Georgia* (Athens: University of Georgia Press, 1976), 64–92; Hurst, *Nathan Bedford Forrest*, 245–51; Henry, *"First with the Most" Forrest*, 431; Carter, *When the War Was Over*, 9; Jordan and Pryor, *The Campaigns of General Nathan Bedford Forrest*, 680–82.

CHAPTER THREE

THE COUNTRY OF THE DAMNED

FORREST'S LIFE AFTER THE WAR meant laying down the sword, but it did not change the man. The struggle continued, as he attempted to rebuild his business and the remnants of his culture. Like many former Confederate generals, he ventured into railroads, insurance, and real estate. But unlike many other veterans, North and South, he was not inclined to create a legacy or myth centered on himself and his exploits. There probably are several reasons, but at least two stand out. First, Forrest's writing skills were limited, so he would not have been well attuned to the impact of the written word on historical memory or able to control that word. If he could not control it, he might well have been dismissive of it or uninterested beyond cooperating with Jordan and Pryor in their preparation of his biography. Further, his ambition was not of a public sort; holding political office would not have suited him. He was in business to make money, not to gain public acclaim or attention.

The attention came anyway, a legacy founded, of course, on the war. There were events after the war that served to build on his reputation, particularly his role in creating the Ku Klux Klan, which probably focused more attention on and sharpened opinions about Fort Pillow. Forrest as a businessman, rebuilding his personal life, finances, home, and society, was pushed to the shadows by the Klan and Fort Pillow, probably oversimplifying the legend by creating two distinct though not necessarily competing stories: Forrest the military genius, and Forrest the racist.

By the end of the war, he was physically beaten, not only from battle wounds but also by physical strain and deprivation. War had left his homeland's economy and infrastructure in shambles, to which he had contributed, ironically, by tearing up the railroads that he subsequently financed and managed. The social and political order had been turned upside down, with a Reconstruction government in place and a Radical Reconstruction governor in office, a governor who saw the former Confederates as a group of traitors.

General Nathan Bedford Forrest. *Courtesy of the Tennessee State Library and Archives*

Just as in war, Forrest was an opportunist and a pragmatist. He knew the state was saddled for the near future with Reconstruction, but he seemed aware that there was opportunity to make money in rebuilding Tennessee. At the same time, he was at work with another of his famous flanking maneuvers, which is one way of looking at the creation of the Klan—a way of fighting the Reconstruction government and rebuilding the old South without attempting to do so by directly taking on the governor and numerous carpetbag officials.

From the start, the transition to peace was not easy for the general. On the return home to Memphis, the train he was riding, filled with soldiers and civilians, left the tracks. Forrest took command of the situation and set to organizing crews. When told that some men were still in the cars and not helping, he furiously declared to the malingerers, "If you damned rascals don't get out here and help get this car on the track I will throw every one of you through the windows." They spilled out and set to work with the others. The train was soon on its way, but getting his business interests and vanquished culture back on track was not so straightforward, and it would take far more than a few sincere threats to get the job done. In many respects, the train incident was a prelude to Forrest's postwar Tennessee—if the South was going to rise again, then the "rascals" had some choices, which were not always mutually exclusive. They could put their backs to the task, join up with the Klan, or align themselves with the factions later symbolized by William Faulkner's Snopes family.[1]

After his return to Memphis, Forrest set to restoring the plantation he owned in Coahoma County, Mississippi. The war had forced him to sell large tracts of land, and he had lost his investment in slaves with emancipation. By September 1865 he had repaired a sawmill on the plantation and was offering lumber to the public. He struggled to find laborers to work the mill, but he had rented lands to seven former Federal officers, who helped him find laborers and oversaw them. In many respects, Forrest was a model of reconciliation. As a practical man—and Forrest was always practical—he knew the most efficient path to rebuilding meant working with former enemies and providing good terms for his workers. At the same time, he managed the operation with military discipline.[2]

Things did not go smoothly, however. Forrest found himself embroiled in two court cases in the spring of 1866, one an extension of his indictment in 1864 for treason, the other a result of his killing of a black man who lived on his plantation. In the treason indictment, he was never brought to trial, but he did have to renew a $10,000 bond in March. The more serious incident involved a man named Thomas Edwards whose bad temper and cruel streak were often directed toward his wife, and he apparently was also generally insubordinate toward the overseer on Forrest's plantation. Matters reached a peak on March 31, 1866, when in the wake of a cholera outbreak Forrest had a crew digging a ditch in order to drain some pools of stagnant water. Edwards walked by, ignoring Forrest's calls for help with the job, and went on to his cabin, where he was heard threatening and cursing his wife. Forrest testified that he told Edwards he had abused his wife too much and must stop. Angered by the rebuke, Edwards then pulled a knife on Forrest, who retaliated by striking him with a broomstick. Edwards lunged at Forrest, wounding him slightly with the knife. They both spied an ax handle in the room, but Forrest beat him to it, striking Edwards behind the left ear and killing him instantly. In October of that year a Coahoma County Circuit Court jury found Forrest not guilty of manslaughter.[3]

While all this was going on, Forrest continued to seek a pardon from President Andrew Johnson, writing him directly in November 1866 and offering to waive all immunity from investigation into his conduct at Fort Pillow, thereby giving Johnson a way to allay the concerns of Northern Republicans. It was nearly two years—July 1868—before the pardon finally came through. In the meantime, Forrest became involved in the paving business, attempting to take advantage of Memphis's possibilities as a transportation hub and its need for improvements to the muddy streets. His company commenced work on the streets, reportedly at a cost of $95,000, and in return received $138,000 in paving bonds from the city. But the city's credit was so poor that Forrest could not find buyers for the bonds and entered into an agreement with the city to hand the work over to another firm. He then quickly turned to a new business, insurance. But this, too, was a struggle, and by February 1868 he had filed for bankruptcy in the U.S. District Court in Memphis.

It was at about this time that Forrest told two former Confederates of a plan he was considering for conquering Mexico, one of a number of such fantastic schemes wafting through American society at the time, perhaps reflecting the sort of psychological decompression that follows any war—it's over, and how can we top that? Forrest figured he could find at least 50,000 young men in the South who did not want to farm for a living but who would fight or dig gold. It is not known whether he actually ever tried to pull the plan together, and the episode may well only reveal something about his mental state, probably resulting from his business struggles. It was also in this period that the seamier side of Reconstruction, involving carpetbaggers and schemers of all sorts, had taken hold. The South was in ruins, the old ruling class pushed aside, and the time ripe for those with a plan to make money; if they lacked scruples, the money came even faster. In the view of many Southerners, devils were in charge of their Eden. It is the era in which Faulkner finds his antiheroes, the Snopeses, who were so

"This Is a White Man's Government." Cartoonist Thomas Nast includes Forrest among Democratic Party stalwarts who would trample the black man and repeal the Reconstruction Acts if they gained the White House in the 1868 presidential elections. Forrest holds a knife symbolizing the Lost Cause and carries his slaver's whip in his pocket. From *Harper's Weekly*, September 5, 1868.

devoid of values that they could not even be called evil. They were without values, without morality. In that context, even flawed values were better than a moral vacuum.[4]

In July 1868, Forrest went to New York as a delegate to the national convention of the Democratic Party, attracting considerable attention both at the convention and on the journey. Wills relates the story of his train coming to a station where a crowd had gathered, perhaps in an unfriendly mood. The conductor asked Forrest to remain on the train in order to avoid trouble, and he agreed to do so. But then a ringleader of the mob stormed onto the car, demanding, "Where's that damned butcher, Forrest? I want him," Forrest leaped from his seat and confronted the man: "I am Forrest. What do you want?" At that, the mob leader promptly fled from the train. Forrest burst into laughter, went out and gave a brief speech, and the train continued peacefully on its way. The episode not only revealed the postwar Forrest in his fury and readiness to do battle but also as a more conciliatory man, who probably would not have found such a challenge humorous in earlier years, and a man willing to stop and calm a crowd that was not all that friendly to him initially. He supported Johnson at the convention but later switched to the ticket for Horatio Seymour and Frank Blair. Though failing to muster the votes to nominate Johnson, Forrest may have helped his own case, getting the pardon he sought from Johnson on July 17.[5]

RADICALISM AT HOME

In the years immediately following the war, Tennessee was on the cusp of war with itself as a result of divisions created during the war. The primary antagonist for the former Confederates was the Reconstruction governor, William "Parson" Brownlow, an openly hostile Radical who declared that he could not blame loyalists for exacting an eye for an eye from the returning Rebels. Brownlow, in 1867, stated that he would uphold the Disenfranchisement Law, which withheld voting rights from unreconstructed rebels, even "if to do so it becomes necessary that there shall be violence and bloodshed." In addition, the black population in Forrest's hometown of Memphis had swelled from about 3,000 in 1860 to nearly 15,000 by 1870. Not surprisingly, reports of clashes between blacks and whites also increased. Though confrontations occurred in other Southern cities, Memphis was the site of some of the worst. On

May 1, 1866, violence broke out after a policeman arrested a black man involved in a disturbance with a white man. A crowd assembled and shots were fired, killing a policeman and a former soldier and wounding several other people. The fight escalated as discharged black soldiers came on the scene and poor whites took up for the police. Later, white mobs took to the streets, and after three days of violence, forty-six blacks, a policeman, and a fireman had been killed.

It was in this atmosphere of racial tension, radical politics, and grinding poverty that white Tennesseans began "night patrols" like those practiced in the antebellum South as a way of keeping slaves on their home plantations; any found off their owner's plantation without permission could be legally whipped. With racial fears mounting after the war, the revived system of patrols soon evolved into a loose-knit system of leagues, "dens," and societies.[6]

WHITE SHEETS AND DARK SHADOWS

The Ku Klux Klan was born in the dark shadows of Reconstruction politics, lawlessness, vigilantism, and racism. As he kept his minority Republican Party in power, Brownlow angered the former Confederates and Democrats with actions that included taking local control of police out of the hands of Nashville, Chattanooga, and Memphis citizens, and shrinking the number of eligible voters to about 50,000 Union sympathizers in East Tennessee. Brownlow called the legislature into special session in July 1868 to combat the Klan by reassembling the state militia. The Klan, he told lawmakers, intended to overthrow state government. He asked that these "organized bands of assassins and robbers be declared outlaws by special legislation, and punished with death wherever found." It was an action that Forrest later turned to his advantage when he testified before Congress that the Klan was organized as a defensive organization, and he cited the threats that Brownlow made against non-Republican, former Confederate Tennesseans.[7]

The Klan's origins are murky, but it appears to have started in late 1865 or early 1866 in Pulaski, Tennessee, where a half-dozen former Confederates organized a fraternity whose activities were devoted largely to riding around in costumes in order to frighten people and to induct new members. Within the year, its membership having outgrown the confines of the rural community, chapters and dens began to emerge in nearby counties. Forrest's role and physical presence in the beginning are unclear, but he apparently joined the Klan in its early days as word of the group was spreading across the state; it seems he was invited to Nashville in 1866 with the idea of assuming leadership. According to Hurst, Klan cofounder James R. Crowe was quoted as saying, "After the order grew to large numbers, we found it necessary to have someone of large experience to command us. . . . So we chose General N. B. Forrest. . . . He was made a member and took the oath in Room No. 10 at the Maxwell House . . . in the fall of 1866. The oath was administered to him by Capt. J. W. Morton." Morton was Forrest's former artillery chief.

The Lost Cause metaphorically shears the "Modern Samson" of his rights under the banner of the Ku Klux Klan. Forrest, second from left, wears a Fort Pillow badge and torches a Bible and other books in this Thomas Nast cartoon. From *Harper's Weekly*, October 3, 1868.

Forrest was just the sort of dynamic figure who would be needed to centralize the quiltwork of dens and chapters that the Klan comprised in its early days. Though he clearly did join the Klan, however, there is uncertainty as to whether he became the Grand Wizard. Before Congress, he denied even being a member and went so far as to say he had tried to suppress the Klan, but at the same time he showed considerable knowledge of the organization and its activities and of orders that were issued and followed. He said he had initiated investigations and reports of the group's activities and ordered arrests. Wills noted that Forrest certainly acted like the commander of the Klan, whatever his title may have been. Hurst gives more credence to the stories of Forrest's election as Grand Wizard in the fall of 1866, though the stories came largely from recollections of Klan cofounders. Whatever Forrest's role, the Klan had begun to proliferate across the South, and Forrest had a substantial presence in that growth. In popular lore, Forrest was the founder of the Klan.[8]

"I HAVE BEEN LYING LIKE A GENTLEMAN"

Forrest's testimony before a congressional committee investigating the Klan in June 1871 was a tactical masterpiece of verbal feints, dodges, assaults, and retreats as he fielded questions on the activities of the Klan, his role in the organization, and his knowledge of it. His answers to pointed questions from the committee more often than not were simply denials of knowledge or involvement, or statements that he was misquoted. Time and again, he was "unable to recall" specifics relating to the origins of the Klan, its activities, organization, or officers. When his memory did kick in, he said his information was based on "generally known" facts or rumors. He was consistent in asserting that the Klan was organized for defense of the community against "outrages" following the war and simply to keep the peace.

News of such violence as whippings he attributed to "newspaper rumors," an accusation possibly sharpened by the fact that much of his testimony was devoted to denying facts published in a newspaper interview in August 1868. Forrest testified that he saw the reporter for only a few minutes, never traveled with the reporter, was unaccustomed to dealing with reporters (perhaps implying that he failed to differentiate his opinions from his facts), and was suffering from a headache at the time of the interview. In the 1868 story, Forrest was quoted as saying that the Klan—which he characterized as a "protective, political, military organization"—was about 40,000 strong in Tennessee, and totaled about 550,000 men across the South. Asked if he were a member, Forrest said, "I am not; but am in sympathy and will cooperate with them." In a reply published in September 1868, Forrest claimed that he had been misrepresented, that he never advised people to resist the law, that the number 40,000 was simply a report that he believed to be true, that the Klan was a peaceable organization devoted to protection of citizens. The same assertions were repeated in his testimony before Congress.

Insisting that he had no idea how or where or when the Klan was organized, Forrest said he had been too busy in the railroad business and trying to build factories in his region. Specifically, he denied any role in organizing it, though he thought it had begun in Middle Tennessee. He was, he admitted, a member of the "Pale Faces," a group he characterized as being akin to Masons and devoted to preventing disorder and helping each other in case of sickness. In fact, Forrest ventured, he believed the Klan had been broken up in 1868. He also asserted that he actually tried in 1867 to suppress outrages—by blacks *and* whites—his object being to keep the peace. He said he had the Klan "broken up and disbanded" by talking to people he believed were connected with it. In all, his testimony was less than forthright. He is reported to have told a friend he encountered after the hearing, "I have been lying like a gentleman."[9]

The committee also was interested in statements attributed to him in which Forrest blamed the Republican Party for the South's ills. When it came to Brownlow, Forrest declared that if the state militia bothered no one, then there would be no fight. He did not believe that would be the case, however; "outrages" would be committed against the people of Tennessee and then, Forrest said, "Mr. Brownlow's government will be swept out of existence; not a radical will be left alive." Of course, the Klan was Brownlow's concern and might have become the provocation for calling out the militia, but Forrest insisted in the interview that he would fight only in self-defense and that he did not want bloodshed.

It was a period in which Forrest seemed at odds with himself. Some of the dissonance, perhaps, resulted from another personal blow in 1868: the death of his mother, to whom he was very devoted. While he publicly spoke in favor of peace, however, he appeared to be planning privately for war against radicalism and Brownlow.[10]

"HIS ACTS WILL SPEAK FOREVER"

From 1868 to 1873, Forrest poured his energy into his railroad business. As president of the Cahaba, Marion, and Memphis Railroad, he was in charge again, overseeing details of construction, raising money, lobbying for favorable legislation, and generally devoting himself completely to the rail line. In the meantime, Brownlow resigned as governor to become a U.S. senator. When his replacement took office in February 1869, Forrest returned to a task he had begun the previous month: on January 25 he had reportedly ordered the Klan disbanded and the costumes destroyed, an order attributed to a "perversion" of the original purpose of the KKK. The order had little effect, but it did distance the chief Klansman from the dens and their activities, which may have been all Forrest wanted to do. In addition, he may have felt it necessary to issue the order because he was no longer able to control the organization. At about the same time, and in yet another newspaper interview, Forrest told a reporter that the South could be successfully repopulated and farmed with freedmen: "They are the best laborers we have ever had in the South." He emphasized his good feelings toward the blacks and even detailed a plan for getting laborers from Africa, since men would not come from Europe or from the North. In 1869, Forrest expanded his immigration advocacy to include Chinese and supported a proposal for "subscriptions" for the labor on his railroad.[11]

For all his hard work and struggles in the railroad business, Forrest believed its financial condition was finally improving by the summer of 1873. When he went to New York to raise more money for the line, however, he found a financial panic under way, undermining his plans. He returned home unsuccessful and was in financial straits again by October. His railroad presidency ended the following April, when he gave up the office. He remained before the public at various reunions and other ceremonies for the Lost Cause, but with his railroad days behind him and having sold his Mississippi land, Forrest had to turn elsewhere to make money. He did so by leasing an island in the Mississippi River, President's Island, which he farmed with convict labor from Shelby County. He built barracks for the convicts, who numbered more than 100, and he and his family resided in a log house on the island. He cultivated cotton, corn, potatoes, millet, and garden vegetables.

Though he seemed to be doing well enough financially, Forrest's health was deteriorating and began to fail rapidly in the spring of 1877. That summer, he traveled to Hurricane Springs, Tennessee, in hopes that the curative powers of the waters would do him some good. Several of his old war comrades came to call on him there, including Wheeler, who noted Forrest's emaciated appearance and pale complexion. By the end of the summer, his condition had deteriorated considerably, apparently due to a combination of ailments, including diarrhea and malaria. He returned to Memphis in spite of his sickness and died there on October 29, 1877. Forrest's last words were more prosaic than Lee's ("Strike the tent") or Jackson's ("Let us cross over the river and rest in the shade of the trees"). He simply muttered, "Call my wife."[12]

His death was front-page news in Memphis. His funeral procession included three militia companies and also a large number of black Americans. The *Daily Appeal* laid the foundation for his legend, recounting his military genius, humble origins, fearlessness, and kindliness. A eulogy by the Reverend G. P. Stainback of the Cumberland Presbyterian Church at the general's funeral, reprinted in both the *Daily Appeal* and the *Evening Herald*, gave a heroic cast to the occasion and the man: "The acts of men never die; they survive the death of the body and live on, and speak and affect others for good or evil ages after the actor has left the field of action. Our deeds make us immortal; and the immortality of our words and actions make our living at all a fearful thing. . . . Lieutenant-General Nathan Bedford Forrest, though dead, yet speaketh. His acts have photographed themselves upon the hearts of thousands, and will speak there forever."[13]

Just as he had evoked radical responses in life, so he did in death. In many Southern papers, his bravery, humility, and role in rebuilding the South after the war played prominently in his obituaries. In the North, the other side of Forrest was often touted. The *New York Times* referred to him as a "great Confederate cavalry officer" but called him a type from the "border country . . . of reckless ruffianism and cutthroat daring," not a trained soldier, and noted his stormy career, which included Fort Pillow. A day later, the *Times* ran a bitterly sarcastic obituary about the "distinguished man," parodying Forrest's defenders by calling the charge of a massacre at Fort Pillow a "wicked Federal lie": "The great Southern cavalryman took part in the late unfortunate civil war from the purest and holiest of motives. He fought to defend his beloved South from the invading Federal troops. . . . The Southern soldiers believed they were right, and hence they were right. Of the misery they caused by taking up arms they must be held blameless because they fought to sustain their honest convictions."[14] The *Boston Globe* referred to him as "General Napoleon Bonaparte Forrest." He was clearly able to provoke both rage and loyalty even in death, as the facts of his life were already being molded to others' purposes and sentiments.[15]

FIGHTING GHOSTLY BATTLES

If literature later helped create the Forrest Myth, it was also present at his funeral, at least in the presence of Lafcadio Hearn, one of the most extraordinary journalists of the nineteenth century. Hearn was born on a Greek island in 1850 and attended Jesuit schools in England and France before coming to the United States in 1869. He wrote reports, editorials, and essays for newspapers and magazines as well as travel sketches, letters, translations, criticism, philosophy, theology, and novels. Later he settled in Japan, where he taught, became a Japanese citizen, and died in 1904. What fascinated Hearn most were myths and superstitions—especially those associated with prehistoric peoples—and popular interpretations of science. He might best be described as a cultural journalist, for he was a man of wide learning and experience and a close observer of different ways of life. His fondness for the exotic and the fantastic is reflected in his poetic prose style.

In the 1870s and 1880s he wrote articles for the *Cincinnati Enquirer*, the *Cincinnati Commercial*, the *New Orleans Item*, and the *New Orleans Times-Democrat*, and it was while he was on his way to New Orleans as a correspondent for the *Commercial* that he happened to be in Memphis on October 31, 1877, to witness and report on Forrest's funeral.

He began by describing the spectacle he observed from a Main Street window as the funeral procession passed by: troops of horsemen, marching Confederate veterans, a brass band playing the *Dead March*, companies of militia, carriages, policemen and firemen, black convicts from Forrest's plantation, members of fraternal lodges and societies, luminaries—including Jefferson Davis—and finally a black-plumed hearse pulled by four ebony horses. Then Hearn gave an assessment of Forrest garnered from street gossip and interviews with a variety of persons who had known him. He reported that the general was admired by many but equally feared and disliked. Forrest's business interests had left him with unpaid debts, the source of much of the animosity. And there was his penchant for violence and invective, including his berating of a tailor who had delivered a moth-eaten suit: he had put a pistol to the tailor's head and threatened to shoot him, according to Hearn's account.

Hearn then told the story of Forrest's early life, finding his character largely derived from the region where he was raised and came of age. "Rough, rugged, desperate, uncultured, his character fitted him rather for the life of the borderer than the planter; he seemed by nature a typical pioneer, one of those fierce and terrible men, who form in themselves a kind of protecting fringe to the borders of white civilization." Hearn called the Forrests "a terrible family," especially Bedford's brother Bill, whom he characterized as little more than a desperado. He visited the site of the general's old slave market where "thousands upon thousands of slaves" were sold, but acknowledged Forrest's reputation as a humane trader. He noted Forrest's war record, pointing out the differing opinions about his ability to cooperate with other officers or command large numbers of troops. He mentioned the general's kindness to children and the affection in which he was held by many Memphis citizens.

Hearn added a disclaimer, admitting he "saw and heard these things only as a stranger in a strange city may observe the last of a long chain of unfamiliar events, and I can not dare to say that the evil out-balanced the good, or that the good outweighed the evil in the dark character of this man of iron." He concluded with a poetic touch: "The same night they buried him, there came a storm. From the same room whence I had watched the funeral I saw the Northern mists crossing the Mississippi into Arkansas, like an invading army; then came gray rain, and at last a fierce wind, making wild charges through it all. Somehow or other the queer fancy came to me that the dead Confederate cavalrymen, rejoined by their desperate leader, were fighting ghostly battles with the men who died for the Union."

Hearn's report probably had no immediate effect on shaping Forrest's reputation, but its appearance in a Cincinnati newspaper shows the controversy that was already brewing as the general was put to rest. Hearn's sense of a myth in the making is keen, and his melodramatic metaphor of the rising storm is telling. Forrest's rest would not be peaceful.[16]

THE LAST REVIEW

In June 1932 some 1,500 surviving veterans of the Confederate armies arrived in Richmond on seven special trains for what was later called the Last Review. They had met forty-one times since the end of the war, and now they were old, weary, and frail but hardy enough for one final parade. There would be other, smaller gatherings, but this was the final grand assembly. For the last time the hoary old soldiers would listen to speeches extolling the Lost Cause.

On the first day of the four-day review the soldiers may have put on wire-rimmed spectacles and strained their eyes to read a somber poem by Allen Tate on the front page of the *Richmond Times-Dispatch*. "I am here with a secret in the night; I am here because the dead wear gray," Tate wrote. The poem was a précis of the Agrarian philosophy: the defeated South had sold out to Yankee lucre; it was better to be a dead soldier than to live under the invader's boot. In one of the concluding stanzas, Tate wrote:

> Soldiers, march! We shall not fight again
> The Yankees with our guns well-aimed and rammed,
> For all are Yankees of the race of men
> And this too, now, the country of the damned.

It is doubtful whether many of the Confederate veterans understood Tate's meaning or welcomed his images of impending death and noble defeat. But perhaps at least some knew in their hearts that wars are never truly lost or never truly won. A few veterans were interviewed by the National Broadcasting Company, the voice of modernity capturing the voices of the past. The radio program began with a Rebel yell, and one old soldier yelled so loudly that his galluses broke and his trousers retreated to his ankles. The interviews went badly. The Confederates were hard of hearing, and some were demented. A veteran called "Uncle Charlie" deflected a question about his uniform and railed against women's attire: "They's a scandal, that's what," he said. "Ah mean short skirts!" When Uncle Charlie started talking about "sporting houses," the interviews were abruptly terminated.

After the reunion, a side trip to Washington had been arranged. Most of the veterans were too exhausted to continue, but one contingent did manage to embark on a special train for the capital. Four of Forrest's doughty, ancient cavalrymen headed a small parade, riding down Pennsylvania Avenue like the Four Horsemen of the Apocalypse. For those with eyes to see, another horse bearing a pale rider well acquainted with Death preceded them. The specter's name was Nathan Bedford Forrest.[17]

NOTES

1. Wills, *A Battle from the Start*, 319.
2. Ibid., 323.
3. Hurst, *Nathan Bedford Forrest*, 328–30.
4. Wills, *A Battle from the Start*, 342–45.
5. Ibid., 347.
6. Ibid., 268, 275–76, 290.
7. Hurst, *Nathan Bedford Forrest*, 268, 277, 307–8.
8. Ibid., 278–79, 284–89; Wills, *A Battle from the Start*, 336–37.
9. Wills, *A Battle from the Start*, 364.
10. Ibid., 351; Hurst, *Nathan Bedford Forrest*, 312–45; U.S. Senate, *Ku Klux Klan Conspiracy: Report of the Joint Select Committee to Inquire into the Conduct of Affairs in the Late Insurrectionary States*, February 19, 1872, 42d Cong., 2d sess., S.R. 41, vol. 13.
11. Wills, *A Battle from the Start*, 356–61.
12. Ibid., 374–78.
13. *Memphis Daily Appeal*, November 1, 1877.
14. *New York Times*, October 30 and 31, 1877.
15. *Boston Globe*, October 30, 1877.
16. Lafcadio Hearn, "Notes on Forrest's Funeral," reprinted in his *Occidental Gleanings* (New York: Dodd, Mead and Company, 1925), 144–55.
17. Virginius Dabney, *The Last Review: The Confederate Reunion, Richmond, 1932* (Chapel Hill, NC: Algonquin Books, 1984), 3, 35, 43–45, 47.

PART TWO

MYTHMAKERS

In the Confederacy there was a particular romanticizing of the ingenious raider, John Mosby, and Nathan Bedford Forrest . . . though the actions of both were in fact based on great physical endurance and fortitude.
—Rupert Wilkinson, *American Tough: The Tough-Guy Tradition and American Character* (1986)

Even seventy-five years afterwards, [Forrest's legend] was still powerful, still dangerous, still coming!
—William Faulkner, "Shall Not Perish" (1943)

This portrait of Forrest is surprisingly flattering given the dislike typically shown for him in *Harper's Weekly*'s pages, especially in the cartoons of Thomas Nast, who often depicted Forrest as a savage killer. From *Harper's Weekly*, February 18, 1865.

CHAPTER FOUR

FORREST AND THE PRESS

THE FORREST OF POPULAR MEMORY is a character starkly drawn, the edges of his character as sharp as the cavalryman's bloodied saber. He has neither nuance nor complexity. Societies create their heroes and villains as they entangle their real and imagined pasts. The press similarly constructs heroes and antiheroes, and Forrest was both. The press created numerous Forrests: a demonic, racist killer for that part of America needing a poster boy for the nation's sinful past; an untutored military genius to remind and instruct the world about the virtues of democracy and the common man; a penitent slave trader who showed redemption at work and the triumph of good; a repentant sinner who found God and tried to atone for his errant ways. To this day, a mention of Nathan Bedford Forrest will often provoke a response that notes little more than his military genius and role in founding the Klan. The more knowledgeable individuals may even cite a few details, such as Brice's Cross Roads and Fort Pillow. But it remains a simple frame of racism, war, and untutored genius that guides even recent recognition of and response to his name. Forrest lived in a limited time and place, and that he gave no thought to a legacy was appropriate for the uneducated man. His purposes were immediate—to build a business, to win a battle. He did not conduct his affairs, military or civil, with careful attention to the pulse of public opinion or to his embryonic legend, although he was not ignorant of their value.

Forrest had more limited press exposure than other important figures in the Civil War for several reasons. First, he was in the Western Theater of operations, which meant he was removed from the East Coast centers of communications, especially New York, Washington, and Richmond; Memphis was the nearest major communications center with respect to Forrest's actions. Other figures in the East such as Colonel John Mosby, the "Gray Ghost of the Confederacy," did far less tactical damage than Forrest but received substantial press coverage, for Mosby was a direct threat to Washington itself, the symbolic heart of the Union. Forrest's exploits were more remote and therefore less visible to a competitive, deadline-driven press and its audience. When he briefly did threaten to menace the lower Midwest late in the war, he was rumored to be moving on Chicago instead of the Ohio River; the Northern press became attentive only when its citadels were threatened. Operating in the West also meant that he was removed from that galaxy of Southern military stars in the East, the brightest of whom was Lee, who had attained the status of a mythic figure in his own lifetime. It also meant Forrest could not shine in the reflected light of the likes of Lee, Jackson, and Stuart. In fact, the Forrest Myth may have been more susceptible to influence by the developing unromantic legacies of some of his adversaries, chief among them Sherman and Grant, both of whom saw and conducted war as a destructive, bloody affair. Clearly, the raw facts of Forrest's life were not well suited to the cavalier myth, probably making it more challenging to build a narrative around him. He did not conveniently or clearly fit any one mythic template.

Second, Forrest's frontier character and lack of education limited his ability to initiate and sustain publicity about himself, had he even been inclined to do so. Being relatively uneducated meant he was not writing about himself to others; he left no substantial archive of personal papers other than battle reports. It also meant he did not write for publication but deferred to others with more literary talent. By extension, this limitation implies a constrained appreciation for the power of the written word; after all, he had been one of the most successful generals of the Civil War in spite of near-illiteracy. As a frontier figure he was not urbane and could not be so. The press of the 1860s and 1870s was already a creature of the city, reflecting those values and ambitions—not the world of Nathan Bedford Forrest.

Finally, his press exposure was limited by the fact that he died in 1877, only a little more than a decade after the war. There was simply too little time for a myth to grow up around the living Forrest, which reduced his press coverage to wartime and a few postwar events. Forrest was not without acumen and sensitivity to the significance of the press in shaping his image—as a soldier, as a businessman, or as a gentleman in the community. His appreciation of the press is evident in his attempt in 1867 to buy the *Appeal*; his bid of $20,000 was nearly successful, but he lost to a competitor by a matter of minutes. He did not likely seek the purchase for the sake of image-building; given the man's business ambitions, he probably saw an opportunity to make money. Still, as a successful public figure he would have been well aware of the benefits of owning a newspaper. His few efforts at publicity and the results seemed at times, perhaps appropriately, somewhat rough and un-refined: moving from backwoods boy to businessman-gentleman, he gained respectability by winning local political office and dress-ing (perhaps overdressing) for his role in polite society. And per-haps Forrest had had his reputation in mind when he employed newspapermen as aides-de-camp at different times during the war. Those aides included, at various times, Henry Watterson (*Atlanta Daily Southern Confederacy, Chattanooga Rebel*, and *Montgomery Daily Mail*), George Adair (*Atlanta Daily Southern Confederacy*), and Mat-thew Gallaway (*Memphis Avalanche*). Barbara Ellis, in her history of the *Memphis Daily Appeal*, notes that numerous Southern jour-nalists applied for commissions in the Confederate Army. One of those was Gallaway, who as press aide acted as Forrest's assistant adjutant general, with the intent of civilizing and polishing the general's rough speech and brutal ways.[1]

Forrest's relationship with journalists became an issue in early 1863, before he had gained military prominence. In fact, he had performed in lackluster fashion in recent campaigns: he had been defeated at LaVergne in Middle Tennessee; he was surprised and nearly suffered disaster at Parker's Crossroads; he made errors at Dover; he was again surprised by the enemy at Brentwood and Franklin. His relations with his commander, General Earl Van Dorn, had deteriorated, and the general even accused him of having one of his aides write an article for the *Chattanooga Rebel* that gave Forrest, rather than Van Dorn, the credit for victory at Thompson's Station.

Although it is unknown whether or not Forrest was respon-sible for such an article, the *Rebel* was being managed at the time by former Forrest staffer Henry Watterson, whose "Shadow" col-umn in the *Appeal* was quite popular. His stories on Bragg's Army of Tennessee studied not only the battles but also camp life, attacks on civilians, and even the execution of spies. Forrest was a com-mander whose temperament and impetuousness appealed to the young, adventure-seeking Watterson, who later wrote that guer-rilla action was "very much to my liking," as opposed to days or weeks in muddy, boring encampments. The *Appeal* closely followed the fortunes of the Army of Tennessee, and its generally favorable treatment of Forrest throughout the war was important because its war coverage and columns were widely reprinted in both America and Europe. Its circulation has been estimated as high as 70,000 (not counting "pass-along" readership) and was noted even by Northern officers for its timely, reliable information. It was a few months after Shiloh that Watterson left Forrest's company to become editor of the *Chattanooga Rebel*. Forrest was easily persuaded that his aide would be of more help to the Southern cause as an editor than as a cavalryman; he once commented that the 80-pound Watterson, who also was afflicted with poor eyesight, was committing suicide every time he went on a raid.[2]

George Adair, owner and editor of the *Atlanta Southern Confederacy*, was an old friend of Forrest who may have been in the slave-trading business with him before the war. In an 1863 interview published in the *Southern Confederacy*, Adair reported meeting up with his "old friend" in Rome, Georgia, where he found Forrest, "plainly dressed," attending to the well-being of a horse; he compared the general's appearance to that of "Old Hickory." Adair went on to recount a story of the bravery and chivalry of this "most agreeable gentleman" during his pursuit of Streight: as Emma Sansom mounted behind Forrest to show him the way to ford the Black Warrior River, her mother warned her that people would talk. But the girl replied that she was "not afraid to trust myself anywhere with a man as brave as Gen. Forrest. Southern men always protect the innocent and helpless." Adair also transformed Sansom into a "beautiful young girl"—as indeed she may have been, but for purposes of Confederate mythmaking only a fair damsel would suffice.[3]

As editor of the *Montgomery Daily Mail*, Watterson again came to the general's defense in 1864 when the *Memphis Appeal* objected to the *Daily Mail's* publication of a short speech by Forrest that was liberally laced with braggadocio, bad grammar, and misstated facts. Watterson acknowledged that the language was brusque but defended its "eccentric eloquence." In Watterson's account, the common man looms large as the editor elevates crudeness to a virtue.[4]

In creating and sustaining the Forrest Myth, however, the coverage following the war was far more important than wartime reporting on the man and his martial exploits, although it drew on wartime reports to shape his legacy. In effect, the press was a critical instrument in reframing the picture of Forrest. For example, whereas before the war, Forrest may have been looked down upon or snubbed in many quarters for being a slave trader, it was not generally proclaimed publicly that such a business was morally

degenerate. After the war, however, in the context of emancipation, slave trading was more than an unappealing enterprise; it had
become both illegal and immoral, but it had to be confronted in
any account of Forrest's life and exploits. His connection with the
Klan and Fort Pillow also continued to haunt him and his legacy.[5]

The nature of the press itself shaped the image of Forrest, too.
The war and postwar years were a period of transition in journalism as newspapers moved away from the traditional narrative-story
form. The increasing use of the telegraph to transmit news and the
rise of "press associations" meant sending the most important news
first, in case the line broke down, and transmitting it in a fairly
impartial fashion, since the information was going to numerous
outlets with differing perspectives. The traditional narrative had
demanded a story with coherent structure and purpose. The new
style favored factuality. But the facts of Forrest's life still begged
for judgment, whether explicitly in the narrative tradition or implicitly by their mere inclusion in the news of the day. And judged
they were.

The press in the first half of the nineteenth century had not
really been much of a "mass" medium; it became so only after the
railroads, faster printing, and the telegraph allowed newspapers
to reach large numbers of people and to do so quickly. By the 1860s,
newspapers had become mass media in the sense that they were
cheap, had a vast audience in urban areas and small towns, and
were easily available. Publishers began treating news as a commod-
ity—active news gathering having displaced the more passive methods of earlier years—as competition increased. Even the definition
of "news" changed as the idea of its being new or "fresh" became
more important. And as it became more factual and more objec-
tive, it diverged from the opinionated material of the old political
press, which had existed for and been supported to a great extent
by political interests and parties. With income now based largely
on advertising and subscriptions, the press was more independent
and less partisan—though the news was not necessarily always balanced or fair. Publishers and editors were often seeking office themselves and were very opinionated about issues. Lorman A. Ratner
and Dwight L. Teeter Jr. point out that newspapers were independent and in positions of power, inasmuch as they could sway opinion, but they had little sense of responsibility to society. Thus, an
era of sensationalism emerged in a press that was generally aimed
at factually oriented news.[6]

Papers north and south used one another's words to launch debates over issues. Northern papers often portrayed Southerners as bullies with whips and without honor: "Eventually, most northern newspapers came to portray all southerners as a conspiratorial, immoral element of society intent on destroying the Republic for the sake of keeping its slave property," according to Ratner and Teeter. Eventually, this view would have an impact on the portrayal of individuals such as Forrest, who could easily fit the one-dimensional stereotype of the slave-holding Southerner, a hardened individual who seemed almost to relish the bloodletting of war. As if that were not enough, he had even taken part in duels. This was often the Forrest one read about in the Northern press, which was offset by a Southern press that saw a different individual and from the same set of facts depicted a man upholding the honor of the South, defending a way of life, and demonstrating the bravery and ingenuity of Southern men. In this way, the press would be both biased and factual. The Memphis newspapers saw the latter individual in command of Confederate troops at Fort Pillow; the New York papers, given the same incident, revealed a murderer who did not abide by the rules of war and was thus without honor. But the disparity of communications systems north and south gave the Northern press an advantage in creating the foundation for the Forrest Myth. The Southern newspapers, though creating a Forrest based on values that resonated across American culture, did not succumb completely to the wealthier, bigger, more widely circulating Northern press. The Southern papers appealed to a national love of individualism and the frontier, which enabled them to depict Forrest's substantial flaws as attributes deeply embedded in a profoundly and genuinely American character.[7]

Forrest was a good story not only because he was an extraordinary individual. As the press had shifted to more entertaining content and away from polemical political essays, it became more event oriented and found its raw material in courts and police stations, in crime stories, and, later, in sporting events. The human-interest story also emerged in midcentury, not only because of the new emphasis on entertainment but also because of the new concern with individuals. Forrest was excellent material on both counts. He was not only extraordinarily individualistic but sensational and entertaining, whether or not one liked him. And he had been a significant figure in the most important catastrophe in American history up to that time.[8]

Though the press in its modern form was taking shape, it was still a distinctly different institution from the one with which modern readers are familiar. "Balance" and "fairness" were not central to the lexicon of reporters, editors, and publishers. Journalism was a business, a rabidly competitive one at times. And though sources may have been cited, they were not necessarily reliable; newspapers frequently republished one another's material, sometimes with attribution and sometimes without. A national press began to have a somewhat industrial look as the creation of press associations meant writing news for multiple outlets rather than personalizing it for the whims of the local paper. The use of the telegraph to transmit information helped standardize the form of news and also meant more diverse news, according to Hazel Dicken-Garcia. The complexity of war caused reporters to use more sources than ever, which increased the diversity of views in the same article, because reporters were cultivating sources as they competed for news.[9]

FORREST'S "WILD BEASTS"

The war news of Forrest's exploits ranged from detailed, factual accounts of his tactical brilliance, such as at Brice's Cross Roads, to wild exaggerations and outright fabrications. In the North the barbarian theme played well. The *Chicago Tribune* admitted that the stories got out of hand at times, noting reports that "the whole country is found to be full of rebel spies," and acknowledging that "another rumor is to the effect that Forrest renewed his attack upon the Fort of Paducah. . . . The wildest and most absurd rumors continually prevail, respecting Forrest and his whereabouts, and no little apprehension has been entertained both in Cairo and Mound City lest he should pay both places a visit. At any time to-day a score of persons were willing to swear he had invaded our State with 20,000 cavalry, accompanied with eighteen pieces of artillery. It is very difficult to arrive at the truth among so many excited rumors."[10]

Only a few days later a *Tribune* writer reported that Forrest and his men were scalping the enemy and using women as shields, promoting even further his image as little more than a savage barbarian: "To show the barbarous character of the foe which we are obliged to fight in this rebellion, I need only say that a rebel was captured yesterday upon the steamer Gen. Anderson, at Paducah, who had in his possession, carefully concealed in a basket, as one would carry home a calve's liver or a loin of beef, a fresh, reeking, bloody, human scalp, which he had taken from the head of either a murdered citizen of Paducah, or from a soldier, killed in bravely repulsing the advance of Forrest's men."[11] Calling the scalp a "rare trophy of Southern chivalry," the report went on to say that five women employed as nurses had been placed in front of a charging column of Rebels, which kept the Union troops, who were apparently more chivalrous than their Confederate counterparts, from firing. The item closed with a rhetorical question: "Are we fighting men or wild beasts? In form and feature, perhaps like men; but in passions, instincts and brutal actions they imitate beasts to perfection."

In Forrest's hometown of Memphis, the general's harshness was acknowledged along with rumors: "We have reliable reports that Gen. N. B. Forrest was killed at Parksville, Ala., on the 13th last, by some of his own command. The circumstances are as follows: The news of Johnston's surrender, though not believed by Forrest, was received with exultation by his worn out soldiers, as it foreshadowed a speedy close of the war. Six of the most enthusiastic were put under arrest, and afterwards shot. The next day four of their comrades, watching an opportunity, fired upon the general, wounding him so badly that he died almost instantly. The act was to avenge the death of their comrades."[12]

The report was not true, of course, and the next day's edition of the *Memphis Bulletin* admitted the error even as it reinforced the notion of the barbarity of Forrest: "The report of his death seems to have been founded on the fact that his life was threatened by an old gentleman from Kentucky, two of whose sons, it is alleged, Forrest had caused to be shot without trial. Their offense was absence from their command without leave." So Forrest's blunt sense of right and wrong became simple necessity, even heroic. In defeat, such an attitude made him even greater. His brutality was measured against a strong sense of justice. In his last address to his soldiers, the *Memphis Bulletin* reported, he admitted "the conditions of affairs," putting him even higher in the esteem of the mass of people than he had been before. Harsh but just, according to the newspaper, which showed Forrest as honest and honorable in negotiations with Federal authorities: "He remarked that he was now as good a Union man as anybody—that the South was whipped."

Forrest was, in short, a commendable realist who squarely dealt not only with the essence of war but also with the consequences of defeat. The press easily transformed the brutal and savage warrior into a savior when the circumstances permitted, and that was the case toward the end of the war when the *Montgomery Daily Advertiser* tried to calm Alabama as Union forces prepared for a final onslaught in February 1865. As Northern troops, horses, and supplies gathered, the paper told readers that "Forrest is watching," even though his troops were spread thinner than ever across both central Mississippi and central Alabama. Similarly, the *Appeal*, in March 1865, exhorted Southerners to keep fighting and drew on Forrest's name as an inspiration: "The will, the will, is alone wanting. Seize your arms, form companies and call upon Gens. Dick Taylor and N. B. Forrest to lead you, and your homes and country are saved."[13]

FORT PILLOW

The brutality and barbarism in the Forrest legend—and perhaps even in reality, depending on which historical accounts one prefers—may well have reached a zenith with the Fort Pillow massacre. Whether or not it was the most brutal and savage episode in his colorful life, Fort Pillow is important in his legend because it is critical to the interpretation of Forrest: a racist killer; a good leader and generally good man who didn't always have control of things (himself, his troops, his business affairs); or a general whose reputation overwhelmed the facts and whose legacy bears a heavier burden for doing the same thing done by many others during the Civil War and other conflicts. Press interest in the event has spanned more than a century, beginning naturally with the massacre itself in 1864 and reappearing intermittently on such occasions as the congressional investigation of the battle, the death of Forrest, and even in 1990, when Shelby Foote's praise of Forrest in the course of Ken Burns's Civil War television series incited recollections of the battle.

One of the earliest press accounts of the battle, from the *Chicago Tribune*, was headlined: "The Butcher Forrest and His Family/ All of them slave drivers and woman whippers." The story on "cowardly butchery" integrates Forrest's past as a slave trader with his growing reputation as a killer, condemning his whole family for being in the business and citing four brothers in particular. Forrest himself was said to be the very personification of meanness: "He is about 50 years of age, tall, gaunt, and sallow-visaged, with a long nose, deep-set black, snaky [*sic*] eyes, full black beard without a mustache, and hair worn long. . . . He was accounted mean, vindictive, cruel and unscrupulous." His slave pen in Memphis was reported to be a "perfect horror," and he was said to have even whipped one slave to death. In case readers had not gotten the point that he was a man without morals, the story noted (wrongly) that he had two wives, "one white, the other colored, . . . by each of which he had two children."

Even one of Forrest's hometown newspapers, the *Appeal*, was somewhat reserved in its praise. It proclaimed the victory a severe blow to the North (which it was not) but acknowledged that the event was a "bloody one." It took the paper about three weeks to run a detailed account of the battle, and then it did not mention that many of the Union troops had surrendered before they were killed, or that two nephews of the *Appeal*'s owner took part in the executions (according to the *Tribune*, the nephews were believed to have killed the white commander and others as they were being taken to a prison camp).[14]

Covering a 1868 congressional investigation of Fort Pillow, the strongly Republican *New York Times* recounted the details of the massacre and also printed Forrest's version, but national politics and the paper's sympathies probably strongly colored the coverage. The paper admitted that it was influenced by the fact that Forrest had become a "shining light" of the Democratic Party and had been a delegate to the recent national convention in New York, but now, "even Democratic friends look upon the Fort Pillow massacre as a blot upon the escutcheon of its author." In revealing the depravity of a prominent Democrat, the *Times* claimed that even women and children were killed. Forrest's political activities were quite useful as well—if one needed a bludgeon to wield against the Democratic Party. The *Times* said "an official letter" signed by General David Stanley, which it reprinted, vouched for the truth of a statement that "throws some light upon Forrest's own exploits as a negro-killer." At Murfreesboro, in the summer of 1863, Forrest reportedly asked a mulatto man what he was doing there. The man said he was a servant to an officer; and "Forrest, who was on horseback, deliberately put his hand to his holster, drew his pistol, and blew the man's brains out."[15]

The *New York Times* highlighted Fort Pillow again in Forrest's obituary. The account is worthy of note not only because of its exaggeration but also because it appeared in a normally reserved and responsible publication of the period:

> It is in connection with one of the most atrocious and cold-blooded massacres that ever disgraced civilized warfare that his name will forever be inseparably associated. "Fort Pillow Forrest" was the title which the deed conferred upon him, and by this he will be remembered by the present generation, and by it he will pass into history. While the flag [of truce] was flying, Forrest's men treacherously crept into positions which they had been unable to take by fight (a trick they had played at other places) and thus were in a situation to make the assault which soon followed under every advantage. . . . The enemy were now within 100 yards of the fort, and at the sound they rushed on the works, shouting "No quarter! No quarter!" The garrison was seized with a panic: the men threw down their arms and sought safety in flight toward the river. . . . Without discrimination of age or sex, men, women, and children, the sick and wounded in the hospitals, were butchered without mercy. The bloody work went on until night put a temporary stop to it; but it was renewed at early dawn, when the inhuman captors searched the vicinity of the fort, dragging out wounded fugitives and killing them where they lay.[16]

So the *Times* wanted his legacy to be based on Fort Pillow—not just as military overzealousness, which might be forgiven, but as an unforgivable moral transgression, felony murder on a large scale and that done treacherously. Such a narrative was a way of taking a verbal shot at Southern pretenses of a chivalric tradition.

Closer to Memphis, the *St. Louis Post-Dispatch* obituary was a marked contrast. "His name was unfortunately connected with the killing of some colored troops at Fort Pillow, after the place had been surrendered, which it was claimed he should have prevented, and did not. It served to create a strong feeling throughout the North against him."[17] With great reliability, the lens through which Fort Pillow was viewed in the press could be predicted by geography. Newspapers in the South, and Memphis in particular, tended to regard the Northern version as a willful misrepresentation of the native son, an aberrant event, and inevitably noted that the congressional investigation had cleared him.

Newspapers north and south may have helped sustain regional animosity by carrying reports from the "other" region, which gave them the opportunity to respond. The *New York Times*, in spite of its hostility toward Forrest, printed a letter datelined Memphis, in which Forrest stated that a speech in New Haven, Connecticut, by General Judson Kilpatrick was untrue and that the general was an "unprincipled liar." Kilpatrick replied that an investigation confirmed his remarks concerning Fort Pillow, and he went on to "reiterate his denunciations of Forrest's unparalleled atrocities." Along similar lines, the *Memphis Appeal* seemed actually to seek out "libel" in order to respond to it, rather like Forrest himself looking for a fight. The *Appeal* published a report from the *Philadelphia Bulletin* and headlined it a "base libel upon a law-abiding citizen." The story said that at a recent meeting in Memphis, held to protest the killing of several blacks in Gibson County by the White League, Forrest had remarked that he would, if he had the authority, "capture and exterminate" the men responsible. But the *Bulletin* story went on to say the killings were merciful compared with what Forrest did at Fort Pillow. Sixteen "unoffending men" were killed in Gibson County, but readers were reminded that Forrest had tortured and murdered 300 men who had surrendered. Men were slain in cold blood, crucified, buried alive, nailed to the floors of houses which were then set on fire: "The murderers of Gibson county have but imitated the example of Gen. Forrest."[18]

Even after the turn of the century, Memphis papers found it necessary to continue to explain Fort Pillow. In a 1901 story describing Forrest's military career at great length, the *Commercial Appeal* turned the blame around: it was the Union troops' fault. Forrest was responsible and moral in his actions; he had urged surrender of the fort and had stopped the firing as soon as possible after the enemy ceased firing, but hundreds of the enemy had already been either killed, wounded, or captured. A few years later the *Commercial Appeal* called the capture of Fort Pillow "daring" but "minor" in Forrest's career and said that an investigation was unable to sustain the charge that Forrest gave black troops no quarter. That defense is not so different from one offered eighty-three years later by the same newspaper, during another episodic uproar over Forrest: "As for the Fort Pillow massacre, [Shelby] Foote says Forrest did everything he could to stop the slaughter of black soldiers and white 'homemade Yankees.' Investigations of the raid cleared him of all wrong."[19]

The controversy over Fort Pillow was not so different in the late twentieth century from what it was in the nineteenth. Relying on gruesome accounts of the incident by Lerone Bennett Jr., the *Tri-State Defender*, a newspaper with an African American audience in the Memphis area, in an August 1985 article pointed to the racism-driven activities of Forrest during Reconstruction and alleged that at the first national meeting of the Klan in Nashville he offered "a plan designed to reduce Negroes to political impotence by economic intimidation, by political assassinations, by the rope, the whip, by maiming, cutting, shootings and murder. By fear." It is an important observation because it draws a clear line linking two significant facts of Forrest's life: Fort Pillow and the Klan. Whatever its merit, it is an easy connection to make: Forrest was in the middle of both, and race was central to each. A few years later the same paper criticized Foote, the city of Memphis, and anyone else defending Forrest's legacy. It compared him to Hitler, Mussolini, and Jack the Ripper, whose historical company he earned because of Fort Pillow, an editorial charged.[20]

Even for a publication not particularly vested in the debate, the issue was a conundrum. In a book review of the Hurst and Wills biographies in 1993, Charles Royster, writing for *Atlantic Monthly*, noted:

> The fort had no strategic importance, and Sherman had ordered that it be abandoned. But that order had not been obeyed, and the attacking Confederates caught in the fort hundreds of black Federal soldiers, as well as many white soldiers, whom the rebels killed in a sustained, purposeful bloodbath. Thereafter the name of Nathan Bedford Forrest was, as he several times acknowledged, permanently linked with Fort Pillow. . . . [Hurst and Wills] explain and apologize. Jack Hurst emphasizes every instance in which Forrest made concessions to the needs or the capacities of black people. He suggests that Forrest deserves credit for striving to restrain the Ku Klux Klan after northern Democrats warned that the Klan's actions were delaying defeat of northern Republicans at the polls. Hurst reminds us that the Civil War included many killings of surrendering, unarmed men other than those at Fort Pillow.[21]

Although the review did not really take sides in the same way as earlier newspaper accounts, even this relatively impartial version found it necessary to link Fort Pillow and the Klan.

POSTWAR COVERAGE

Both the *New York Times* and the *Memphis Daily Appeal* carried an 1869 Forrest interview that was remarkable—whether one was pro- or anti-Forrest—because of his observations about the critical role of black Americans in revitalizing the South. The interviewer said he was on his way down the Mississippi when he found that his company included Forrest. The conversation turned to the defeated South, and, when asked how the land could be repopulated, Forrest said "with negroes," whom he praised as hard workers. When the reporter alluded to Fort Pillow, Forrest said that it had been investigated and he was found not to blame. He went on to say that Europeans and Northerners would not come to repopulate the South, but blacks would; he even proposed bringing people from Africa. "It's my country," Forrest concluded, "and I don't intend to give it up as long as I can do anything to build it up. I am an American, and from the day I surrendered have been for the United States."

The remarks show, if little else, that Forrest's attitude was not one-dimensional or static and that he was just a simpleminded hater of blacks. The *Daily Appeal* may well have picked up the interview for those very reasons, as well as to promote a Memphis native son as a national figure. A few years later the *Times* showed a similar response when, in July 1875, the paper reported on a July 4 speech in Memphis by Forrest at which a "remarkable" scene occurred: blacks applauded him, and he was presented with a bouquet by one of the societies of black women present. He said he accepted it in a spirit of reconciliation and that he was the friend of "colored people," whom he exhorted to work hard and be industrious. Perhaps the remarks merited no further comment, which the *Times* did not provide, because Forrest was addressing such a fundamental American value and in fact saying that blacks were part of the value system, one in which hard work and industriousness would be rewarded.[22]

THE POSTWAR FORREST

In the years following the war, press accounts of the man and his battlefield exploits promoted the Forrest Myth, particularly Southern accounts, but even Northern newspapers could unintentionally contribute. For example, the *New York Times* probably meant no acclaim when, in its 1877 obituary, it gave Forrest credit for creating modern guerrilla warfare. At that time, it could well have been a muttered insult, because guerrilla warfare was contrary to the chivalric, romantic tradition of which the South was so enamored. Ambushes and hit-and-run fighting were not gentlemanly or courageous. Still, the paper did recognize ingenuity and innovation in the conduct of war:

> He proved himself the most regularly successful of all the Southern cavalry leaders. This was due as much to good fortune as his own talents. He never had a good officer sent against him, and he seldom attacked except where he greatly outnumbered his enemy. As a scientific commander, he was much the inferior of Wheeler or Stuart; but he had all the qualities of a guerrilla chieftain, and the history of his exploits abundantly proves that he displayed them. He was swift and daring in his advance, stubborn and defiant in retreat, cool and ready in face of temporary disaster and skillful in wielding the large force he commanded.[23]

One could read that paragraph in much the same way American culture has read Forrest's life—in whatever way best suits one's purposes. Unlike accounts from the South, the *Times* gave great weight to "good fortune," which is not to say that Forrest was less than a military genius but which does dilute that claim—no special genius is required if one always outnumbers the enemy. The issue of whether Forrest was or was not a mere "guerrilla chieftain" is central to evaluating his role in the war, and many subsequent writers have challenged almost every word in the *Times* account.

The Memphis newspapers immediately saw things otherwise and across the decades promoted Forrest as a figure of national historical significance. From their perspective the only objection might be that the national spotlight was not large enough for this figure; it would take the stage of world history to accommodate the drama and the impact of Forrest. The *Memphis Daily Appeal*'s assessment contrasted sharply with that of the *Times*: "He was born a military hero, just as men and women are born poets. Though not familiar with history, he seemed to understand the methods of the Crusaders, and would adopt the tactics of Saladin or [Richard] Coeur-de-Lion, as the exigency required. He knew nothing of the cunning strategy of the wily Fabius or the daring Hannibal, but he adopted the policy of either by intuition when the emergency presented itself." The *St. Louis Post-Dispatch* had similar sympathies and, unlike the *New York Times*, saw guerrilla warfare as another way of showing genius and daring: "His name was at one period of the late war a very familiar one, and will rank among the most dashing and successful of Confederate cavalry officers. Like Morgan, his greatest exploits were raids and independent expeditions, cutting off communications and capturing supply trains."[24]

The *New Orleans Daily Democrat* made similar claims for the Forrest legend, giving him credit for innovations that both North and South adopted and fitting his accomplishments to the emerging industrialism by touting not only his victories but also his "efficiency": "No other command in the Confederate army could record more victories, more extraordinary escapes and larger results achieved with so small a force. To Forrest is due the new organization which was finally adopted by both armies; superseding the clumsy old system of cavalry, heavily mounted and armed, fighting on foot as skirmishers and infantry, with the horses tethered, and kept out of reach of bullets and shells, but ready to be mounted for pursuit and retreat. He reduced this to a system and illustrated its efficiency in many brilliant campaigns."[25]

In these obituaries, Forrest began to emerge as an iconic figure for the South and Southern masculinity. Like those of the South itself, Forrest's forces are "smaller" than the foe's in numbers, matériel, and support. The stories of an impoverished youth defending and providing for his family segue easily into the legend of a man defending his homeland, one who succeeds not because of material superiority but because he is innately superior, endowed by nature and environment with special abilities. In the frontier tradition of self-reliance and tall tales, he is almost radically individualistic. These themes, emerging in the obituaries and earlier news about Forrest in the 1860s and 1870s, are those that endure. Three decades later, in 1901, the *Commercial Appeal* deemed him the "South's Military Prodigy," a man of "preeminent . . . genius . . . among the great captains known to the world." And the theme of native intelligence remained: "He showed an appreciation of the highest art of war even if he knew nothing of its science." In a twist that elevated Forrest and, by extension, the individual Southern man, the defeat of the South was called the "Confederate wreck," implying that the fault was not with individuals but with government. The newspaper still insisted that "the world has been forced to recognize the abilities of the great cavalry leader. In the last few years Gen. Forrest has become better known to the student of history than ever before, and those who saw nothing specially brilliant in his record before are beginning to acknowledge him one of the greatest generals that fought on either side."[26]

In 1905, on the occasion of dedicating Forrest's statue in Memphis, his role as symbolic Southerner is apparent in the *Commercial Appeal*'s reference to "the great Southern chieftain" and in remarks from a speaker who refers to Forrest and "his people." The phrase makes him sound like a tribal leader, with perhaps an unintended intrusion of the noble-savage myth into his legend. The idea of Southern nobility and chivalry had been undiminished by the passage of a few decades; in fact, it seemed to have been resurrected with more passion than ever by the turn of the century. Forrest also remained more than ever a "natural" genius, admittedly untutored but with martial talent linked to things greater than mere academies. He was destiny writ large; more than emblematic of the South, he represented anything noble about the United States. He was the frontiersman in fact and in spirit. He was soiled and rough, strong and clever, taking his place in world history by virtue of his deeds and that which was "native" to him—his destiny.[27]

The *Commercial Appeal* also declared that Forrest "made for himself a name that will go down in the annals of history as an example of faithfulness in duty, heroic bravery and strategic warfare." It contrasted him to West Point officers and touted his backwoods roots:

> The monument stands for the greatest cavalry leader and the greatest strategist the world has ever known. Not the polished cadet with medals of honor, upon a steed of war caparisoned with gaudy colors and fighting beneath a banner upheld by a nation as an emblem of trained military education, but under the stars and bars—a rough diamond, without the gold and glitter, but the simple honest devotion to duty and natural genius all his own. He was the prototype of the immortal Washington in bravery, devotion to duty and insight into the intricacies of war. He had the bravery and determination of Friedrich Wilhelm of Prussia, the dash of Napoleon, the calm judgment of Washington. He understood the war game, the Kriegspiel, before the Prussians ever thought of it and before Japan made use of it.[28]

The writer went on to quote a *Commercial Appeal* story from a few months earlier, which not only had made the same points in putting Forrest in the company of Napoleon and Hannibal but opined that under "more favorable circumstances, he would probably have been universally recognized as the central military figure of American military history. . . . What a romantic figure . . . this dashing and intrepid Rough Rider and his merry men. When the passions of the war have completely subsided, and sectional hatred has grown pale, the romance writer of the future—some American Scott—will find in the exploits of Forrest fit material for novels that will rival 'Ivanhoe' and the 'Legend of Montrose.' "[29]

The malleability of Forrest's legend was shown again when the same newspaper only a few days later shifted from the romantic myth to declare Forrest "an intuitive General," one "guided by a masterly 'common sense' that, perhaps, has not been surpassed in American history, unless it be by that of Andrew Jackson, in many respects a similar type of man." Here he is compared not only to a major figure in American history but to one who also was from Tennessee, from the frontier, a man of minimal education whose accomplishments grew from natural rather than learned talents. Hyperbole in the tradition of the American tall tale asserted that Forrest's victory at Brice's Cross Roads "is conceded by historians to be the greatest piece of strategic warfare in the annals of history." Putting up a monument to him could be done without apology, for "Forrest will stand out in history as one of the world's military geniuses. He was born a soldier. . . . His career will always adorn one of the most romantic pages of history."[30]

In short, his commonness made his greatness even greater. In 1921 the *Commercial Appeal* quoted the acting mayor of Memphis as stating, "Gen. Forrest is, without question, one of the greatest men that Tennessee has produced in its history. He was a born military genius, and his like is not found once in a century. Though untrained in technical warfare, he used military tactics which were followed in the late Bore [*sic*] war." It seemed again that his tactics were even more brilliant because he was untrained.[31]

Especially in the local paper, time and events appeared only to increase the potency of the Forrest Myth. In 1940 the *Commercial Appeal* credited him with being the inventor of blitzkrieg warfare: "What Forrest did on horses, the Germans are doing in planes and tanks." In particular, this article pointed to the fact that Forrest's troops "were known as infantry even though they rode horses," because Forrest believed them more effective fighting on foot with guns than being on horseback with guns. After World War II the newspaper still claimed that Forrest's tactics were "studied by military men the world over" and insisted, into modern times, on Forrest's place in military history. In 1985 the paper cited Foote's assurance that General Rommel never toured battlefields to study Forrest's tactics; however, "the German blitzkrieg was nothing more than a Forrest cavalry charge on tanks instead of horses." Acknowledging in that same decade the civil rights protesters' challenge to the Forrest statue, the *Commercial Appeal* held its ground on the general's place in history: "Though controversy has always swirled around Forrest, there never has been any question of his bravery or his ability as a general whose campaigns are still studied from West Point to Europe."[32] The modern challenge to such statements came, naturally, from a Northern publication, *Atlantic Monthly*, which in 1993 dismissed Forrest as a "minor player in some major battles and a major player in minor battles. He could never have been an important theater commander. The picture of Forrest in command of a Confederate Army is about as plausible as a picture of Robert E. Lee beating his subordinates with his fists and threatening to kill Jefferson Davis."[33]

At times, newspapers seemed to step back from lionizing or demonizing Forrest to take measure of the man with a detailed accounting of the warrior's exploits. The *Commercial Appeal* in 1901 provided the tally from the Johnsonville raid: "Forrest had killed, wounded or captured two officers of his own rank, 1,100 prisoners, half a million dollars worth of army stores, most of which he carried off, 60 wagons, 200 head of stock and four guns, with a loss of only eighteen killed and thirty wounded." The story said that in the twenty-one days from the time Forrest entered Tennessee until his return to Corinth, he had marched 500 miles; had killed, wounded, or captured 3,500 of the enemy; had captured eight pieces of artillery, 900 horses, 100 cattle, and as many wagons; had destroyed 100 miles of railroad; had captured a number of gunboats; and was credited with a "$2,000,000 blaze of glory" at Johnsonville. In another raid, by an accounting attributed to his biographer, Thomas Jordan, Forrest was credited with destroying fifty bridges, capturing or killing 2,500 of the enemy, and seizing fifty wagons, 10,000 guns, and one million rounds of ammunition, among other things.

As if that recital of the warrior's worthiness were not enough, the newspaper turned to the enemy to confirm Forrest's value: "Sherman was offering a major-general's commission to the man who should kill Forrest, even if it cost the lives of 10,000 men and all the money in the United States treasury." His wounds, horses, and the men he personally killed were also specified: "In the engagement at Town Creek he received his third wound in battle, a severe shot in the right foot. . . . Ever in the thickest of the fight Forrest killed three men in personal combat, had the hammer cut from his pistol by a saber, received several sabre [sic] slashes and escaped only by jumping a wounded horse over an overturned wagon. . . . This prodigy of war . . . had twenty-nine horses shot from under him."[34] The *Commercial Appeal* never settled on the exact number of horses brought down while carrying Forrest, but it was a lot: "Twenty-seven horses are said to have been shot from under him, and that not fewer than thirty of the enemy fell beneath his individual prowess during the four years of war." By 1921 the paper was reporting even higher numbers: "It is said that during Forrest's military career his outfit captured 31,000 prisoners. . . . Gen. Sherman, of the Union forces, asserted that the famous leader's capture and destruction of $6,000,000 worth of federal supplies and a gunboat fleet at Jacksonville was a feat of arms that excited his admiration."

At one point the *Commercial Appeal* abandoned such accounting in favor of simply asserting that "Memphis' greatest Civil War hero . . . is reputed by historians to have killed more men in hand-to-hand combat than any commander since Richard the Lion Hearted." (Actually, the source of that comparison was General Richard Taylor, Forrest's commanding officer at the end of the war, who made it in his 1879 memoir.) The story went on to make even a rather odd image—if not a downright cartoonish one—sound heroic: "At Tupelo, Miss., when a wound in his foot made it impossible for him to ride in the saddle, the dauntless general took to a buggy and led his cavalrymen in a dashing charge." Not many men in history could be dauntless, dashing, and fearless while seated in a buggy.[35]

By the 1940s and 1950s, the Memphis paper's accounts of Forrest may have reflected a resurgent regionalism, putting Forrest forward as a Southern symbol. He was never beaten, according to the paper in 1940; he did retreat several times, but even then his raiders always bounded back. Ten years later, at the dawn of the nation's modern civil rights movement, the *Commercial Appeal* recounted Streight's mission to capture Forrest "at any cost," which ended with Forrest chasing the Union general out of Alabama. The story also recalled the "most daring exploit" of Forrest's small band, riding into occupied Memphis, garrisoned by 5,000 Federal troops, on a foggy August dawn in 1864, "riding low in the saddle and shooting as they came."[36]

In the 1950s the federal government had the South in its sights again, this time armed more with attorneys than with troops but occupying Southern cities all the same. With governors vowing never to surrender to new racial integration laws and calling out their own forces to defend against the new federal incursion, the Forrest Myth could take on a new dimension.

THE KLAN

The Klan, like Fort Pillow, is problematic in dealing with Forrest's legacy, particularly if one is attempting to salvage or build a reputation for a man who becomes, for some, a symbol of Southern ingenuity, toughness, patriotism, and devotion. In the nineteenth and early twentieth centuries, Southern papers often had defended him and his role, or non-role, in the Klan, whereas Northern papers condemned the "butcher of Fort Pillow" for the lawless, vigilante Klan and pointed to the logical extension from massacring blacks during the war to helping create and lead the Klan after the war. Coverage of Forrest's testimony before Congress in 1871, often surprisingly brief and without comment, tended to characterize him in extremes: a heroic Forrest defending fellow citizens, or a villain continuing his ways. The *Galveston Daily News*, for example, concluded, "Forrest knows whereof he speaks . . . . It is about time to disbelieve the exploded story [of the Klan's existence]." The *New York Tribune* saw his testimony otherwise, as demonstrating "the hero of Fort Pillow in his true colors—his admissions and contradictions for the Congress committee." Other papers, too, charged that Forrest contradicted himself, while his memory seemed conveniently to fail him at times.[37]

The Klan was the indelible dye in the fabric of the Forrest story, and it had to be acknowledged. In many instances, Forrest was allowed to address the issue himself, and papers reiterated his denial of having said 40,000 Klansmen were in Tennessee, his claim that he knew nothing positively of the organization's strengths or objectives, and his belief that its purpose was protection of people from the injury and violence of, presumably, the state's Reconstruction government. Much Southern press coverage of Forrest's testimony was similar to reports in the *Memphis Daily Appeal*, putting blame for any organized movement on the shoulders of Governor Brownlow, whose forces Forrest accused of such marauding that people were led to organize for protection. Like Forrest himself, the papers often dodged any direct dealing with the topic, quoting his declaration that he "had failed to ascertain that any such Klan exists. . . . He did not believe in its existence." Furthermore, the North

was still to blame for unrest in the South because greedy Northerners who came south employed blacks and elevated them to office.
Admittedly, according to such accounts, some violence had occurred, but the cases were few and the Klan probably was a scapegoat, if indeed there was such an organization.[38]

With the turn of the century, a Southern newspaper in a resurgent South of rekindled racism no longer needed either to defend
or to dodge the Klan issue. It could even be celebrated, which the
Memphis Commercial Appeal did:

> The Kuklux order was formed at the house of Gen. John C. Brown
> in Pulaski, Tenn. and spread with wonderful rapidity. Forrest
> became the "Grand Cyclops" of the order and when the national
> government got close on the trail of the organization he sent to
> President Grant through Senator Oliver P. Morton of Indiana and
> Gen. John T. Wilder full information as to his connection with the
> affair, showing the secret correspondence and making the point
> that he took the leadership of the organization solely to prevent
> it from going to excesses and to be in position to effect its dis-
> bandment as soon as the members could be convinced that the
> necessity for the organization no longer existed. Grant appreci-
> ated the situation and the congressional investigation committee
> justified the existence of the Kuklux by the statement that no State
> was ever reduced to such humiliation and degradation as that
> unhappy commonwealth (Tennessee) during the years Brownlow
> ruled over her.[39]

In that period of American history, the racism and even lynchings that reached new heights made the Forrest legend–building
easier with the chance to dismiss the issues of slave holding, Fort
Pillow, and the Klan. The mythmakers could focus anew on Forrest's
embodiment of American and Christian values, an approach embraced by the Nashville Agrarians in the 1920s.

OBITUARIES (1877)

In rituals of remembrance, death is an occasion for life's accoun-
tants to calculate the dead one's deeds—with specific purposes in
mind. When Forrest died, the making of his myth was already well
under way, and so his obituaries were devoted to fleshing it out,
whether heroic or demonic. In his hometown the *Memphis Daily
Appeal* heralded his patriotism, military genius, and humble
beginnings:

> Starting life as a poor boy, . . . he hewed his own destiny by the courage of his heart, the valor of his principles, and the energy of his character . . . without fear of anything earthly . . . yet tempered by the kindliest and best disposition that ever animated human action. A manhood which, scorning all that was wrong, but allied to the true and the right, defied the temptations of wealth and power. . . . The very type of manly chivalry, the marvel of military genius, the untutored champion of patriotic chivalry, and the perfection of manly nobility . . . frank and sincere, rigid and honest, . . . decisive and positive. . . . It may truly be said of Gen. Forrest, as it has of other men, that his mind was entirely free from THE WRETCHED METAPHYSICS which too much enslave the politics and morals of the day.[40]

The obituary also cited his devotion, self-sacrifice, self-reliance, and integrity in business affairs and, as though anticipating the sentiments of those less enamored of the Forrest legend, noted the "genuine sorrow" of the "hundreds" of black men, women, and children who asked to view Forrest's remains. Following a veritable catalogue of Forrest's life and military career, the paper concluded: "We leave to history the duty of committing to an imperishable record a faithful detail of those brilliant military achievements which . . . will become a precious portion of the legacy of this great republic. The fame of N. B. Forrest will ever reflect luster upon the American name. Posterity will keep bright the splendor of his heroic deeds."[41]

The *Charleston News and Courier* expressed similar sentiments, including reference to the poor boy who rises above his beginnings by means of his own hard work and ingenuity. But it went further by giving Forrest's name alone the power to frighten enemies and embolden allies:

> Born of humble parents—poor and untutored in youth—he was successful in civil life, and was the noblest specimen of a citizen-soldier. With unconscious power, he began his military career a private in the ranks. With increasing consciousness of strength, he passed through the gradations of command until he stood at the head of a cavalry corps, the terror of one army and the admiration of the other. With the intrepid dash of Murat and the dauntless courage of Ney, he possessed a native strategy second to no man. In battle his name alone was a tower of strength—his presence ever inspriring courage in the weak and confidence in the strong, and he will live in history as Nature's military genius.[42]

Forrest's infamy was not ignored in Southern papers, but it was admitted in the context of heroism. The *St. Louis Post-Dispatch* said, with some understatement, "His name . . . will rank among the most dashing and successful of Confederate cavalry officers. . . . His name was unfortunately connected with the killing of some colored troops at Fort Pillow, after the place had been surrendered, which it was claimed he should have prevented, and did not. It served to create a strong feeling throughout the North against him." The *Memphis Daily Appeal*'s response to Fort Pillow was to reprint the correspondence with President Johnson in which Forrest requested a pardon and claimed that his reputation had been unjustly demeaned, especially in connection with Fort Pillow. According to an accompanying editorial note, Johnson kept the letter as a model of how one should conduct reconciliation. The *Atlanta Constitution* was similar in its praise of humble origins, devotion to family, and "some of the most daring and brilliant chapters of confederate war history." It explained Fort Pillow in the context of the pardon letters, citing one supporting letter from Frank Blair (later a Democratic candidate for vice president), who wrote that Forrest ordered no executions, that he tried to save the prisoners, and that "his courage, displayed in more than a hundred battlefields, ought to convince any man that he is incapable of the dastardly outrage alleged against him." In this case, the American myth is employed as defense by arguing, indirectly, that an individual so emblematic of American values could not be capable of murder and cruelty.[43]

The accounting in other papers, especially in New York, was less kind. In a bitter, sarcastic article headlined "In the Light of Conciliation," the *New York Times* derided Forrest's achievements and everyone defending his actions at Fort Pillow; reconciliation had been imposed on the land, and justifying people like Forrest and his atrocities was no longer possible. The paper noted that Forrest was a "great guerrilla" with a "stormy career," which included Fort Pillow. Though working with the same facts as the Southern papers, the *Times* showed an individual who was antithetical in the worst way to the Virginia aristocracy and the romanticized South: "While Virginia, and what might be called the 'old South,' produced gallant soldiers and dignified gentlemen, the Southwest, the rude border country, gave birth to men of reckless ruffianism and cutthroat daring. The type of the first was Gen. Robert E. Lee; that of the latter, Gen. Bedford Forrest," who was "notoriously bloodthirsty

and revengeful. . . . Forrest was well known as a Memphis specula-
tor and Mississippi gambler. . . . He was known to his acquaintan-
ces as a man of obscure origin and low associations." Of Fort Pillow,
the *Times* said, "Without discrimination of age or sex, men, women,
and children, the sick and wounded in the hospitals, were butch-
ered without mercy." It added that Forrest's principal occupation
since the end of the war had been to explain away Fort Pillow: "He
seemed as if he were trying always to rub away the blood-stains
which marked him." Militarily, the *Times* concluded, he was inferior to Wheeler or Stuart as a "scientific commander," though he
"had all the qualities of a guerrilla chieftain": "Gen. Forrest's sudden dash through Memphis, with no more result than the killing of
a few men on either side, was the recklessness of the mere guerrilla
chief—which Forrest essentially was."[44]

The *New York Tribune* also cited the guerrilla tactics, Forrest's
"distinguished gallantry at Fort Donelson," his "bold attack on
Murfreesboro," and his "dreaded brigade." But Fort Pillow, it said,
was "deliberate, wholesale massacre of prisoners of war after they
had surrendered—many of them long after—and for the naked reason that some of them were black." In a city farther removed from
the still simmering North-South feelings, the *San Francisco Chronicle*
probably summarized the contradiction in as balanced a fashion as
was possible: "The late Gen. Forrest was a brilliant cavalry leader,
but his gross inhumanity at Fort Pillow leaves a dark shadow on
his otherwise fair name."[45]

LOOKING BACK: A HERO FOR
THE TWENTIETH CENTURY

Creating a Southern hero for the twentieth century meant that a
newspaper had to rely on more than the memories of Southerners.
It would not be enough for a man to have been a great leader of
fellow Southerners in the Lost Cause. He had to be more than a
fighter, more than a general. He needed to be an exemplar not just
of Southern values but of values that transcended place and time—
even though some might see the South as unique in producing a
people who demonstrated courage, patriotism, hard work, self-
reliance, and devotion to family and faith. The *Memphis Commercial
Appeal* in 1901 made such an icon of Forrest: "His manner in personal intercourse with his fellows was easy and dignified, his words
well chosen and his conversation chaste. Possessed of an imperious

temper, he swore when under the influence of great excitement, but there was in his mental make-up absolutely nothing of the rowdy. His personal habits and private life were exemplary, he eschewing liquor and tobacco in all forms." It went on to point to a lynching that Forrest reportedly prevented in Memphis because "he was ever a partisan on the side of law and order. This was equally true of his connection with the Kuklux order during reconstruction days." He was described as being loved by his men and contemptuous of cowardice and neglect of duty. Catching two deserters, "he asked them if they intended to return and they said they did not. He promptly had them shot."[46]

A few years later, the newspaper staked a claim to Forrest's role as a national legend, not just a local or regional hero: "What can we say of such a hero whose meteoric dash across the firmament of life made both the North and South hold their breath in silent admiration? What words of praise are fitting for such a hero whose whole life was spent in loyalty and sacrifice for home, for loved ones and for his country? Praise is too weak, eulogies too shallow and words too feeble to do his sacred ashes justice."[47] Moreover, he looked the part: "Gen. Forrest was considered a much handsomer man than would be judged by any of his pictures, he was 6 feet 1 1-2 inches tall, he had broad shoulders, full chest and symmetrical, muscular limbs, and his carriage was erect. He weighed 185 pounds. His eyes were grey, bright and searching, he had dark hair, mustache and beard, his features were clear cut and browned by the sun." Some of the conclusions are questionable such as that there was "nothing of the rowdy" about him—other than his tendency to get into gunfights and knife fights and to end up killing people.[48]

Even the most mundane of incidents could be resurrected and elevated to the level of a morality play, such as the time he apparently helped some women whose carriage was stuck in mud and cursed other men who did not assist them. One of the ladies was Mary Montgomery, whom he later married. That chivalrous act was linked—yet again—to a story of his saving a criminal from the lynch mob, literally cutting the rope with his knife.[49]

All such unqualified praise was diluted within a few decades; by 1940 the *Commercial Appeal* admitted that he was a man of contradictions: "At home, he was soft-spoken, gentle, ever-smiling and virtually a total abstainer from profanity. In battle, he was bombastic and ruthless in both words and action; his ordinarilly [sic] sallow countenance became livid. But the battle over, no one was gentler and more understanding," wrote one of his officers, Dr. J. B. Cowan. Despite his facility for violence and his uncultured early life, Forrest never smoke or drank. He was deeply pious, so much so that he often held religious services before battle. Scrupulously clean in his personal appearance, even in the field, he was considered nearly "prudish." He also demonstrated that great Christian value of charity. In preparing to conduct war and to pay for some of its consequences, "he exhausted most of his fortune outfitting his troops during the war and supporting his men's families afterward."[50]

In 1958, only a few years after the critical *Brown v. Board of Education* decision eliminating the "separate but equal" concept in education, the *Memphis Press-Scimitar* carried a story in which the city was scolded for not celebrating Forrest's birthday in Forrest Park. It quoted a speaker who saw in the general a worthy figure: "As New England points with pride to Paul Revere and Virginia to George Washington, so does the South point with pride to Nathan Bedford Forrest."[51] A change in attitudes about race meant a reevaluation of Forrest, but it did not mean abandoning him. In 1985 the *Commercial Appeal* acknowledged a dark side to this "most successful cavalry commander of the war" as it weighed his achievements. His slave trading and role in the Klan were noted, as was the massacre at Fort Pillow; however, "some historians and close students of the war say he was as much a villain as hero."[52]

"FIRSTEST WITH THE MOSTEST"?

A legend's shadow inevitably obscures something in his life. Forrest's lack of education could be problematic for the mythmakers: Was he an ignorant, racist killer or a clever, hardworking man who transcended his beginnings? The *Memphis Daily Appeal* chose the latter assessment in its 1877 obituary of Forrest, who was "deprived of an opportunity to receive even a rudimentary education. In 1836 and 1837 he had an opportunity for attending school, which he turned to a good account, as he rapidly learned to read and write, and the value of figures, in which he was an expert in his immense business transactions."[53]

In the early twentieth century this aspect of Forrest again became a point of honor, rather like his defeating the West Point officers of an earlier generation. The *Commercial Appeal* considered Forrest's education at length.

It is the current belief of the day that General Nathan Bedford Forrest was a very illiterate man. He was not an educated man, he held no diplomas from Harvard or Yale, and was not disciplined and trained at West Point. He was a backwoodsman, a slave trader before the war, but letters . . . written in Forrest's own hand writing, do not bear out the idea that he was an ignoramus. His letters are not so beautiful as those of Addison and he was not versed in Belles Lettres. He used the provincial language of his Southland. He had not the forensic power that distinguished Burke, Pitt and Chatham, but whatever he said or wrote was from the heart.[54]

In this twist on the topic, given the conviction in his writing, his lack of education was elevated to a matter of pride. Better yet, "he was taught in the best of all schools, the school of experience. . . . His letters are deep, clear, decisive, full of great truths, and are almost entirely void of grammatical errors." A few days later the newspaper declared that Forrest's "native endowments, both mental and physical," took the place of a formal education.[55]

New York papers also noted Forrest's lack of education but did not cloak it in the virtues of a frontiersman rising by way of hard work and ingenuity. Instead, the *New York Tribune* and the *New York Times* focused briefly, in 1918, on Forrest's alleged remark about getting there "firstest with the mostest." The *Tribune* complained that Forrest was incorrectly quoted by General Maurice, a newspaper columnist on military strategy, who had Forrest saying in reply to a lady's inquiry about his recipe for success, "Ma'am, I got there first with the most men." According to the *Tribune* writer, "The text of the quotation does injustice to Forrest. This great soldier never spent more than six months inside a schoolhouse. He remained all his life a stranger to book learning and talked what might be called a 'cracker' Southern dialect. What he really said in an answer to the question put him was 'I got there firstest with the mostest men. . . .' No one would have been more amused than he at the unimpeachably academic form given by a cultivated British brother-in-arms to one of his pithiest and most characteristic sayings."[56] The *New York Times* responded to the article, reiterating that Forrest was uneducated but insisting that the *Tribune*'s version relied on words chosen by someone who thought he knew Southern dialect but apparently did not. Instead, according to the *Times*, Forrest said, "Ma'am, I got thar fust with the most men." A sample of his writing was attached to show "how he really talked."[57]

The discussion was not flattering, in any case, and certainly not intended to further the myth. It soon began to sound like a modern-day debate between two scholars with opposing interpretations of runic script. As late as the 1940s the *Commercial Appeal* continued to insist that the quotation revealed depth, virtue, and intelligence. In an article headlined " 'Git Thar Fustest': Forrest Probably Said It Differently," it noted that Forrest's military tactics had been adopted in World War I and by Nazi Germany. " 'But whatever the military virtues of gittin' thar fustest with the mostest men, it just isn't grammar and it's not the kind of words Gen. Forrest would have used,' asserted his only living grandchild, silvery-haired Mrs. Mary Forrest Bradley. 'My grandfather received little classroom education, but he had a real gift for using words correctly as a study of his papers, speeches and orders will show.' " The article discussed Forrest's written and oral skills and cited examples. Although "all his writings show utter disregard for proper spelling," many saw in him a "born orator" with a "wonderful command" of the language.[58]

Apparently it did not matter how or even whether he made the remark, according to the *Commercial Appeal*: "Perhaps he did not give utterance to the colloquialism widely attributed to him, 'Git there fustest with the mostest,' but certainly he was the exemplification of that successful military operation." The quotation has endured, curiously enough, because it must symbolize something more than bad grammar or great common sense. The *Commercial Appeal* in 1985 was not willing to forgo it but could compromise in almost dismissive fashion: "Forrest is sometimes said to have said he won battles by 'getting there fustest with the mostest.' [Shelby] Foote said Forrest, an uneducated but far from illiterate man, actually said: 'I just got there first with the most men.' "[59]

The uneducated man was naturally tied to another figure of mythic virtue, and that was the frontiersman. The *Memphis Daily Appeal*'s obituary had said as much when it noted that Forrest was unencumbered by the "routine of red-tape and the teachings of West Point. . . . The scholar lives too much in his closet, depends too much on what he has learned to always correctly act when thrown on his native resources." The *New Orleans Daily Democrat* concurred: "Without education or a profession, reared in a rude and somewhat violent community, pursuing modes of life and business which exposed him to constant perils and severe trials of his many qualities, and compelled a reliance upon his personal courage and prowess, he always proved ready for every emergency and shrank from no danger or responsibility."[60]

After the turn of the century, when the frontier had taken on a more romantic hue, the *Commercial Appeal* praised in verse Forrest's backwoods upbringing:

> . . . It may be that the rugged scenes
> In which his early life was cast, had shed
> About him such an air of independent boldness
> That his nature was imbued with something of
> The ruggedness of his environments. A gem
> Of priceless value, though without the fickle
> Glitter of artificial polish, and though rough-
> Hewn, a light shines forth, of steady and
> Effulgent ray, which has descended to us
> And will brighten history's pages.[61]

Fortunately for Forrest, his legacy did not rest on the quality of the poetry dedicated to him.

The 1905 unveiling of the Forrest monument in Memphis saw similar sentiments, romanticizing the rudeness of Forrest's early life, weighing his circumstances against hope and courage. It was a point of pride that Forrest was not "the polished cadet" but came instead "from people who hewed their way into dens [sic] wildernesses, letting in the sunlight where it had never before penetrated, and leading the onward march of civilization, felling the mighty forests for the foundations of great cities and making a road for the approaching wheels of commerce to pass over, and also making for themselves a name that shall last as long as the grinding wheels of time shall turn."[62]

NOTES

1. Hurst, *Nathan Bedford Forrest*, 369; Barbara G. Ellis, *The Moving Appeal: Mr. McClanahan, Mrs. Dill, and the Civil War's Great Newspaper Run* (Macon, GA: Mercer University Press, 2003), 121, 401, 564 n. 54. In 1858, Gallaway started the *Avalanche*, which became a rival to the *Appeal*.

2. Ellis, *The Moving Appeal*, 116–17; Ellis, ibid., 1–4, 233; Joseph Frazier Wall, *Henry Watterson: Reconstructed Rebel* (New York: Oxford University Press, 1956), 35–37.

3. Hurst, *Nathan Bedford Forrest*, 126.

4. Ibid., 231.

5. Ibid., 361–63.

6. Lorman A. Ratner and Dwight L. Teeter Jr., *Fanatics and Fire-eaters: Newspapers and the Coming of the Civil War* (Urbana: University of Illinois Press, 2003), 1–28.

7. Ibid., 118.

8. Hazel Dicken-Garcia, *Journalistic Standards in Nineteenth-Century America* (Madison: University of Wisconsin Press, 1989), 30–42.

9. Ibid., 55–57.

10. *Chicago Tribune*, March 31, 1864.

11. Ibid., April 3, 1864. About two weeks later the *Tribune* recanted slightly and said that Forrest was not with his troops as was reported in the earlier story.

12. *Memphis Bulletin*, May 18, 1865.

13. Ibid., May 19, 26, 28, 1865; Ellis, *The Moving Appeal*, 340, 346.

14. *Chicago Tribune*, May 4, 1864.

15. *New York Times*, September 13 and 14, 1868.

16. Ibid., October 30, 1877.

17. *St. Louis Post-Dispatch*, November 11, 1877.

18. *New York Times*, November 3 and 12, 1868; *Memphis Commercial Appeal*, September 10, 1874, quoting *Philadelphia Bulletin*.

19. *Memphis Commercial Appeal*, May 30, 1901, May 17, 1905, May 7, 1988.

20. *Tri-State Defender*, August 10, 1985, June 11, 1988.

21. Charles Royster, "Slaver, General, Klansman," *Atlantic Monthly* (May 1993): 125, 128.

22. *Memphis Daily Appeal*, March 12, 1869; *New York Times*, March 15, 1869; *New York Times*, July 9, 1875; a similar report was carried in the *Memphis Daily Appeal*, July 6, 1875.

23. *New York Times*, October 30, 1877.

24. *Memphis Daily Appeal*, October 30, 1877. See also October 31, 1877; *St. Louis Post-Dispatch*, November 1, 1877.

25. *New Orleans Daily Democrat*, October 31, 1877.

26. *Memphis Commerical Appeal*, May 30 and 31, 1901. See also April 5, 1905, which states that "Forrest is recognized by competent military men of Europe as being one of the greatest military geniuses of all time."

27. Ibid., May 11, 1905.

28. Ibid., May 14, 1905.

29. Ibid., quoting the *Commercial Appeal* of January 29, 1905.

30. Ibid., May 17, 1905.

31. Ibid., July 13, 1921.

32. Ibid., July 13, 1940, July 13, 1947, July 13, 1985, May 7, 1988.

33. *Atlantic Monthly* (May 1993): 126.

34. *Memphis Commercial Appeal*, May 30, 1901.

35. Ibid., May 17, 1905, July 13, 1921, July 13, 1937. The memoir was Richard Taylor, *Destruction and Reconstruction: Personal Experiences of the Late War* (New York: Longman's, Green and Company, 1955).

36. Ibid., July 13, 1940, July 13, 1950.

37. *Louisville Courier-Journal*, June 28, 1871; *Chicago Tribune*, June 28, 1871; *Cincinnati Daily Enquirer*, June 28, 1871; *St. Louis Globe Democrat*, June 28, 1871; *Charleston Courier*, June 28, 1871; *Memphis Daily Appeal*, June 28, 1871; *New York Times*, June 28, 1871; *Galveston Daily News*, June 30, 1871; *New York Tribune*, June 28, 1871.

38. *Memphis Daily Appeal*, April 15, 1870, June 25, 1871.

39. Ibid., May 30, 1901; Hurst, *Nathan Bedford Forrest*, 297. See also Joel Williamson, *The Crucible of Race* (New York: Oxford University Press, 1984).

40. *Memphis Daily Appeal*, November 1, 1877.

41. Ibid., October 30, October 31,1877.

42. *Charleston News and Courier*, November 1, 1877.

43. *St. Louis Post-Dispatch*, November 1, 1877; *Memphis Daily Appeal*, November 3, 1877; *Atlanta Constitution*, October 31, 1877.

44. *New York Times*, October 30, October 31, 1877.

45. *New York Tribune*, October 30, 1877; *San Francisco Chronicle*, November 1, 1877.

46. *Memphis Commercial Appeal*, May 30, 1901.

47. Ibid., May 14, 1905.

48. Ibid.

49. Ibid., May 17, 1905. On the rash of lynchings in the decade before this story, see Williamson, *Crucible of Race*, 181–82.

50. *Memphis Commercial Appeal*, July 13, 1940.

51. *Memphis Press-Scimitar*, July 14, 1958.

52. *Memphis Commercial Appeal*, July 13, 1985.

53. *Memphis Daily Appeal*, October 30, 1877.

54. *Memphis Commercial Appeal*, May 14, 1905.

55. Ibid., May 14 and 17, 1905.

56. *New York Tribune*, May 27, 1918.

57. *New York Times*, May 28, 1918.

58. *Memphis Commercial Appeal*, July 13, 1940.

59. Ibid., July 13, 1947, July 13, 1985.

60. *Memphis Daily Appeal*, October 30, 1877; *New Orleans Daily Democrat*, October 31, 1877.

61. *Memphis Commercial Appeal*, May 30, 1901.

62. Ibid., May 14, 1905.

CHAPTER FIVE

MONKEYS AND MANIFESTOES

THE SOUTH HAS MANY HISTORIES—real, imagined, and mythic. As agricultural America withered in the smoke and heat of industrialism, a select cadre of Southern intellectuals looked backward for cultural sustenance. They found it in the reality of war, the romance of the cavalier, and the myth of the garden.

The Nashville Agrarians had their beginnings in a loosely organized literary discussion group in 1915 at Vanderbilt University. Their intellectual indulgences were interrupted by world war, their faculty and student members dispersed by the conflict and personal circumstances, but they reconvened in 1919. The group eventually revolved around sixteen figures, among them John Crowe Ransom, Allen Tate, Andrew Lytle, Donald Davidson, Frank Owsley, John Gould Fletcher, and Robert Penn Warren. At first they had focused their energies on new poetry with an emphasis on form and complex content. Their genesis publication was a small poetry magazine, *The Fugitive*, which began in April 1922. Those associated with the project were called Fugitives, and some continued in the Agrarian movement. The magazine's demise, only a few months after the end of the notorious Scopes "monkey trial" in July 1925, was not from lack of interest or support but from lack of time on the part of the Fugitives.

A legend grew up that the Scopes trial catalyzed the thinking and writing of the group, provoking a defensive reaction and, eventually, publication in 1930 of *I'll Take My Stand*, which became their manifesto. This is only partially correct, however. Davidson, a book columnist for the *Nashville Tennessean*, later found it useful to remember the trial as the affront to Southern pride that launched the movement, a shot fired at the Fort Sumter of Northern political arrogance by a cohesive partisan intellectual brigade. In a sense, then, the trial became a creation myth for the Agrarians after the fact, although undoubtedly it seemed at the time to be provocative. Just why it was so important to them has to do with what the trial came to represent.[1]

The Scopes trial grew out of a larger fundamentalist crusade in the early twentieth century. By the end of the nineteenth century, fundamentalists had begun to insist on reading the Bible literally, especially the creation story in Genesis, as the inspired word of God. Like the Agrarians, the fundamentalists were reacting to new scientific ideas, especially Darwinian evolution theory and its incursion into traditional religion and beliefs. At one level the Scopes trial concerned the teaching of evolution in public schools. But at a deeper, more important level it was a reaction against new ideas about the origins of humanity in a society shifting from rural to urban, from an agricultural economy to an industrial one. The trial was also a symbolic attack on critical elements in Southern mythology, particularly Christianity and the yeoman farmer.

The assault on the former was mounted in Clarence Darrow's famous debate with William Jennings Bryan during the trial. Bryan was lambasted in the writings of *Baltimore Sun* journalist H. L. Mencken, who delightedly savaged the South as a vast intellectual vacuum, barren of civilization and inhabited by hillbillies, rubes, rednecks, and morons. To him, the agrarian Southerner was "a poor clod . . . deluded by childish theology, full of an almost pathological hatred of all learning, all human dignity, all fine and noble things." The South had once been, according to Mencken, the seat of American civilization as it had been inherited from Europe, but after the Civil War the coastal aristocracy had been replaced by a gaggle of oafs. The furor over the trial helped galvanize the Agrarians because it was an embarrassment, not just for Tennessee but for all of the South. The image that emerged did not complement the South's self-image as a paragon of Jeffersonian democracy, home of the the noble yeoman farmer. Moreover, Darrow and Mencken were Northerners.[2]

The Agrarians responded to both prongs of the attack on their culture and its myths. In defending the South, some of them were merely answering an insult, as opposed to building an intellectual foundation on a usable past. They knew the South could not be defended only on the strength of its literary tradition. Instead, they turned to what F. Garvin Davenport Jr. called an "illusory fiction," criticizing science and industry and responding to Mencken and his ilk not because they attacked cherished institutions but because the South in general was under assault again by outsiders. In retrospect, planning to do battle against industrialism with mythology seems about as anachronistic as engaging in a war without a sufficient number of cannon factories—which, of course, the South had done from 1861 to 1865.

The timing for the release of *I'll Take My Stand* in 1930, however, could not have been better for the Agrarians. Industrialism appeared to be in retreat in the wake of the stock market collapse and the onset of the Great Depression. Ransom's introduction criticized the "cult of science," which he charged with enslaving "our human energies to a degree now clearly felt to be burdensome." He and the authors of other essays in this collection took issue with suppressing the mystery of nature and what they saw as the scientific presumption of having answers to everything. It was a provocative volume and perhaps in that respect was most true to a Southern tradition dating back seven decades. Like Forrest, they answered the attack on Southern society and tradition with action. "It was," wrote John Egerton, "in the most profound sense, a reactionary document, a lashing out at foreign forces (industrialization, communism, the North) and a defense of hoary Southern virtues, real and imagined. . . . Industrialism was the paper tiger that all the writers were exhorted to confront with whip and chair, and most of them dutifully did so, calling up criticisms from as far back as the Iron Age."[3]

A USEFUL MYTH: FORREST AND THE AGRARIANS

When the Old South sought to expand its plantation culture into the emerging western territories, it fell back on a fictional image of a settled, feudal society. As Henry Nash Smith explained, however, literary plantations "are almost always in the older South, and when they are situated in the new, developing Southwest, they are unhistorically depicted as duplicates of the Virginia and Carolina estates on which the convention was first based. Such symbols could not be adapted to the expression of a society like that of the West, either South or North, where rapidity of change, crudity, bustle, heterogeneity were fundamental traits." Actually, the coastal plantations themselves were imitations of the Italian Renaissance culture based on the classical civilizations of Greece and Rome, so the plantations of the Southwest—including the lands southwest of the Appalachians as well as the lands beyond the Mississippi River—were imitations of an imitation. The Southwest was a long way geographically, chronologically, and culturally from Greece and Rome. The folk literature of the Southwest, made popular by newspapermen such as Mark Twain, survived the Civil War and was important to American literature but was, according to Smith, "of little or no use politically because while it depicted a society containing slaves, it dealt with slavery only incidentally and had no case to make for the institution." In other words, it was an unusable past, an unmalleable myth. So the challenge for Lytle and the other Agrarians was to construct a usable past, a useful myth into which a character such as Forrest could be inserted and rendered acceptable. Lytle in particular helped build the Forrest Myth by providing its intellectual foundation.

Some of the Agrarians became philosophical and moral alchemists in their "discovery" that a vein of lead in Southern history— violence and slavery—was in fact purest gold, setting the South apart and above the rest of the country. They were looking not for a factual history but for a history that aggrandized their Southern culture. A mythical approach to the problem justified the past, clarified the present, and damned the attackers. Like the South of the 1860s, the Agrarians' South of the 1920s was defined not by a substantial history but by a mythical one. It was a society defined more by what it opposed—modernism and industrialism—than by what it valued. Like the South of old, many in the New South opposed certain aspects of liberalism, especially as it affected race relations and industrialism. Both Ransom and Tate defended myth as a struggle with science, and thus the opposition to industrialism became almost necessary for those fully committed to "essential history": that is, history as myth, not as narrative based on fact. And for some Agrarians, race was the essence of that myth.[4]

Put in this context, Forrest, for Lytle and others, was a deeply flawed man but an excellent Southern man; his personal history might be tainted, but the profound moral truth that was his essence transcended such niggling detail. So his slave trading and his alleged murder of black soldiers at Fort Pillow were inconsequential in the context of a greater moral lesson, congruent with fundamentalist Christianity: that Forrest forgave and was forgiven. He forgave by calling for people to put the war behind them and to work in concert. He was forgiven by former slaves, as evidenced by their coming to work on his farm after the war and the testimony of at least a few that if he was a racist, at least he was a benevolent one. Framed with an emphasis on the right facts and Christian ideals, the real Forrest, the historical Forrest, could become a parable of Christian redemption. In this way, the historical issues surrounding Forrest were submerged in the greater or essential "truth," which was discernible only in a mythic interpretation of his life. In speaking to the validity of biblical myth, Ransom argued that "religious myths, including those of the Bible, are unhistorical and unscientific, precisely as our gallant historians and higher critics have recently discovered; but . . . their unhistorical and unscientific character is not their vice but their excellence, and that certainly was their intent." For Ransom, the key point was that myth is memory and remembering a creative process. "The mythmaker is a desperate man, for he has a memory. He remembers the remarkable individual in the richness of his private existence. He sees very little relation between that individual and the dry generalization into which science would fit him." Though Ransom was not speaking directly to the Forrest Myth, his words are applicable in understanding the myth—but not the life—of Nathan Bedford Forrest.[5]

THE SOUTH RISES AGAIN—ALMOST

Numerous groups emerging from the 1920s through the early 1940s were devoted to studying the South. The Agrarians were among the most conspicuous of those groups, which ranged in interest across diverse fields: language, history, political science, economics, music, and sociology. The South Atlantic Modern Language Association was founded in 1928; the Southern Political Science Association and the Southern Economic Association in 1929; the Southern Historical Association and the Southeastern Chapter of the American Musicological Society in 1934; the Southern Sociological Society in 1935; the South Central Modern Language Association in 1939; the Southeastern Regional Conference of the College Art Association in 1941. Such activity is indicative of something more than literary quibbling over esoterica; it involved an effort to understand an emerging South. The new interest was more than a reaction to the Scopes trial, essentially a parody, and more than the Agrarians, a small but disproportionately important literary and political movement. These groups were expansive in their interests, goals, and motivations. The response to them reflected a long-simmering interest in and demand for an understanding of Southern culture and society.[6]

Indicative, too, of a broader interest in the South was the involvement of journalists in the Southern revival. Perhaps the most important journalist of the period in that regard was Wilbur J. Cash of the *Charlotte News*, author of the classic *The Mind of the South*, which he worked on during the 1930s. Like the Agrarians, he believed that the yeoman farmer was the foundation of Southern society and history. Davidson cited another journalist, John Temple Graves of the *Birmingham Age-Herald*, as offering consistent editorial support for the Agrarian cause and ideas. Graves published *The Fighting South* in 1943, which may well have pleased Davidson not only because of its congruency with Agrarian philosophy but also because Davidson saw in Graves a fellow provocateur, as evidenced by the title of the book.

Allen Tate worked with Herbert Agar, editor of the *Louisville Courier-Journal*, to produce *Who Owns America? A New Declaration of Independence*. Published in 1936, the volume criticized "large corporate property." One of the pieces even rebuked farmers for leaving an agrarian economy in order to "deliberately . . . share in the great profits of a money economy dominated by finance capitalism." Like the rebels of 1860, the Agrarians were radicals who saw themselves arrayed against an external threat to a way of life: industrialism bearing down on the farmer. But unlike the radicals of 1860, the Agrarians were men of the pen, not of the sword. When it came to helping the small farms and farmers, they had little practical effect. With some exceptions, they left it to a variety of New Deal agencies, the Farm Bureau, the Federal Writers Project, and tenant farmers' unions to find solutions.[7]

Another sign of interest in the South came in the work of writers and photographers. Erskine Caldwell and Margaret Bourke-White's *You Have Seen Their Faces*, published in 1937, dramatized the plight of the Southern poor. Much in opposition to the style of this book was the peculiar antijournalistic manifesto *Let Us Now Praise Famous Men* by James Agee and Walker Evans. Agee, a disaffected journalist on leave from *Fortune* magazine, and Evans, a roving documentary photographer with the Farm Security Administration, went to Alabama in 1936 to portray the lives of some tenant farmers. The original assignment, which was intended for publication in *Fortune*, gradually mutated into a screed against what they saw as the patronizing style of Caldwell and Bourke-White—the kind of journalism that exploits the lives of the poor for profit—and against the entire reformist ethos of the New Deal, which, in Agee's mind, reduced human lives to statistics and stripped them of their spiritual essence. Agee and Evans saw none of the grandeur of the Old South envisioned by the Agrarians. Their tenant farmers are the by-products of the Civil War, less interested in the Lost Cause than in lost lives, condemned to relentless toil on land they neither own nor revere. By the time their work was published in 1941, however, national attention was diverted by the gathering storm of war, and the book was a financial flop.[8]

CRITTERS AND CONTROVERSY

Agee and Evans may have been destined for financial failure because they offered an antidote to myth—probably an unwelcome curative in a time bracketed by the twin illnesses of depression and world war. Another work, in sharp contrast to their anti-myth, was an unabashed glorification of the Forrest legend and the Old South. Andrew Lytle and Donald Davidson sought epic Southern heroes who could illustrate the virtues of the Old South. Davidson had envisioned an epic poem about Forrest but gave it up because he saw the subject as too familiar for a poet, though worthy of a biographer or novelist. "You can't find a hero that you can use, nor can you invent an adequate one at this time," he wrote. "Any hero you might take won't do for an epic, partly because he's been too well documented." The phrase "a hero you can use" is significant. Davidson was interested in propaganda for a cause; he was interested in myth, not history. Perhaps he was thinking of the biographies written by his fellow Agrarians, such as Allen Tate's *Stonewall Jackson, The Good Soldier* (1928) and *Jefferson Davis, His Rise and Fall* (1929). Lytle attempted to dispel the Mencken-catalyzed myth of Southern "white trash," portrayed as ignorant, hookworm-ridden hillbillies. To do so, he needed an alternative myth, one that cast the agrarian tradition and values as an antidote to industrial modernism and its inevitable spiritual corrosion.[9] In Forrest, Lytle found the man to personify that myth, a man through whom he could celebrate the frontier, the garden, the yeoman, the cavalier, and Southern tradition. Lytle favored the western rim of the South, the frontier that had produced men like Jackson and Forrest rather than the plantation aristocrats. In Forrest, Lytle resurrected the mythology he favored—and its sins—while elevating Forrest to the Confederate pantheon.

Lytle's biography was a contribution to the Forrest Myth; his Forrest personified an idealized yeoman farmer. A mythologic scheme that grew out of the Agrarians' discussions came to life in

Lytle's Forrest: the common man of uncommon heroics and uncommon intelligence; a slaver who is humane and caring, even to
the extent that former slaves remain with him during the war and
as freedmen; a primitive figure, out of the wilderness, conquering
the frontier. In Lytle's hands, he is also a fitting symbol for all the
Reconstruction-era South. Forrest becomes involved in a number
of business ventures, most notably perhaps railroad building, but
he fails and eventually returns to farming, though on a much diminished scale compared with the antebellum days. In the course
of the railroad ventures he is impoverished while less worthy men—
capitalists and industrialists, men devoted to "progress"—become
wealthy in those enterprises.

An indebted Forrest, though, pays off his debts in full. He and
his railroad venture are, for Lytle, the South and industrialism, a
noble entity sullied by amoral carpetbaggers. Forrest, like the South,
is an innocent who is taken advantage of, goes down in defeat, but
is heroic and honorable in failure. The only way to redemption is
the way Forrest chooses—going back to the land, the farm, which
carries with it not only the image of the yeoman farmer but also
the suggestion of the garden myth and spiritual traditions. The
garden myth uses the symbols of the Garden of Eden and the Hel-
lenic Arcadia as metaphors that can be adapted to the plantation.
The enlightened Southern planter becomes a natural man of the
soil, a man of letters and culture, in contrast to his New England
counterpart, the Yankee industrialist. But the garden in this sense
has a serpent—slavery. Redemption in the garden, then, is spoiled
by the serpent of slavery. [10]

Charlotte H. Beck interprets *Bedford Forrest and His Critter Company* as Lytle's first novel, not a biography but a way of "combin-
ing regional pieties, identification with the particular hero of Lytle's
own region of birth, and training in the inclusion of dramatic elements in his first important narrative project." Walter Sullivan earlier made much the same point when he noted the curious structure
of the book. He characterized the first hundred pages as a historical study, mere preparation for the narrative that is the heart of the
book. In the first section, Lytle supports a thesis: Forrest emerges
from these preliminary pages as a doomed hero. When Bragg enters the story, according to Sullivan, he becomes the "enemy and
betrayer of Nathan Bedford Forrest, . . . a villain as distinctly identified as those in any novel. . . . Ideology is put aside for the sake of
drama."

As history, the book fails dismally, a point made by the noted historian Henry Steele Commager in a review published in the *New Republic* in 1931. Lytle's contention, said Commager, was "that the failure of Davis to recognize in time the genius of this homespun cavalryman was fatal to the Confederacy" and that the mistake was not so much an error in military judgment as it was a "deliberate ignoring of the plain people from whom Forrest sprang." Commager criticized the "unsupported generalizations" in the book (which indeed omits citations) and disputed both Lytle's "facts" and his conclusions about what might have occurred if Forrest had been given command of the western armies earlier in the war. He praised Lytle's writing and his "portrait of a frontiersman," adding, however, that the portrait "would hang just as comfortably in San Francisco or Minneapolis or Chicago as in Richmond." As for the facts, Richard H. King viewed the book as "less interesting for what it says about Forrest than for what it says about Lytle's vision of the past. He whitewashed Forrest's role as a slave trader and excused Forrest's lack of control over his troops, which led to the Fort Pillow massacre of black troops. Leaving nothing to the imagination, Lytle ended the biography with a panegyric to the Ku Klux Klan."

Among other critics, Mark Lucas pointed out the "one-dimensionality of its portrayal of Forrest. For instance, Lytle writes straight apologia for Forrest's role as grand wizard of the Ku Klux Klan. . . . Thus, ostensible complexities in the character of Forrest go unplumbed so that 'a son of the gods' can emerge in unshadowed heroism." Court Carney saw the book as meeting the desire for a more defiant Forrest in the 1930s. Lytle, he said, "depicted a dashing and reckless leader capable of incredible military successes and possessing almost supernatural strength. Lytle also turned Forrest's 'reckless ruffianism' into a positive attribute that provided the basis of the writer's admiration for the general." Emory Thomas took issue with Lytle's contention that Forrest saved Southern culture by embracing the Klan and, by inference, feudalism and Western culture. "Thus," he wrote, "in the cause of unreconstructed apology, Lytle manages to thrash Western culture, Southern culture, feudalism, and Forrest all at once."[11]

The book has its defenders as well, however, not so much as biography or history but as story, myth, and drama. Even Lucas thought King's attack on the book simplistic: he said Lytle's views on Reconstruction, for example, showed competent scholarship and was not out of line with what prominent historians of his time (and even Lucas's) were writing about the period. Furthermore, Lytle was closer to a still visible past than his later critics: "To be morally indignant with Lytle for his not being morally indignant with Forrest is, in a sense, anachronistic, a failure to see Lytle in his time and place." And Lytle was an "embryonic novelist" inclined to polemics—in other words, an Agrarian with a polemical sword to sharpen, and Forrest was the grinding stone upon which he sharpened it.

Walter Sullivan concluded his preface to a new edition of Lytle's book with the hope that it "can remind us of what we have forgotten and help to restore in our society some of the virtues that we seem to have misplaced." J. O. Tate, in the *Southern Partisan*, described the book as "a vigorous and idiomatic account of Forrest's life in the context of the Old Frontier, seeing him as a symbol of Southern Feudalism; and connecting him with the point of view that sustained the Agrarians." Alphonse Vinh, reviewing the new edition for the *Southern Partisan*, agreed that the book reads like a novel and credited Lytle with some Tolstoyan description. He called the story a classical epic, a morality tale, and a foray into the vortex of the Forrest Myth. Benjamin B. Alexander, also writing in the *Southern Partisan*, agreed that the subject is of mythic stature, the "Achilles of the Confederacy," with roots in Homer and Virgil. He praised Lytle for recognizing the importance of clan, kin, patriarchy, and familial values and saw in Forrest's story a conceptualization of nationalism based on the folk. He gave the book contemporary value, seeing its relevance to an understanding of what went wrong during the Vietnam War, and warned (in 1987) that Islamic fundamentalism would present a challenge to American nationalism. A knowledge of Forrest could be of value, he argued, in comprehending American military and political power.[12]

In his own introduction to the new edition, Lytle tells how his grandmother, as a child, was shot by a Union soldier; he thus makes the war personal. He discusses the nature of the hero, and describes "the community into which I was born and in which memory called Forrest the great hero. The hero saves not only by his prowess; he saves by the divinity within himself. Indeed his prowess depends upon this divinity. The hero's most perfect image is, of course, Christ the man-god." He describes Forrest's family as "a part of that vast restlessness which had spread over Europe after the breakdown of medieval life, and which, because it could not be contained entirely by the rigid discipline of nationalism, continued by overflowing into the Americas. Here, in the newly occupied continent of North America, the Europeans set about to appease their nostalgia for feudalism." Thus, Forrest is descended from tribesmen of the European forests and would not submit to despotism. Lytle begins by telling the story of how Forrest stalked and slew the panther that had slashed his mother. Right away the myth is established. Forrest slays a snake, fights wild dogs and local toughs, and stands down a neighbor whose ox he had slain on his family's property. This is the same story that Aileen Wells Parks would tell in *Bedford Forrest: Boy on Horseback*, but Lytle's Forrest is not a hero for children. This Forrest is a hero for an entire civilization that Lytle believed was under attack, and when he lays down his sword at the end of the war and becomes the Grand Wizard of the Invisible Empire, he stands as the last ruler of the Old South, the last knight of the old feudal order, and, in Lytle's mind at least, the first Agrarian.[13]

Lytle's Forrest was the response to Mencken's stereotype of an ignorant, white-trash South. Lytle created a figure of natural intelligence, ennobled by tradition, who could face down again the Northern infidel intruders.

FACISM, RACE, AND THE AGRARIANS

Uncertainty pervaded the 1920s and 1930s. The vitality of urban life—its business, its art, its culture—was both embraced and damned across American culture. Americans knew they were in a transitional era of new ideas, new economics, even a new morality, but the politics, economics, and values of an agricultural culture were still alive and well. The Scopes trial exemplified the clash of cultures, an event in which faith battled data. Even Henry Ford, symbol of American ingenuity and ambition in the new era, could condemn history as "bunk" but unabashedly spend a small fortune recreating his own history, his childhood home. Science and technology were challenging not only the farm economy but religious traditions grounded in a literal reading of the Bible. Many found themselves between eras—coming into the "modern" age but not yet being there, leaving the rural standards but not yet having left them behind. In the 1930s some saw the Great Depression as the failure of capitalism; others, as nothing less than the failure of democracy. Some saw radical change as the solution; others turned to radical retrenchment. Some Agrarians, as acutely aware as anyone of living in two times, saw the latter as the solution. They looked backward as they looked forward. In searching for a place in time, they dabbled in strange ideologies. Fascism and communism were in the wind, and the wind was blowing across the South as much as any other region.

By about 1936, with the rise of totalitarian regimes in Europe, the Agrarians became susceptible to charges of fascism—in part because of their association with Seward Collins, a controversial New York publisher who enlisted most of the Agrarians, principally Tate and Davidson, as contributors to his journal, *American Review*, in 1933. About the time of the group's meeting with Collins to settle editorial matters, Davidson, historian Frank Owsley, and the future Pulitzer Prize–winning poet John Gould Fletcher—the most enthusiastic neo-Confederates among the Agrarians—began considering other outlets for their views, which in Fletcher's case included anti-Semitism. Fletcher, whose views were highly changeable, at one point called for an established national church and the restoration of the monarchy, and had even tried to interest Tate in forming a Southern political movement. Tate, according to Richard H. King, had come "awfully close" to a proto-fascist reading of Southern history in his biography of Jefferson Davis. Daniel Aaron alleged that James W. Jackson, a historical character rendered sympathetically in Tate's novel, *The Fathers*, was in reality "a kind of Confederate Horst Wessel," a Nazi hero.

Fletcher and Owsley proposed a campus organization at Vanderbilt to be called the Grey-Jackets, whose members would march in Confederate uniforms and resist those who sullied the memory of the Lost Cause. Fletcher suggested that they destroy a monument to Cyrus McCormick, whose reaper, they thought, had hastened the Northern victory. Other schemes they considered involved actions against chambers of commerce and participation in neo-pagan harvest festivals. Curiously, the movement was to be open to blacks, who were to be rewarded with land ownership as part of the effort to expel the hated Northerners—although Fletcher worried that the Grey-Jackets could turn into Brown Shirts (a reference to Nazi storm troopers) and begin shooting the blacks. Davidson and Owsley, perhaps not willing to go as far as Fletcher, quietly set up a pro-Southern semisecret student organization at Vanderbilt called the Phalanx, which attracted about two dozen members. Owsley gave a radio talk denouncing communist subversion of blacks, and he developed a reading list for members of the Phalanx, giving special attention to *American Review*. Some Agrarians were horrified by these antics.[14]

When the journal began publishing openly pro-fascist articles in 1934, critics, including Mencken, attacked Collins and the Agrarians. Collins was seeking to end parliamentary government, or set up some kind of monarchy or fascist state headed by a strong man who might be an imperial president—perhaps even Roosevelt. Hesitant to be identified as propagandists for any political movement, most of the Agrarians repudiated both fascism and communism. The Phalanx officially disappeared from Vanderbilt, perhaps continuing for a short time with a few members as an underground movement. But Owsley, fearing communism and what he saw as New Deal attacks on the South through anti-lynching legislation, suspected that fascism could be useful in putting down "human rats" who threatened the region. He proposed a constitutional amendment dividing the United States into self-governing economic regions with powers of nullification, reminiscent of John C. Calhoun. He died in 1955, denouncing integration (the "mongrelized state with its contempt and suspicion of tradition and gentility") and communists.

Fletcher had drowned in 1950, a probable suicide. Davidson, who "expressed the brutal underside of Agrarian racial views," in King's words, became a vocal opponent of communism, even calling for a loyalty oath for Tennesseans during the Cold War, and an increasingly strident defender of segregation. His attacks on blacks were often vile; blacks were, he said, "a grinning barnacle tucked away in all the tender spots of Southern life." In *Attack on Leviathan* (1938) he asked, "What did a few lynchings [in Georgia] count in the balance against the continual forbearance and solicitude that the Georgian felt he exercised toward those amiable children of cannibals, whose skins by no conceivable act of Congress or educational program could be changed from black to white." Rejected by most of his old friends in the Agrarian movement, Davidson became, according to Daniel Joseph Singal, "little more than a local curiosity at Vanderbilt, an angry old man keeping the Agrarian flame burning long after the movement had died." Davidson himself died in 1968, leaving behind a complex legacy, his gifts as a poet, teacher, and philosopher and his personal decency tarnished by his racism. Larry Daughtrey, one of his students at Vanderbilt and later a reporter for the *Nashville Tennessean*, wrote in a column for the newspaper in 1997 that Davidson, "hat[ing] blacks," had "become a sort of metaphor for the university itself: the intellectual richness diminished by a moral flaw embedded deep in its soul."[15]

Despite these manifestations of radical thought and certain affinities with elements of fascist thought, one should take care in identifying the Agrarians with fascism. In general, the Agrarian movement was far more antifascist than fascist; certainly, most of its members were not fascists. Cash said as much: "It is not true, as was foolishly charged by the Communists and others who should have known better, that [the Agrarians] consciously inclined to Fascism." Cash, indeed, was mindful of genuine fascist elements in the South, such as the Ku Klux Klan, which he saw as "an authentic folk movement—at least as fully such as the Nazi movement in Germany." In Chapel Hill, University of North Carolina sociologist Howard W. Odum was warning of deadly parallels between the South and Nazi Germany and possible revolutionary symptoms. Thus the necessary elements for a native fascist movement were in place. It is easy to see how isolated statements by the Agrarians and some of the more foolish ideas that percolated at the fringes of the movement could be exploited by those opposed to the general thrust of Agrarian thought.

Fascism itself was based on a myth, a perversion of classicism and nationalism. The image of goose-stepping Grey-Jackets and neo-Confederate racists and resistance fighters is almost irresistible in that regard. But the truth is otherwise. The journalist Ralph McGill, a celebrated Southern reformer, who began as a reporter for the *Nashville Banner* and was later the editor and publisher of the *Atlanta Constitution*, was exposed to the Fugitives and the Agrarians at Vanderbilt University. He came to see the Agrarians as sentimentally and naively attached to the myth of the Old South. He dismissed *I'll Take My Stand* as a "composite, posturing plea for a return to the economy and the culture of the plantation. *I'll Take My Stand* did not quite advocate slavery. It did, however, most earnestly recommend a return to a paternalistic system in which civilized planters would halt the writing of a poem to turn smiling faces to Uncle Tom, who, hat in hand, had a request to make." This characterization fails to appreciate the diversity of viewpoints expressed by the Agrarians, but McGill, though critical, stops short of calling the Agrarians fascists.[16]

The neo-Agrarian Richard Weaver even argued in 1944 that the South was the first region in the United States to intuit a threat in fascism, although in debate "the South would have been hard put to distinguish between some of the slogans of the New Order and the tenets of its own faith, sealed with Confederate blood and affirmed in many a postbellum oration. That the Southern whites considered themselves *Herrenvolk* in relation to the Negro is one of the obvious features of our sociological landscape, and belief in the influence of blood and soil is powerful with them, as with any agrarian people. . . . The restoration of medieval concepts in Europe might almost have seemed the Confederate's dream of reversing history and regaining the way of life which he lost in 1865." But, Weaver argued, the South, more than other regions, instinctively resisted fascism and other movements that challenged its protective myths and called for the creation of a mass state. Rather, the South "realized that as soon as the first encroachment is made, the battle is on, and there can be no cessation until a victor has been decided." The Civil War was about decentralization, not centralization. The South sought to establish a regional power, separate from national values, so when it saw "society threatened by the new and extreme proletarian nihilism, it expresse[d] once more the conservative reaction and gird[ed] for battle."[17]

As a poster boy for the Agrarian movement—sacred to Lytle, Davidson, and Caroline Gordon, in particular—the protean Forrest, then, could be interpreted either as the Southern equivalent of a fascist Aryan Superman leading a rebellion of the *volk*, or, in Weaver's sense, as a folk hero who could be summoned from memory when "the battle is on, and there can be no cessation until a victor has been decided." In either sense, Forrest is the metaphoric man of the hour, ready to be summoned from his plinth in the South's hour of need. Lytle called his biography "an attempt to show General Forrest as he developed into the most typical strong man of the Agrarian South," battling the Northern industrialists who broke Southern feudalism by conquest.[18] "Strong man" is a curious phrase in retrospect, in that it has come to be associated with the likes of Napoleon, Hitler, Mussolini, Franco, Stalin, Juan Perón, Fidel Castro, and the leaders of untold juntas—not, presumably, what Lytle meant. But it is suggestive of the potential for a fascist state in the South, harking back to some phony mythology of the Confederacy.

Fiction writers such as David C. Poyer have plowed this ground often enough. In his novel *The Shiloh Project*, Poyer creates a fascist movement that threatens to undermine a modern, independent Confederate empire. A rogue agent provocateur rails against "Dixie socialism" and predicts that some day the South "will be purified—by the gun, the rope, and by fire. . . . Now we goin' to be a nation, by God. One party—the Kuklos League. One leader. One flag, and one aim—the unshakable superiority of the white race." It is a chilling vision, a fiction with feet walking on the ground of Confederate myth.[19]

McLUHAN AND THE AGRARIANS

A little-known fact about the Agrarians is that one of the movement's earliest proponents was the Canadian media and literary scholar Marshall McLuhan, whose later books—*The Mechanical Bride: Folklore of Industrial Man, The Gutenberg Galaxy: The Making of Typographic Man*, and *Understanding Media: The Extensions of Man*—became influential explorations of the emerging mass communications industries in the twentieth century, giving rise to such popular expressions as "the medium is the message" and the notion that the media are the "extensions of man." McLuhan saw the media as creators of myths, so it is understandable that he was attracted to the mythic South and the Agrarians. He traveled to Nashville to meet Davidson and Owsley, carried on a correspondence with Tate, and published eight articles and reviews in the *Sewanee Review* from 1944 to 1947 under Tate's editorship, including "The Southern Quality." Through the mid-1940s, according to Jonathan Miller, "McLuhan seems to have stagnated in a well-recognized form of cultural nostalgia. The familiar themes of conservative agrarianism repeat themselves like a monotonous fugue" in his essays. McLuhan argued that the South was a residue of the European classical humanist tradition and stood in opposition to profane rationalism. He had written Tate in 1945 that the American use of atomic bombs against Japan justified rejection of the Allies' "exceedingly dubious 'cause,' " the end point of rationalism.

Like Tate, who encouraged him and widened his appeal, McLuhan embraced Christianity and Catholic Christian culture. He saw the South as a chivalric bulwark against modernity, the North as a barbarous region corrupted by commercialism and its handmaiden, advertising, estranged from the values of Saint Thomas Aquinas. Industrialism and science and all forms of specialization had divided mankind from its spiritual roots, in McLuhan's dualistic thinking. But he, like many of the Agrarians, particularly Lytle, ignored the problem of race while casting the South in the role of defender of Christian values.[20]

In his later thought, McLuhan regarded the media as potential allies in the retrieval of wholeness and the recovery of an oral tradition predating Gutenberg and the coming of Industrial Man. He believed that the Civil War had in some sense protected the South from fully embracing the modern world and allowed it to preserve at least a memory of civilization and agrarian values that might yet be harvested. And yet the communications philosopher McLuhan overlooked the salient point that the South had declined in part *because* it lacked a communications system appropriate to its size. His theories have come under attack from many quarters. Miller, for example, pointed out that far from being "the stable civic paradise painted by McLuhan, the Old South was a caldron of rampant rural individualism. It was restless, plural, and, above all, thinly settled. The volatile expansion of its population prevented that steady consolidation of shared human interests so essential to the growth of organized knowledge. If the South remained technologically backward it was not, as McLuhan implies, because it was *too* civilized, but, more direly, because it was not civilized *enough*."[21]

THE AGRARIAN LEGACY

The Agrarians have their explainers, defenders, and apologists, including Eugene D. Genovese, who attempted to counter charges that the Agrarians and other Southern conservatives were fascists, agreeing with Weaver that they staunchly opposed fascism. He pointed out that identifying racism with fascism "is a dangerously misleading half-truth, for racism has done nicely in democratic regimes." Mark G. Malvasi has written that the Agrarians' "dark pronouncements about the fate of the Republic at the hands of entrenched bureaucrats, untrustworthy politicians, greedy capitalists, and corrupt citizens have come true with a vengeance." Speaking more broadly of the Agrarians and their conservative progeny, Malvasi concluded that "they honor their ancestral dead and keep their tireless vigil, awaiting the moment when man's fall from grace into history shall be redeemed."[22]

Among the South's myriad histories and myths, the Agrarians' legacy has been as important and as malleable as the Forrest Myth. They exploited and elevated mythology, and Lytle in particular helped create the Forrest Myth. The Agrarians aggrandized the individualist myths that Forrest actually lived. The meaning and morality have faded and blurred around the edges, but like sunset shadows, they have grown darker and more gray.

As an intellectual movement, the Agrarians suffered the same fate as the Confederacy itself. Paul K. Conkin, a noted Vanderbilt University historian, well described the Agrarians as "a loose circle, with vague outer boundaries and frequent shifts in membership." Although they have received "much loving attention" from scholars, according to Conkin, the story of how the group struggled and matured and "ultimately suffered decline and defeat" has been neglected. The Confederacy, too, also both more and less than the sum of its parts, was a loose circle, never fully unified politically or intellectually. The Confederacy and the South were not identical regions; the inherent contradiction in a "unified Confederacy" is evident in a gaggle of writers and university professors aggrandizing the agrarian life. The Confederacy tried to defend and justify a vast region that produced characters as different as Forrest and Lee. The greater South, including the border state of Kentucky, was the birthplace of both Lincoln and Davis. The Agrarians included personalities as diverse as Ransom, Warren, Fletcher, and Owsley. That there never was *one* South is a fact the Lost Cause myth often overlooks. There never was one Agrarian movement, either. Although both the Agrarian cause and the Lost Cause have received "much loving attention," perhaps both causes were ultimately unwinnable.[23]

NOTES

1. Daniel Aaron, "The Neo-Confederates," in Aaron, *The Unwritten War: American Writers and the Civil War* (Madison: University of Wisconsin Press, 1987); Twelve Southerners, *I'll Take My Stand: The South and the Agrarian Tradition* (New York: Harper and Brothers, 1930); George Brown Tindall, *The Emergence of the New South, 1913–1945* (Baton Rouge: Louisiana State UniversityPress, 1967), 575–80; Paul V. Murphy, *The Rebuke of History: The Southern Agrarians and American Conservative Thought* (Chapel Hill: University of North Carolina Press, 2001), 146–47.

2. For a fuller treatment of the Scopes trial, see Edward J. Larson, *Summer for the Gods: The Scopes Trial and America's Continuing Debate over Science*

and Religion (New York: Basic Books, 1997); Edward Caudill, *Darwinism in the Press: The Evolution of an Idea* (Hillsdale, NJ: Lawrence Erlbaum, 1989); H. L. Mencken, *Prejudices: Fifth Series* (New York: Alfred A. Knopf, 1926), 68; Fred Hobson, *Serpent in Eden: H. L. Mencken and the South* (Chapel Hill: University of North Carolina Press, 1974); F. Garvin Davenport Jr., *The Myth of Southern History: Historical Consciousness in Twentieth-Century Southern Literature* (Nashville, TN: Vanderbilt University Press, 1970), 52–53.

3. Twelve Southerners, *I'll Take My Stand*; Tindall, *The Emergence of the New South*, 576–78; John Egerton, *Speak Now against the Day: The Generation before the Civil Rights Movement in the South* (New York: Alfred A. Knopf, 1994), 64–65.

4. Smith, *Virgin Land*, 151–52; Alexander Karanikas, *Tillers of a Myth: Southern Agrarians as Social Critics* (Madison: University of Wisconsin Press, 1966), 160–64; Raimondo Luraghi, *The Rise and Fall of the Plantation South* (New York: Franklin Watts, 1978), 15–19; Davenport, *The Myth of Southern History*, 65.

5. John Crowe Ransom, *God without Thunder: An Unorthodox Defense of Orthodoxy* (1930; reprint ed., Hamden, CT: Archron Books, 1965), 55, 65.

6. Tindall, *The Emergence of the New South, 1913–1945*, 588–99.

7. Ibid., 576–91; Wilbur J. Cash, *The Mind of the South* (1941; reprint ed., New York: Vintage Books, 1969); Herbert Agar and Allan Tate, eds., *Who Owns America? A New Declaration of Independence* (Boston: Houghton Mifflin, 1936); George Marion O'Donnell, "Looking Down the Cotton Row," in *Who Owns America? A New Declaration of Independence*, 162, cited in Tindall, *The Emergence of the New South*, 581.

8. Erskine Caldwell and Margaret Bourke-White, *You Have Seen Their Faces* (New York: Modern Age Books, 1937); James Agee and Walker Evans, *Let Us Now Praise Famous Men* (Boston: Houghton Mifflin, 1941). For more on Agee, see Paul Ashdown, ed., *James Agee: Selected Journalism* (Knoxville: University of Tennessee Press, 1985, 2004); and "Prophet from Highland Avenue: Agee's Visionary Journalism," in *James Agee: Reconsiderations*, ed. Michael A. Lofaro (Knoxville: University of Tennessee Press, 1992), 59–81.

9. Allen Tate, *Stonewall Jackson, The Good Soldier* (New York: Minton, Balch, and Company, 1928); Allen Tate, *Jefferson Davis: His Rise and Fall* (New York Minton, Balch, and Company, 1929); Lytle, *Bedford Forrest and His Critter Company*; R. R. Purdy, ed., *The Fugitives' Reunion: Conversations at Vanderbilt* (Nashville, TN, 1959), 62, quoted in Aaron, *The Unwritten War*, 296.

10. Lewis P. Simpson, "Garden Myth," in *Encyclopedia of Southern Culture*, ed. Charles Reagan Wilson and William Ferris (Chapel Hill: University of North Carolina Press, 1989), 1108–9.

11. Charlotte H. Beck, *The Fugitive Legacy: A Critical History* (Baton Rouge: Louisiana State University Press, 2001), 132–33; Walter Sullivan, preface to Lytle, *Bedford Forrest and His Critter Company*, xvi; Henry Steele Commager, "The Terror of the Damnyankees," *New Republic*, July 22, 1931, 266; Richard H. King, *A Southern Renaissance: The Cultural Awakening of the American South, 1930–1955* (New York: Oxford University Press, 1980), 58; Mark Lucas, *The Southern Vision of Andrew Lytle* (Baton Rouge: Louisiana State University Press, 1986), 9; Court Carney, "The Contested Image of Nathan Bedford Forrest," *Journal of Southern History* 67 (August 2001): 618–19; Emory M. Thomas, foreword to Wills, *A Battle from the Start*, xv.

12. Lucas, *The Southern Vision of Andrew Lytle*, 10–11; Sullivan, preface to *Bedford Forrest and His Critter Company*, xvii; J. O. Tate, "On Nathan Bedford Forrest (and the Death of Heroes)," *Southern Partisan* 4 (Summer 1984): 13–19; Alphonse Vinh, "Southern Agrarian Warrior Hero," *Southern Partisan* 14 (4th Quarter 1994): 42–45; Benjamin B. Alexander, "Nathan Bedford Forrest and Southern Folkways," *Southern Partisan* 7 (Summer 1987): 27–32.

13. Lytle, *Bedford Forrest and His Critter Company*, xix–xxvii.

14. Paul K. Conkin, *The Southern Agrarians* (Knoxville: University of Tennessee Press, 1988), 108, 110–11, 118; Aaron, *The Unwritten War*, 304; Allen Tate, *The Fathers* (New York: G. P. Putnam's Sons, 1938); King, *A Southern Renaissance*, 104; Daniel Joseph Singal, *The War Within: From Victorian to Modernist Thought in the South, 1919–1945*, 249; Albert E. Stone Jr., "Seward Collins and the *American Review*: Experiment in Pro-Fascism, 1933–37," *American Quarterly* 12 (Spring 1960): 3–19; Ben F. Johnson III, *Fierce Solitude: A Life of John Gould Fletcher* (Fayetteville: University of Arkansas Press, 1994), 202–3.

15. Conkin, *The Southern Agrarians*, 109, 114, 119–22, 145–46, 160; Donald Davidson, *Attack on Leviathan: Regionalism and Nationalism in the United States* (Chapel Hill: University of North Carolina Press, 1938), 142; King, *A Southern Renaissance*, 59; Singal, *The War Within*, 231; Larry Daughtrey, "Moral Flaw Diminishes VU's Glory," *Nashville Tennessean*, May 23, 1997, quoted in Mark Royden Winchell, *Where No Flag Flies: Donald Davidson and the Southern Resistance* (Columbia: University of Missouri Press, 2000), 298.

16. Cash, *The Mind of the South*, 344, 391; Singal, *The War Within*, 150; Ralph McGill, *The South and the Southerner* (Boston: Little, Brown and Company, 1964), 82.

17. Richard Weaver, "The South and the Revolution of Nihilism," *South Atlantic Quarterly* 43 (April 1944): 194–98.

18. Lytle, *Bedford Forrest and His Critter Company*, 395.

19. David C. Poyer, *The Shiloh Project* (New York: Avon Books, 1981), 212–13.

20. Marshall McLuhan, *The Mechanical Bride: Folklore of Industrial Man* (New York: Vanguard, 1951); Marshall McLuhan, *The Gutenberg Galaxy: The Making of Typographic Man* (Toronto: University of Toronto Press, 1962); Marshall McLuhan, *Understanding Media: The Extensions of Man* (New York: McGraw-Hill, 1964); Jonathan Miller, *Marshall McLuhan* (New York: Viking, 1971), 58; Marshall McLuhan, "The Southern Quality," *Sewanee Review* 55 (July 1947): 357–83; Murphy, *The Rebuke of History*, 148–49; Marshall McLuhan to Allen Tate, August 10, 1945, folder 6, box 29, Tate Papers, Manuscript Division, Department of Rare Books and Special Collections, Princeton University Library, Princeton, New Jersey, quoted in Murphy, *The Rebuke of History*, 149; Philip Marchand, *Marshall McLuhan: The Medium and the Messenger* (New York: Ticknor and Fields, 1989), 66–68.

21. Miller, *Marshall McLuhan*, 55.

22. Murphy, *The Rebuke of History*, 85–86; Eugene D. Genovese, *The Southern Tradition: The Achievement and Limitations of an American Conservatism* (Cambridge, MA: Harvard University Press, 1994), 125. For a discussion of Genovese's thought, see Murphy, *The Rebuke of History*, 255–64; and Mark G. Malvasi, *The Unregenerate South: The Agrarian Thought of John*

Crowe Ransom, Allen Tate, and Donald Davidson (Baton Rouge: Louisiana State UniversityPress, 1997), 252, 254.

23. Conkin, *The Southern Agrarians*, ix, 2.

ı

CHAPTER SIX

HYDRA AND HERACLES

SO MANY GROTESQUE CHARACTERS strut through Southern fiction and myth that it has become something of a cliché to say that Southern writers are virtually obsessed with monsters. In a 1959 essay on Southern literature, Richard Weaver tried to explain this obsession. Monsters, he said, make literature relevant because belief in monsters is closely related to the belief in heroes. For every Centaur, there is a Theseus; for every Hydra, a Heracles.[1] In Forrest, Southern fiction discovers both its Hydra and its Heracles. He is the monster and the hero, the dragon and the dragon slayer.

As a fictional character, Forrest is not exclusively the creation of Southern writers. He appeals to all who interpret in fiction the Civil War and its aftermath. Of necessity, the issues engaging these writers are predominantly Southern ones, yet they touch larger themes. Although some find Forrest worthy of the *Iliad*, capturing him in fiction has not always succeeded. Eileen Gregory writes of the problem of reconciling romance, literature, and history. For Civil War novels, "almost by definition, are romances, characterized by tendencies which are deadliest to the serious novelist—idealization, sentimentality, and polemicism." Forrest falls captive to these tendencies and more, for he is, in his heroic incarnation, a projection of the writer's prejudices toward unresolved memory. "The desire to chronicle the hero is hard indeed for any novelist to fulfill," Gregory insists. "The naturalism at the roots of the novel is essentially skeptical, resistant to the easy appeal of public beliefs and of heroic gestures: irony is its dominant tone."[2] Novelists as different as William Faulkner and Elmore Leonard have struggled to find something universal in Forrest. The character who emerges is a variegated, mottled hero, and sometime monster, with the collective weight of a genuine American myth.

Myth may be congruent with history, at least in the eyes of the historical novelist, yet Andrew Lytle was skeptical of the term "historical novel" because its "ambiguous specification" confuses the reader. If a novel fails as fiction, he asked, can it succeed as history?

Or if the history is flawed, can it succeed as fiction? "And how often does criticism pass over blocks of history in a book, lumps of yeast which have not worked the dough, or public figures so briefly and, at the same time, so obviously public; or moving over the scene stiffly like papier-mâché figures, or poorly disguised in some quasi-mythological dress." History, he said, is a method of investigation requiring artistry and imagination. Historical figures are not mythical beings but human creatures. For this reason, "the well-wrought novel is the only way of recovering the illusion of past time." So the question isn't whether the story is historically sound but whether it faithfully represents human behavior in a particular situation.[3]

Lytle notwithstanding, fiction offers a kind of supplemental history that may clarify or further obscure the past, putting history to work for the present. Myths will transcend narrative in any case. A "true" story may gild a myth as readily as a "false" one, leaving myth as the only "story" granted to fallible voyeurs of the past.

Distinguishing between the "real" Forrest of history and the "unreal" Forrest of fiction is evident in attempts to reveal the man through his own words. According to those who knew him, Forrest frequently mangled the English language with a mixture of frontier idioms, idiosyncratic invective, and singular figures of speech. He was, in some respects, the Yogi Berra of the Civil War, known as much for the way he said things as for what he had to say. Action ignites a myth, and language propels it. A Mark Twain could perhaps get this kind of fractured talk into credible dialogue, but lesser writers often turned Forrest into the village idiot rather than a homespun hero. Some, sensibly, trod lightly on dialect and gave Forrest the plausible speech of a frontiersman with a patina of literacy. He was no Lincoln in eloquence, but neither was he a buffoon. For a mythic figure, *presence* is more important than eloquence. The truest stories are those that let myth have its way and find the right words to fit the myth. Many stories have been written about Nathan Bedford Forrest. Some of them may even be true.

"BURIED ALIVE"

Possibly the first story in which Forrest appeared as a fictional character was published even before the end of the war. Titled "Buried Alive," it showed up in *Harper's Weekly* on May 7, 1864, just a few weeks after the assault on Fort Pillow, which is its subject (*Harper's*

Weekly was decidedly pro-Union in its editorial content, mixing war news and some 100 fictional narratives during the conflict.) A black Union soldier, Daniel Tyler, survives the battle and recounts its horrors from the safety of a Union hospital. Tyler was working in a field in Alabama when he saw a column of Union cavalry approaching and ran away to join them. Taken to Louisiana, he enlists in a black regiment and is among the fort's defenders when Forrest's troops attack. After the Union soldiers repulse several charges, Forrest calls a truce and then breaches the fort's defenses when the Federals honorably lower their guns. The Rebels, described as savages, devils, and monsters, then wantonly slaughter the black troops. Tyler is shot, clubbed, blinded, captured, and buried alive in a ditch. He claws his way out, swoons, awakens in the hospital, and tells how most of his companions "were murdered in cold blood only a week ago by Forrest's rough-riders."[4] Like most *Harper's Weekly* stories, "Buried Alive" did not carry the name of its author. Accordingly, readers probably did not distinguish between fictional and purported eyewitness accounts of the assault. Tyler is inexplicably literary in his narrative, sounding more like Frederick Douglass than an Alabama fieldhand. Forrest is more an unseen evil wraith than an actual flesh-and-blood character, a pattern often repeated in Forrest fiction. On one extraordinary occasion, however, "Forrest" did appear in the flesh, with fatal consequences.

"EF EVER A MAN LOOKED LIKE A DEMON HE DID"

William Forrest, Nathan Bedford Forrest's son, reportedly was attending a performance of *The Clansman*, a play adapted from a novel by Thomas Dixon Jr., in Memphis in 1908 when he had a fatal stroke at the moment an actor playing his father appeared on stage. If the story is true, his stroke was the neurological equivalent of the shock to the national nervous system brought about by Dixon's trilogy of Reconstruction novels and the play that became the basis for D. W. Griffith's 1915 film, *The Birth of a Nation*. Born in North Carolina in 1864, Dixon was ordained as a Baptist minister, practiced law, and served as a state legislator. His family's sufferings during Reconstruction and their experiences with the Ku Klux Klan became the basis for *The Leopard's Spots: A Romance of the White Man's Burden, 1865–1900* (1903), *The Clansman: An Historical Romance of the Ku Klux Klan* (1905), and *The Traitor: A Story of the Fall of the Invisible Empire* (1907).

The play was a sensation. In it, the Klan is extolled for restoring order to the South. Villainous Northern politicians, carpetbaggers, and scalawags conspire to bring further ruin to the region. The South is righteous, democratic, defiant, and pure, and has a mission to restore national innocence. Dixon's concern, according to F. Garvin Davenport Jr., was "a national crisis in which an older set of basically agrarian values was threatened by subversive alien forces represented specifically by the Negro threat and generally by a gamut-running, urban-industrial-scientific-capitalistic syndrome of materialism and racial degradation." Dixon's attitude toward blacks was patronizing at best and execrable at worst. Blacks in his stories are sexual predators and the helpless dupes of the Northern despots, changed "from a legal abstraction into an organic threat." Forrest again appears obliquely, as befitting the head of a secret society. In *The Clansman*, he is called the "Grand Wizard of the Klan at Memphis."

The Traitor begins with Forrest's order to disband the Klan. His cameo appearance is consistent with his role in so much Southern myth and fiction. He is usually on the fringes, a character who draws a sword and leaves a scar but is seldom the Shakespearean Brutus who delivers the killing blow and defines the tragedy. According to Everett Carter, Dixon was trying to write an epic glorifying what he called the history of the Aryan race, a theme Griffith expounded upon in *The Birth of a Nation*.[5]

Joel Chandler Harris, the prolific Georgia journalist best known for his Uncle Remus stories and local color folktales of the Old South, wrote contrasting profiles of Forrest in two novels he completed after he retired in 1900 as associate editor, editorial writer, and columnist on Henry Grady's *Atlanta Constitution*. Harris was born in 1848 and joined the *Constitution* in 1876. His first collection, *Uncle Remus: His Songs and His Sayings*, was published in 1880, and soon brought him international literary acclaim and the support of Mark Twain. The tales were popular fare during the Gilded Age, as Americans embraced the romance of reunion and were becoming receptive to a sentimentalized version of the Old South in which race had little to do with the Civil War. Uncle Remus, in one story, is a faithful slave who both defends his master and then saves a wounded Union soldier, becoming, according to David W. Blight, "the ultimate Civil War veteran—he fought on both sides."[6]

The first of Harris's novels, *A Little Union Scout*, appeared after its serial publication in the *Saturday Evening Post* in February and

Joel Chandler Harris described the change in Forrest when he led soldiers into battle: "His face, which was almost as dark as an Indian's when in perfect repose, was now inflamed with passion and almost purple." Illustrator George Gibbs attempted to capture Forrest's fury in this scene. From Joel Chandler Harris, *A Little Union Scout* (New York: McClure, Phillips, and Company, 1904).

March of 1904. Immediately popular, the book sold 4,000 copies in only a few weeks. A generous review in the *New York Times* praised Harris for transcending the bitterness of the war while telling "a good, straight tale about human, likable people." Here Forrest shines as a chivalrous, avuncular, laughing figure given to homespun aphorisms. "It ain't what people think of you—it's what you are that counts," he tells his scout, Carroll Shannon, the novel's narrator, who says Forrest's advice "rings true every time I repeat it to myself. It covers the whole ground of conscience and morals."[7]

Shannon is telling his wartime adventures to his daughter, who has just returned home from college. He and a companion, Harry Herndon, and Herndon's slave, Whistling Jim, join Forrest's command near Murfreesboro. Jim wounds a Union soldier, Jack Bledsoe, an old friend of Shannon and Herndon. While taking Bledsoe through Union lines so he can receive medical attention, Shannon meets Jane Ryder and her brother Tom, a Union colonel. Unknown to Shannon, Jane disguises herself to become the fabled Yankee spy Frank Leroy, whom Forrest has read about in the *Chattanooga Rebel*. Forrest orders Shannon to find Leroy, but a civilian tells him Leroy is the invention of a reporter. "There ain't a word of truth in all this stuff you hear about Leroy. He's in the newspapers, and he ain't anywhere else on top of the ground." Shannon later unmasks Jane and a romance develops.[8]

Shannon fights on with Forrest as he covers Hood's retreat from Nashville, which Shannon calls "the most remarkable episode of the war . . . and all because the leader was Forrest. Nothing but death would have prevented us from responding to his summons." Chivalry and honor triumph, and the Southern soldier lives to tell the tale, able to endure defeat because of the nobility of his commander. Forrest is a transcendent figure standing above the travails of Shannon, who personifies and practices the honor and chivalry so manifest in Forrest. The novel is in the romance-of-reunion tradition and a parable for the Gilded Age, with Whistling Jim fighting for the Confederacy, remaining loyal even after winning his freedom, and accompanying Shannon and Jane, who marry.[9]

Harris's *The Shadow between His Shoulder-Blades* appeared in 1909, following the success of *A Little Union Scout*. The story first ran serially in three November 1907 issues of the *Saturday Evening Post*. Billy Sanders, Harris's alter ego in this novel, tells tales as an old man about his wartime encounters with Forrest. The main action occurs sometime after July 28, 1864, when Forrest had reportedly died from lockjaw. Sanders first sees Forrest riding in a farm buggy with his injured foot propped up on a rack extending over the dashboard: "I never seed a sicker-lookin' man in all my born days than that man in the buggy. He was thin as a rail, an' his cheekbones stuck out like they was tryin' for to come through his skin. He was dark-complected to start wi', an' his skin was so yaller that it had a greenish look. Thar wa'n't nothing well about him but his eyes, an' they was jest blazin'." Interestingly, Robert Henry, in his

"What are you doing here?" Forrest gruffly asks an elderly slave in this illustration by George Harding. From Joel Chandler Harris, *The Shadow between His Shoulder-Blades* (Boston: Small, Maynard, and Company, 1909).

biography of Forrest, ostensibly quoting Harris, rendered this description of him as "sick-looking, thin as a rail, cheekbones that stuck out like they were trying to come through the skin, skin so yellow it looked greenish, eyes blazing," thus cleaning up the dialect in the original. Henry's version appears also in Hurst's biography, with the additional notation that the description is that of an "eyewitness." This may be a case of fiction becoming fact, a not uncommon symptom of mythmaking. Also, there is a sort of deference to the classical idea that the eyes are the mirror of the soul.[10]

Harris's Forrest, like a sort of military Uncle Remus, explains his technique not only of getting to the battle first with the most men but also of pushing harder at the crucial moment when the troops "git the idee that they've done e'en about all they kin do an' might as well quit." As for tactics, he says, "A good hand wi' a pen kin write 'em all down in less'n a minnit an' have time to spar'." Forrest is a tough customer, a man who has never liked or trusted blacks and never forgets a slight or a betrayal. When aroused, says Sanders, Forrest could be brutal. "I wish you could 'a' seed Gener'l Forrest as I seed him then," he says. "I know'd then why ever'body was afear'd of him; ef ever a man looked like a demon he did. I believe ef he'd 'a' blow'd out a long breath you could 'a' seed it smoke!" When Forrest hangs a turncoat and former business partner, Sanders says that "for days an' days—I could feel the shadder of that black, swingin' thing right betwixt my shoulder-blades, an' when I'm off my feed I can feel it yit; sometimes it's cold, sometimes it's hot."[11]

Irvin Cobb, another journalist who used Forrest in his stories, was the son of a Confederate soldier. Born in Kentucky in 1876, Cobb became the editor of the *Paducah Daily News* and wrote columns for the *Louisville Evening Post* before reporting on the First World War for the *New York World*. He joined the staff of the *Saturday Evening Post* and also wrote regularly for *Cosmopolitan*. Cobb's "Judge Priest" stories appeared in newspapers and magazines and were adapted for radio and cinema. He wrote these stories as a rebuttal to Northern stereotypes of Southern life, which he claimed focused mainly on the gentry. "I wrote," he said, "what I conceived to be a series of pictures, out of the life of a town in the western part of Kentucky, that part of Kentucky which gave to the nation, among others, Abraham Lincoln and Jefferson Davis."

Judge William "Fighting Billy" Priest first appeared in the *Saturday Evening Post* in 1911 and continued to amuse readers in some forty short stories and two novels. They are tall tales, not unlike the Joel Chandler Harris pieces. The judge is a former sergeant who rode with Forrest's cavalry, became an attorney after the war, and served some four decades into the 1920s as a circuit judge. He presides over his domain as a benevolent despot with folksy wisdom and country humor, solving the problems of a cast of outrageous smalltown characters.[12] Most of the judge's cronies had served with him under Forrest. For these old soldiers, according to Wayne Chatterton, "Forrest is deified, and the war is a shrine which they must visit and revisit in their memories. There, nothing ever changes." Although Judge Priest shares the prejudices of his times, he always fights for justice. In one story he saves two black men from the Klan. In another, "Forrest's Last Charge," he rallies the veterans to save a group of Sicilian laborers from a lynch mob. Cobb died in 1944, leaving behind a reputation as one of the great American humorists of his generation.[13]

"I NEVER READ ANY HISTORY"

William Faulkner, winner of the Nobel Prize for Literature in 1950, is especially noted for his experiments in the form and style of his short stories and novels, which are a mixture of romanticism and realism, set in the South, and Southern history. He grew up in Oxford, Lafayette County, Mississippi, which he recreated as Yoknapatawpha County. Faulkner often wrote about the conflict between tradition and the modern world. Yoknapatawpha County was a small place in a large context. At a time when many American writers were looking beyond American borders, Faulkner was looking within. To him, modern society was as much an invader in the 1920s and 1930s as the Union armies were during the Civil War. His work endures and gains strength as modernity continues its intrusion into regions and local communities, especially in the South. The contemporary mantras of globalism and multiculturalism are not without consequences, although Faulkner knew some changes were beneficial and necessary. The conflict between tradition and modernity is represented in many of his novels by two families, the Sartorises and the Snopeses. The latter are amoral and successful, people without a code who just show up in the community and gradually gain wealth and power. They are like the carpetbaggers of an earlier era. The Sartorises, with a long history in Yoknapatawpha County, are traditionalists but doomed, outwitted, and conned by the Snopeses time and again.

Faulkner's great-grandfather, Colonel William C. Falkner (the spelling was changed in later generations), fought at First Manassas and commanded a small force of Confederate rangers in parts of Mississippi and Tennessee where Forrest was active; he may have had some contact with Forrest's forces, who sometimes made their headquarters in Oxford. Some evidence suggests that Colonel Falkner fathered a child by a former slave near the end of the war, and named her Fannie Forrest Falkner in homage both to his sister,

Frances, and the general. Faulkner knew the family secrets and wove them into his fiction. Forrest was one of a number of figures Faulkner used to represent the South, scrapping for its very existence, intoxicated by myth distilled in primitivism and brutality that is bottled and labeled as well-aged, sweet civility—either way, an intoxicant. Other American authors have used the cavalier myth to dig into the meanings of American culture, but Faulkner adopted events of the Civil War, such as Pickett's Charge at Gettysburg, as metaphors for demarcation in American history.[14]

Faulkner's Forrest, a part of the novelist's own family history, is a man of the South, helping define and, paradoxically, mystify the region. Cleverly, Faulkner uses the character to impose himself even more intimately on the history of the South and into his family's blood. In the words of one critic, he depicts the South as a "frontier echoing both primitive and civilized heritage," in which Forrest, representing the primitive, is an ideal subject. But Forrest is never the symbol or figurehead for the balance of the fate of the Confederacy, as is the case for Pickett in *Intruder in the Dust*. Instead, Faulkner's use of Forrest is rather like the general's Memphis raid when his brother Bill rode straight into the lobby of the Gayoso Hotel, where General Hurlbut had a room. Luckily for Hurlbut, he was staying in other quarters that night. And so the South had ridden a beast into civilization's lobby but did not find civility. Bedford's brother Jesse headed for the headquarters of General Washburn, who escaped in his nightclothes, but the Confederates did get his uniform.[15]

Stealing the uniform had great symbolic promise. The South did not capture the real thing, the Union general himself, or the civility he symbolized, but only the trappings. The South wore those trappings in its chivalric mythology, making heroes of Forrest and his brothers. Like Jesse Forrest, Faulkner found a uniform in the closet, and his ancestor presumably on hand at the Memphis raid. Treating the Southern myth rather as Forrest must have handled the captured uniform, Faulkner tries to "capture" its owner, who has already departed. The novelist parades about with the uniform, worries over it a bit, and then returns it to its owner. Throughout American history, the South has been attempting to capture civilization but inevitably finds it elusive.

Like a literary raider, Forrest flits in and out of Faulkner's fiction, never the principal of a major novel or engagement but fitting well the literary tactics of a novelist immersed in the past who engaged his subject not with a conventional narrative approach but with modern and innovative stylistic assaults; these are often risky but ultimately triumph. Although he is mentioned in nine novels and eight stories and essays, Forrest is a principal subject in only one Faulkner story, the humorous "My Grandmother Millard and General Bedford Forrest and the Battle of Harrykin Creek," published in 1943. Grandmother Millard, mother-in-law of the absent Colonel John Sartoris, attempts to save the family silver from the Yankees by putting it in the privy, with an attractive young cousin posted to divert the plundering soldiers by claiming that a young woman is inside. The Yankees batter down the privy, only to find there really is a young woman, seated and screaming. But one of Forrest's officers, Lieutenant Philip St.-Just Backhouse, shows up to save the girl and immediately falls in love. Given those circumstances, the girl becomes hysterical at the mention of her rescuer's name. His subsequent reckless conduct provokes Forrest, who arrives at the summons of his old friend, Grandmother Millard. Together they contrive a fictitious report that the lieutenant, breveted major general, has been "killed" at the putative "Battle of Harrykin Creek" during which he had rescued the girl. He is "replaced" by Lieutenant Philip St.-Just *Backus*, and a wedding soon follows. Forrest is the only nonfictional character in the story, a spoof of the romanticism so dear to the South's self-image and myth. Faulkner describes Forrest as a "big dusty man with a big beard so black it looked almost blue." The general is crude in appearance and language but gallant and gentlemanly. This Forrest could have been created by Harris. Mythical magnolias and lace are set, tongue in cheek, against the harsh history of slavery, violence, and illiteracy.[16]

"Grandmother Millard" is fiction with some history. Faulkner's dates are off by a couple years, the real historical time being August 1864, not April 1862, when Forrest was recuperating in Memphis from a wound received at Shiloh. "Harrykin Creek" is apparently Hurricane Creek near which Confederate troops were deployed. Elmo Howell calls it typical of Faulkner's use of history, which is concerned not with facts but with the meaning that could be imposed on them. " 'I never read any history,' [Faulkner] once said, 'I talked to people. . . . When I was a boy there were a lot of people around who had lived through it, and I would pick it up— I was just saturated with it, but never read about it.' " Faulkner used Forrest to comment on the South at war, the unlettered general becoming a dash of cold reality on the South's mythical romanticism.

"The name of Forrest," Howell writes, "carried a special meaning in Faulkner's country, even beyond the war, for Sherman never caught him and he continued his devilment up to the very end. The strange contrasts in his character and situation appealed to the novelist and made him a natural subject for the comic irony that Faulkner was master of in his lighter moments."[17]

Forrest appears obliquely in "Shall Not Perish," one of Faulkner's most beautiful stories. Early in the Second World War the Grier family receives word that their 19-year-old son and brother, Pete Grier, has been killed soon after enlisting to fight the Japanese. The Griers are poor farmers but accept their loss bravely and attempt to comfort the wealthy banker Major de Spain, whose son has died by crashing his aircraft into a Japanese battleship; the major, embittered, believes his son died for nothing. The Griers then visit a museum where they see pictures of people from other small towns across America, brave people like themselves who had tamed the continent and died for the nation. They recall bringing an aging, senile grandfather, a former Confederate soldier, to see a cowboy film. The old man had dozed off, and when he awoke to see charging horses in the film, he rushed from the theater shouting "Forrest! Forrest! Here he comes! Get out of the way!" When the old man is ridiculed, Mrs. Grier says, "He wasn't running from anybody! He was running in front of them, hollering at all clods to look out because better men than they were coming, even seventy-five years afterwards, still powerful, still dangerous, still coming!" This, then, was the elusive "meaning" of Pete's death and the death of Major de Spain's son. The American people—like Forrest and his cavalry, better men—were irrepressible, still powerful, still dangerous, still coming.[18]

Faulkner, like many other writers, was also taken by the historical evil of the South, not only in war but also in the culture at large. In *Sanctuary* he "discovers evil," according to Daniel Joseph Singal, who believed that Faulkner was dealing with a crude story told to him in 1926 of a gangster raping a woman with a mechanical device and forcing her into a brothel for several weeks. As evil thus becomes tangible and visible, the lurid assault is not only on the woman but on the reader's expectations about the content and sensibilities of serious literature. More than a few critics were taken aback. It may have been the case, too, that the image carried over to war, especially the Civil War, in which an agrarian South is symbolically "raped" by the mechanical, industrial North and stuck, unwillingly and forcefully, in the "brothel" of industrialism and capitalism.[19]

As Wills has observed, Forrest's history as a slave trader and sometime Klansman rendered him made to order as a character in Faulkner's fiction. Wills calls attention to Forrest's presence in *Go Down, Moses*, in which he sells a slave to the McCaslin family in 1856. This brings, in Faulknerian terms, the curse of slavery down upon the family, with Forrest the unwitting agent of evil. And yet Forrest is a man of rectitude in the Faulknerian canon, a cut above the Snopses and the swindlers who tried to cash in on the war.[20]

Faulkner's stories in *The Unvanquished* have been criticized for their commercial slickness, but such concern looks at Faulkner in a narrower literary vein and neglects his important role as creator and communicator of mythology, popular and otherwise. Of the seven stories in *The Unvanquished*, five were originally published in the *Saturday Evening Post*. Their primary theme is historical, following the transition of Bayard Sartoris from childhood to manhood. In the evaluation of historical legend, Sartoris recalls events of many years before, and reality gradually seeps into the boy's consciousness. In the early stories, "Ambuscade" and "Retreat," Faulkner focuses on the gap between the naive romanticism of the child and the reality. The war is heroism and glory. The breach widens in the next story, "Raid," and Sartoris, now fourteen, begins to understand the excitement and tragedy of former slaves—the thrill of freedom, but the inevitable difficulties that follow. It is, in many respects, the South of the 1920s and 1930s, Faulkner's South, in which the Klan is resurrected and the Nashville Agrarians begin to create a heroic legend of Forrest and other Confederates. The change that Faulkner chronicles in *The Unvanquished* is the change of the South in the 1920s, in which modernism intrudes and whites cling to a mythical past.[21]

When Faulkner has Bayard Sartoris recall the roots of Southern racial problems—carpetbaggers putting former slaves up for elective office and in effect taking control of local government away from whites—it is parallel to the loss of control that agrarian-minded traditionalists felt in the 1920s when Northern industrialists intruded anew, threatening history and culture again. Sartoris and other whites turn violent and steal election boxes. Faulkner points to Northern culpability in creating the lawless, modern South. His genius is his ability to be enveloped, willingly, by the South but to see starkly the reality of its mythology. He sees the

North as curing the sin of the South at the point of a bayonet and then recreating that sin in the interest of modern economics. Characters such as Forrest might have remained ignorant, even innocent, backwoods farmers had the North not forced the South to rationalize an evil and put uniforms on its peasantry.

DEATH HAD ALWAYS BEEN WITH HIM

None Shall Look Back by Caroline Gordon, the granddaughter of one of Forrest's soldiers, was published in 1937, one year after the publication of Margaret Mitchell's *Gone With the Wind*. Perhaps Gordon's novel has remained in the shadow of Mitchell's celebrated work because it was never brought to the screen. *Gone With the Wind* remains the iconic Civil War novel, the popular culture's homage to lost causes, hopelessly mixed up in the public mind with Hollywood hokum and its attendant kitsch industry. Gordon's novel, although it skirts some of the same territory as Mitchell's tale, is much richer.[22]

Gordon was born in Kentucky in 1895. As a reporter for the *Chattanooga News*, she wrote about the Fugitives, forerunners of the Agrarians, and later married Allen Tate. They spent time in Paris, where they met many of the "Lost Generation" writers. When they returned in 1930, their Clarksville, Tennessee, home soon grew into a sort of utopian writers' colony; there Lytle began writing his biography of Forrest. In this atmosphere, it is not surprising that Gordon would begin a Civil War novel. In 1934 she wrote to Maxwell Perkins at Scribner's and sketched the outline of the proposed book. Perkins was already one of America's most celebrated editors, having mentored such writers as Hemingway, Fitzgerald, and Wolfe. Gordon presented Forrest as an archetypal man of the Southern states west of the mountains. She supported the general Agrarian thesis that Virginia had exerted too much dominance over the South before and during the Civil War. "Lee lost the war because he wasn't committed," she wrote in a letter. "Forrest was replaced after every battle he won. . . . It would have been better for the South—and for the nation—if the South had won." Gordon's novel was to be based in part on her family's own story. "I rather want to have Forrest a character in the action, in somewhat the same way Napoleon is in *War and Peace*," she wrote to Robert Penn Warren, perhaps indicative of the epic she had in mind. In another letter she "wanted Forrest to be like a god."[23]

Scribner's had intended to publish her novel in 1936 but post-poned it to avoid direct competition with Mitchell's. The book eventually appeared in February 1937, but *None Shall Look Back* never became a best seller. Reviewers compared it to *Gone With the Wind*, which Gordon called "half a dozen of the best plots in the world wrapped up with the Civil War as cellophane." Although the two books touched on many of the same themes, Mitchell was better able to address the cultural concerns of the ordinary Southerners for whom she was writing. Jim Cullen observed that Mitchell made "slaveholding whites the true victims" of the war "at a time when racial questions were beginning their long ascent to the top of the national agenda." If Mitchell was interested primarily in race and Reconstruction, Gordon, according to Walter Allen, declined to examine slavery as a moral issue. Critics have seen her work as primarily concerned with the nature of the hero and the possibility of heroic action.[24]

None Shall Look Back begins predictably enough with a Kentucky planter reposing in a summer house and sending a slave child scurrying off to fetch a julep. A large, interconnected family serves as a microcosm of the wider social order. Belles with fluttering eyelashes frolic in the rose garden and gambol beneath the leafy boughs of the hemlock trees with young fops—but soon the war pierces this Eden like a bayonet, and the novel turns dark and bloody. They "had been playing a waltz and everybody was dancing and then suddenly they had heard the hoof beats down the road and a few minutes later the place was full of mounted men" with the "black-browed Colonel," Nathan Bedford Forrest, in command. Soon the young men are off to war; the women and the old men and the slaves and the men with no fight in them stay behind to protect their homes and provender as best they can.[25]

Gordon renders Forrest's famous battles in sanguinary detail. He becomes the great mythical hero of the war, fighting the hated invader despite great odds, his ferocity growing legendary among his men: "They said old Forrest himself carried a sabre big enough for any two men and ground against all military regulations to a razor edge. A man in the Tenth had seen him whirl it in both hands and slice off a Yankee's head as if he'd been a gobbler on a block." Southern soldiers are ennobled by their endurance and their allegiance to a great cause, as one female character explains: "There's just two kind of people in the world, those that'll fight for what they think right and those that don't think anything is worth fighting for." At Murfreesboro on December 7, 1864, Forrest seizes the colors from a fallen scout, Rives Allard, the scion of one of the principal families in the novel, and charges into the Union lines against the tide of retreating Confederates. "He raised amazed eyes to the milky sky. Death. It had been with him, beside him all the time and he had not known. . . . The rose-colored flag danced above him, then dipped. It veiled his face for a moment from the men's sight but they heard his voice sounding back over the windy plain and saw him gallop toward the fort." Forrest carries the fight to the enemy but even he can't save the South.[26]

It was especially this scene that critic Ashley Brown admired, as Allard is "caught up in the larger action of which Forrest is the representative, and for this to be credible Forrest must participate in the pathos himself." This larger action harks back to the book's title, for the biblical prophet Nahum tells of soldiers fleeing from the defense of Nineveh in 612 B.C.: "Stand, stand, shall they cry; but none shall look back." In the novel it is Forrest who shouts at his retreating troops: "Rally, men, rally! For God's sake, rally," but "they would not listen. They broke around him and fled, orphan chickens scudding before a hawk over the plain." Forrest always appears in someone else's memory until at the end the point of view shifts, and in the final charge we see the battle through Forrest's eyes. "Everything seems to lead up to that moment," Brown said. "Forrest, then, is more than a public figure who fills out the composition and gives it historic credibility. His presence has meaning" as in classical tragedy, "where something comparable happens: for instance in the *Oresteia* when Orestes' fate is taken up by Apollo."[27]

Eileen Gregory observed a parallel between the novel and the biblical text, which "clearly suggests that the defeat of the South is a kind of retribution, that it collapses out of some ultimate weakness of spirit," a misguided piety, a failure to consider any ends beyond self-perpetuation and an abstract devotion to family and land rather than to a wider community. Set against this tragic flaw is the hero Forrest. While the novel ends, like the *Iliad*, "with an austere and uncompromising sense of loss and grief, it also, like the *Iliad*, wholeheartedly praises the hero, whose central task is to act as fully and selflessly as possible, with awareness of the ultimate stakes of his action." As a hero, Forrest is always associated with the horse, and the image of Forrest on King Phillip is a "culmination of the constant presence of horses throughout the novel.

. . . The horse and the hero are inextricable, joined especially in battle as a sign of intensity, power, and mysterious spiritedness." The novel's ending, therefore, "clearly points to the endurance of its heroes and its heroic gestures in the face of death. Forrest on his powerful horse, always obscure and unaccountable, partially veiled from our vision, enters into memory here, joining other, ancient heroes on the 'windy plain.' "[28]

"IN LOVE WITH DEATH"

Alfred Leland Crabb's *A Mockingbird Sang at Chickamauga*, published in 1949, presents a more folksy Forrest who sounds like a straight man on the Grand Old Opry radio program popular at the time the novel was written. Despite the contrived dialogue, Crabb gives a good account of the strategies that led up to the clash at Chickamauga and capably provides what so many war novelists omit: a sense of terrain. The story involves spies and scouts who gather intelligence for "Ol' Bed" through stealth, guile, and deception, even appropriating the identity papers from a couple of *Leslie's Weekly* reporters. Forrest seems the only competent commander in either army, and he and his men loom larger in the novel than they did on the field of battle. Whatever Crabb picks from the pocket of history, he deposits in the bank of narrative. Charles Dana, the *New York Tribune* managing editor who had been appointed assistant secretary of war and sent to snoop on Union generals for Secretary of War Edwin Stanton, appears as a character in the book and tells General William Rosecrans: "The Rebel Forrest has become quite a myth in Washington. Really he keeps Washington nervous. Does his genius warrant that?" Crabb left no doubt that it did.[29]

Nor did Shelby Foote, who wrote one of the most famous novels about Forrest. Faulkner called Foote's *Shiloh* "the damnedest book I have ever read and one of the best," ranking it above *The Red Badge of Courage* by Stephen Crane. Published in 1952, *Shiloh* was Foote's fourth and most successful novel and his best-known work before the historical trilogy *The Civil War: A Narrative*, begun in 1958 and completed in 1974. The success of the trilogy and Foote's appearances on Ken Burns's *The Civil War* television series in 1990 enhanced the novel's subsequent popularity and reputation. A native of Greenville, Mississippi, and the great-grandson of a Confederate cavalryman who fought at Shiloh, Foote served in the U.S. Army and the Marine Corps during World War II. After working briefly for the Associated Press in New York and then for a radio station and a newspaper, the *Delta Democrat-Times*, in Mississippi, Foote turned to writing fiction, first selling a story to the *Saturday Evening Post* in 1946. He began working on the novel *Shiloh* in 1947.[30]

Shiloh is told in the voices of eighteen soldiers who fought in the fields and woods above Pittsburg Landing, Tennessee, in 1862. The novel's seven sections alternate the perspectives of Union and Confederate combatants. The speaker of the opening monologue, Lieutenant Palmer Metcalfe, an aristocratic aide-de-camp on General Albert Sidney Johnston's staff, reappears in the final chapter, and the penultimate chapter comprises a dozen monologues by members of a single squad of Union soldiers. The collective voices serve as a doomed chorus moving through the landscape of battle as the soldiers occasionally encounter one another as well as the generals, including Forrest, who seem to control their destinies. Foote's prose is sometimes spare and laconic, befitting the prosaic and sometimes bemused reflections of unlettered young privates; sometimes Shakespearean; sometimes ironic, as if a cosmic tragedy were being invoked by a Greek poet and orchestrated by indifferent gods.

Both Metcalfe and Sergeant Jefferson Polly, one of Forrest's scouts, observe the cavalryman's martial zeal with wonder. Polly recalls how he knew from the first time he saw Forrest that he was "looking at the most man in the world" and how he "followed him and watched him grow to be what he had become by the time of Shiloh: the first cavalryman of his time, one of the great ones of *all* time, though no one realized it that soon except men who had fought under him." Others believe the wild talk they have heard about Forrest, that he was little more than a fearless bumpkin who fights only by instinct, a story that "made good listening. But it was just not true." They did not know Forrest had amassed a fortune and gained stature in Memphis politics, says Polly, "so when people say Forrest came into the war barefoot and in overalls, they aren't telling the truth; they're spreading the legend."[31]

Polly, however, embellishes the legend even as he tries to contain it. Forrest is the only commander who understands that Grant's army is being reinforced and that the Sunday successes of the Confederate army at Shiloh will be negated unless a night attack is launched. Yet when the next day's battle indeed does turn against the Confederates, Forrest's cavalrymen "were not downhearted and we never failed to do whatever was required of us as long as the colonel was out front in his shirtsleeves, swinging that terrible sword. That was his way."

At Fallen Timbers, Metcalfe, now "unattached" after Johnston's death on the field, comes upon Forrest as he prepares his defense against Sherman's pursuing brigade. The fight is "one of those things you would have to see to believe. But it was true, all right, and I was in the middle of it." After his horse is shot, Metcalfe is pitched to the ground, has the wind knocked out of him, and sees "something that made me forget that breathing had anything to do with living."[32] Helen White and Redding S. Sugg Jr. noted that Metcalfe "sees Forrest in mythic perspective and does not need breath. He is Metcalfe still, reacting to events as his nature and breeding dictate, and history has been melded with fiction." What he observes is Forrest racing ahead into Sherman's lines and then extricating himself from the clutches of the enraged Union soldiers with a bullet near his spine, the last projectile "that drew blood in the battle of Shiloh." Metcalfe begins to breathe again, as if Forrest's charge had been supernatural, suspended in time and space, and his survival so improbable as to give some kind of benediction to the battle. On the subsequent retreat to Corinth, Metcalfe recalls Sherman's prophecy that the South's cause would fail and discovers "the oversight in his argument. He hadn't mentioned Forrest or men like Forrest, men who did not fight as if odds made the winner, who did not necessarily believe that God was on the side of the big battalions." Metcalfe fights on even though his father warned him that the South bore within itself the seeds of its own defeat because of "incurable romanticism and misplaced chivalry. . . . We were in love with the past, he said; in love with death."

Giving Metcalfe the final word in the novel, said White and Sugg, leaves the reader "with some thinking to do." By fighting on with Forrest, he and the South make a choice, opting perhaps for the less rational but more honorable course of action. If divine intentions are not discernible to mere mortals, if the South is wrong and the poison of defeat is its inevitable cup to drink, it is still preferable to live existentially with passion than to submit to a mechanistic logic and a cosmic determinism that might makes right and that the outcome is beyond human control.[33]

Foote's novels, according to critics Edward C. Reilly and Thomas H. Landess, are often preoccupied with the theme of masculinity. In *Shiloh* the individual soldier, obsessed with pre–Civil War sentiments of individual heroism, confronts what is arguably the first modern battle in the first modern war, perhaps the turning point of that war, and learns that the individual is strangely powerless in this new kind of war. Yet Forrest contravenes modernity, becoming in essence "a mythic hero who embodies the ultimate virtues valued by society. In the person of Forrest one sees the ideal against which to measure not only the lesser figures in *Shiloh*" but also the emasculated characters who appear in Foote's other Southern fiction, according to Landess: "One need only look at the contemporary world to measure the decline of Southern society since its earlier era of greatness. And because of these final scenes of unmitigated heroism *Shiloh* is unique as a twentieth-century chronicle of war."[34]

OUT–FORRESTING FORREST

Elmore Leonard's *Last Stand at Saber River*, published in 1959, brought one of the premier western and mystery genre writers into the circle of talented authors who have used Forrest as creative source material. Leonard's story is set in the Arizona Territory during the last days of the Civil War. Paul Cable, a wounded captain from Forrest's command, has been discharged and returns with his family to reclaim his homestead. He finds his home occupied by Union sympathizers who work for Vern and Duane Kidston, brothers who supply remounts to the Union Army. A former Confederate soldier, Edward Janroe, who runs guns to the Southern forces, tries to maneuver Cable into killing the Kidstons. Although Cable wants to avoid trouble, he is drawn into several gun battles, each of which he fights by "out-Forresting Forrest" with the general's own tactics. "God, and Nathan Bedford Forrest, I need help," thinks Cable. "God's smile and Forrest's bag of tricks."[35]

Duane goads Cable by calling Forrest a bushwhacker, but Cable senses he can reason with Vern if he can separate him from his hotheaded brother. Struggling with his moral code, he passes up an opportunity to kill Vern, laments the necessity for killing, and meditates on the war itself. Like the struggle with the Kidstons, the war was not a matter of absolutes but of perceptions. When Janroe learns the war has ended, he murders Duane out of revenge, provoking Vern to track down Cable, whom he thinks responsible. But Cable figures out that Janroe killed Duane and persuades Vern that they should make common cause against the gunrunner. The two men slay Janroe in a final fight. Leonard shows the ambiguity of the war and the promise of reconciliation among combatants. If Cable and Vern Kidston, good men who have fought in a dirty war, can put aside their differences, there is hope for a better life on the frontier. Cable transcends his mentor, Forrest, who taught him how to fight but not how to forget.

Leonard revisited Forrest in *Tishomingo Blues* (2002), his thirty-seventh novel. Denis Lenahan, a former professional high-diving champion working the carnival circuit, sets up his act at a casino resort in Tunica, Mississippi, witnesses a murder, and gets mixed up with Detroit gangsters trying to take over the drug business from the "Dixie Mafia." Walter Kirkbride, a sleazy home builder and Civil War reenactor blackmailed into laundering money for the Dixie Mafia, is obsessed with Forrest: "I never feel so alive as when I'm Old Bedford." Kirkbride, the other crooks, the diver, and even a cop dress up in Union and Confederate uniforms and shoot it out with live ammunition during a reenactment of the Battle of Brice's Cross Roads. Although the novel mocks the reenacting craze and the gaming industry with all their attendant vices, Forrest is again portrayed as a high-minded avenger of mythical proportions. Kirkbride postures as a Forrest expert but passes on only legends and canards. He dresses up to look like Forrest, his hero, but behind the beard and the uniform he is just a counterfeit Confederate adrift, like the South, in a fetid cultural swamp far removed from the noble cause he thinks Forrest fought for.[36]

"HE IS A MONSTER"

The best novel about Forrest grew out of a student's honors thesis at Kenyon College. As a boy growing up in Alabama, Perry Lentz saw what he later described as a "lurid contemporary engraving" of the Fort Pillow massacre reproduced in a biography of Forrest. There is such a drawing from *Harper's Weekly* in Robert Selph Henry's 1944 biography, and it is indeed lurid, although Henry's caption dismisses it as "highly imaginative." Perhaps what most appalled young Lentz was the image in the foreground depicting two Confederate soldiers slitting the throat of a black Union soldier. Thus began what he called "a curiosity, a hunger, a frisson, a yearning" awakened by the engraving and the incident behind it. What became *The Falling Hills* was written in the summer of 1963 and the spring of 1964 during the Civil War centennial and the gathering storm of the civil rights movement. "My principal intention," he wrote, "was to recreate, with all the vividness and the historical accuracy that I could muster, what was once the most famous racial atrocity in a war that was caused by racist beliefs and by the peculiar institutions and cultures that had been built upon them in this nation." But at the time, Fort Pillow "seemed to have slipped from the American imagination."[37]

The Falling Hills is the story of Captain Leroy Acox, a reluctant officer in Forrest's cavalry, and Lieutenant Jonathan Seabury, a New England idealist who seeks to improve the lot of the black soldiers at Fort Pillow. Their progressive disillusionment with the war reaches its climax at the ill-fated battle. Forrest again is more a force of nature than a human figure. To Union soldiers stationed in the Tennessee forts, he is "wrathful and animal-like, his bare hands tearing through the doorway to get at the young men inside." In the quiet hours, "it was absolutely natural to assume that Forrest was coming at them, just as a man in the dark, when he knows there is something there, figures it is stalking him." Forrest sees Fort Pillow as a "cankering, infested boil on the men's minds and it stood for everything they hated and he was going to take them in swift and hard and they were going to lance it. It would be a relief and a purgation."[38]

The Confederates' blood lust stems from what they see as the treachery of the Unionist Tennesseans manning the fort: behind the ramparts are "their own renegade flesh and blood." When the attack is ordered, Forrest's face is "a mask of anger and weary resignation and hatred, and the mood of the Tennessee woods . . . was upon him." The slaughter ensues, Seabury is killed trying to save a terrified black soldier, and Acox, while feeling a "great horror and a great guilt," succumbs to the violence because he believes it is "Forrest's orders that we kill them all . . . I suppose because it might as well have been true. We killed them as if it had." The slaughter was right, he reasons, because the fort stood for something and needed destroying. Forrest's culpability is implicit—true to history, perhaps, if not to myth, because whatever happened at Fort Pillow is crucial to the way Forrest is perceived. If not guilty, he can be portrayed as something of a hero; if guilty, he is a monster. Lentz doesn't find many heroes in this story. What brings this novel to the forefront of Civil War fiction is its rich, uncompromising language and its understanding of the complexity of the war and the forces that lead rational men to irrational passion.[39]

Also touching on Fort Pillow is Frank Yerby's best-selling *The Foxes of Harrow*, the story of unsavory Louisiana aristocrats, who are contrasted with morally superior slaves in the antebellum South. Lieutenant Colonel Etienne Fox, the scion of a plantation-owning family, serves with Forrest. "He's an uppity Frenchified sonofabitch but, Gawddamnit all, he fights," says the general. Fort Pillow changes the South for Fox. "Life now would have to be lived out in memory. In dreams in the night, nightmare screaming. In forever backward-looking."

James Sherburne's *The Way to Fort Pillow* also probes the battle. Hacey Miller, who teaches at a Kentucky college, joins a Union cavalry regiment, eventually commands black troops at Fort Pillow, and survives. Sherburne sticks closely to eyewitness accounts and official reports. Forrest gives the order for the attack and leaves the scene while the butchery continues. Again, he is more presence than character. When the evil deed is done, he simply steps off stage while lesser players bewail the carnage. The worst atrocities are committed later by bushwhackers who move in "like hyenas in the darkness, to torture the living and rob the dead." Sherburne doesn't try to resolve historical controversies but shows the horror of the battle and the general political situation in Kentucky and Tennessee that preceded it.

Allen B. Ballard's *Where I'm Bound* considers the war from the point of view of black soldiers and their families. Forrest is variously described in slithery, reptilian terms. He is damned directly by a Confederate colonel who tells his wife that Forrest ordered the massacre after the Fort Pillow garrison was clearly defeated. Forrest makes an appearance during an account of the atrocities committed at Brice's Cross Roads. [40]

Jesse Hill Ford's *The Raider* interjects the Forrest Myth into a Faulkneresque epic about West Tennessee settlers before, during, and immediately after the Civil War. Ford grew up in Nashville, attended Vanderbilt University, and studied under the Agrarians Donald Davidson and Andrew Lytle. *The Raider* is the story of Elias McCutcheon and his family as they settle on the West Tennessee frontier and become wealthy but are eventually destroyed by the war. McCutcheon enters the narrative as a drifter after his family in Middle Tennessee is wiped out by cholera, "wandering, as it were, seeking his God again in the woods." He serves in the war reluctantly, abandoning his Union sympathies only because he feels an obligation to fight with his neighbors against the Yankee invaders. Thereafter, his service as the leader of a Confederate cavalry unit is congruent at many points with Forrest's, but a mythic Forrest: the Federal commanders begin to believe McCutcheon is a wizard riding at the head of a huge force of "demons mounted on race-horses," and is responsible for most of the mayhem throughout West Tennessee. McCutcheon gradually becomes more savage, "sad and scarred and scratched-like," as the war brutalizes the region. He "lives with sorrow and by the saber; butchering and shooting enemies in raid and battle, assault and pursuit, pushing himself always to the forefront." Having looked "for a fate that only him and maybe God, between them, knew anything about," he survives the war, isolated and demented, while peace returns to the land.

John Alvis viewed McCutcheon as "a hero in the vein of Odysseus" and saw the character as a rarity in modern fiction, "an integral man capable of endurance without complaint and of effective action without rapacity." The novel shows the roots of sectional conflict on the frontier and the truly evil nature of any civil war. McCutcheon is not Forrest but represents the Forrest Myth in fiction.[41]

OF GRANDFATHERS AND GRANDSONS

Two Pulitzer Prize–winning writers, in addition to Faulkner, have each included Forrest in a short story. Both stories are about young men growing up with grandfathers who served with Forrest. Robert Penn Warren, the most notable literary figure among the Agrarians, included "When the Light Gets Green," first published in 1936, in *The Circus in the Attic and Other Stories* (1947). Peter Taylor, who studied under Tate, Ransom, and Warren and was influenced by Lytle, was not an Agrarian but was sympathetic to their ideas. "In the Miro District" was published in *The New Yorker* in 1977 and included that year in *In the Miro District and Other Stories*.

In Warren's story a young Southern man recalls his grandfather, Captain Barden, who served with Forrest and now has "a long white beard and [sits] under the cedar tree." Captain Barden, a reader of history, thinks the South might have won the war if it had followed Forrest's advice and "cleaned the country ahead of the Yankees, like the Russians beat Napoleon." He also fought at Fort Pillow and talks disparagingly about drunken black soldiers massacred under a bluff. In 1914, Captain Barden has a stroke and dies four years later, his own physical and emotional paralysis spanning another war. The paralysis is symbolic. Captain Barden talks of Forrest as "right" and "a genius," but like the South he is paralyzed—emotionally by tradition, physically by Northern conquest. As a child, the narrator sees his grandfather reflected in a mirror, "green and wavy like water," but is indifferent to the old man, who seems caught up in a refracted reverie in the boy's imagination. Warren's story is existential in nature, and the child sees the past as something unimaginable in the present moment. Captain Barden is an emissary from Forrest's world who can be recalled only in the tangible accouterments of his existence, like the corncob pipe he smokes; his essence, like Forrest and the war, is as obscure as the reflection in the mirror.[42]

"In the Miro District" similarly explores a generational response to the men who fought in the war. The setting is a Nashville upper-middle-class neighborhood in about 1925. The narrator recalls this year, when he was eighteen and his grandfather, Major Basil Manley, was an old man, from the perspective of late middle age. Looking back on his youth, the narrator examines what had been the custom of the 1920s—the pairing off of the young and the old—which he finds curious in retrospect. Men of his age who are the grandsons of Confederate veterans "are likely to seem much too old-fashioned to be believed in almost—much too stiff in their manner to be taken seriously at all. They seem to be putting on an act. It is as if they are trying to *be* their grandfathers."[43]

As a young man, however, he resented the grandfather with whom he was expected to bond by his social-climbing parents. Having a Civil War veteran around was considered socially desirable, but the major did not quite fit the expected role. He declined to speak about his service with Forrest, except for an occasional anecdote about shooting off a man's hat outside the Gayoso Hotel or the time Forrest forced him off the road into a ditch when he was riding a mule to enlist in Forrest's cavalry. He had been offended and had cursed Forrest: "Likely I'm the onliest man or boy who ever called Bedford Forrest a son-of-a-bitch and lived." But as the narrator recalls, that "was not, of course, the kind of war story I wanted." The major's son-in-law, too, tries to question the old man about Forrest's grand strategy and asks whether the war might have been won if Jefferson Davis had been attentive to the fighting in Tennessee. Major Manley would say, "I don't know about any of that. I don't know what it matters." He was likely to dwell instead on a more recent incident when he was kidnapped in 1912 by night

riders, escaped, and wandered through a swamp for ten days. This
was the kind of authentic experience that mattered to the old man,
who avoided Confederate reunions, "that gathering of men each
year to repeat and enlarge upon reminiscences of something that
he was beginning to doubt had ever had any reality." Authenticity,
therefore, was not useful in social climbing and status building.
What was wanted was plantation romanticism, not swamp crawl-
ing and redneck rascality.[44]

Besides, there is the major's appearance, "an old country grand-
daddy who came to town not wearing a tie and with only a bright
gold collar button shining where a tie ought to have been in evidence." He lives by his own code, unable or unwilling to recognize
the same individuality in his grandson. Their conflict widens after
Major Manley unexpectedly intrudes upon his grandson's hijinks
with young women "of the other sort," very different from those
well-heeled young ladies who attend the prestigious Ward Belmont
School. The major is stern but tolerant, since the natural moral order of the Old South has not been violated. But after finding the
boy in a state of deshabille and hiding a girl from Ward Belmont,
Major Manley has had enough, for his grandson is symbolically
violating the idealized order by mating with the "real" and modern South, the one that has given itself over to making money and
embracing the Northern value system.

After this incident, Taylor explained in an interview, Major
Manley realizes that his grandson "no longer has any of the values
he has. . . . See, the parents have been very conventional people,
and they wanted him to be the peacock on the lawn and all that. So
he had put all his confidence in the boy. Then he saw that was use-
less, that the world he had tried to be realistic about had lost its
values." The grandfather then assumes the expected role: he grows
a long white beard like Captain Barden in the Warren story, begins
attending Confederate reunions, and talks freely about the war,
entertaining the friends of his daughter and son-in-law and his
grandson's classmates. Now, "he would even speculate about
whether or not the War in the West might have been won if Bragg
had been removed from his command or whether the whole War
mightn't have been won if President Davis had not viewed it so
narrowly from the Richmond point of view." All adore this "new"
old soldier, but the grandson senses that something has been lost
between them: the old man is doing the same kind of whoring that

the young man had indulged in. The old generation becomes the child of the new. [45]

In a 1974 letter to Warren, whose story he was certainly familiar with, Taylor said there were "subjects that are accessible to me now and that never seemed so before. One of them is about my grandfather's kidnapping by the Nightriders, at Reelfoot Lake. It may be more about me than about Grandfather, but it is fun making use of the stories he used to tell—even about his first meeting with General Forrest." "Did the character of the grandfather, in his new identity, become more like Tate or Lytle than Warren," asks Charlotte Beck, "always rehashing the war and assuming a privileged status as its historian?" Perhaps so. References to Forrest, so important to Lytle and Gordon, Beck suggests, "constitute by the time of Taylor's usage a coterie symbol for the fiction of the Fugitive legacy."

These stories give insight into the meaning of Forrest and the Civil War for the generation that came of age in the early twentieth century. Warren and Taylor were both writing about the South in confrontation with modernity. Their grandfathers had been the link with the war but had been expected to perform a ritual they may not have wished to perform. The war for them was real, unromantic, something to be accepted and forgotten; Forrest had been a hard-fighting commander, morally complex, not a symbol but a presence. The sons and grandsons, though, wanted a heroic war that might have been won and might still be won if the South could hold to its agrarian values. The old soldiers, who retained a code and an independent spirit not necessarily compatible with the new century, were expected to play the role of old soldiers. Grandsons, beginning to understand their grandfathers in a way their fathers could not, form a bridge to a future in which men like Forrest become myths, not men. Myths are powerful. Men are merely men.[46]

A FOOL NAMED FORREST

Winston Groom's novel *Forrest Gump*, published in 1986, became much better known after the movie of the same name became a great favorite in 1994. Forrest Gump, "a idiot since I was born . . . but probly a lot brighter than folks think," is "kin to General Forrest's fambly someways." The general, his mother tells him, was a great man "cept'n he started up the Ku Klux Klan after the war

was over an' even my grandmama say they's a bunch of no goods.
. . . So whatever else ole General Forrest done, startin up that Klan
thing was not a good idea—any idiot could tell you that. Nonethe-
less, that's how I got my name." Like his putative ancestor, Forrest
Gump has a talent for survival and for showing up at all the significant events of his time through a series of remarkable coinci-
dences. Gump the holy fool is more rational than the historical
events at which he is present. Nathan Bedford Forrest implicitly is,
like Forrest Gump, a fool for a Lost Cause, and neither a better nor
a wiser man than his idiot namesake who, at least, knows the world
is as mad as he is.[47]

B-Four, by Sam Hodges, is similar in some ways to Forrest Gump.
This time, a hapless, befuddled teenage reporter named Beauregard
Forrest is an unwilling fool for the Lost Cause. His father, an Alabama banker whose home is a shrine to the Confederacy, looks like
Robert E. Lee and urges his sons always to consider "what Lee
would have done" before determining a course of action.
Beauregard struggles to get a front-page story in the Standard-
Dispatch, where he is considered something of a joke, writing Pet-
of-the-Week stories and employed only through his father's influence. But Beauregard, who has been raised on Confederate lore and
reenactments, wants to escape from his father's obsessions and expectations and becomes suspicious of all the "pathetic subcultures"
that find their way into his newspaper's "Style" section. Asked by
a young woman if he is related to General Forrest, he says, "We're
not related. My dad paid a genealogist a lot of money, but the guy
turned up nothing on us and Nathan Bedford"; disappointed, his
father "went through a 'Forrest was overrated' phase, but it didn't
last long." Beauregard eventually breaks a story about school board
officials using a stolen portable classroom for a deer lodge where
they show porn films and entertain exotic dancers provided by a
firm run by his brother. The Southern fascination with the Civil
War is the target in this book, whose author was a reporter for the
Birmingham Post-Herald and the Orlando Sentinel.[48]

FIGHTIN' WITH FICTION

Many authors interested in writing fiction about the Civil War have
turned to smaller publishing houses or so-called vanity presses to
publish their works, novels that vary in quality but are often well
researched and competently written. Forrest is well represented,

and just how these stories are told gives some indication of the nature of the Forrest Myth.

Charles Gordon Yeager's *Fightin' with Forrest* mixes fiction and history in an odd way. Yeager said he wrote the novel to remedy the fact that Forrest was relatively unknown, which is hardly the case. Although he claimed to be skeptical of historical accuracy, he relied heavily on Wyeth's biography, supplementing that account with "more logical recordings of particular incidents," inventing dialogue, and including characters from his own family tree. Yeager introduces fictional characters, then credits the real persons who inspired them in footnotes. He runs into many of the problems with "ambiguous specification" that Lytle warned against, and the novel might better be titled "Fightin' with Fiction." The extensive documentation in the footnotes suggests he would have been better off writing a biography.[49]

Never to Quit, by Bob Armistead, is the story of James Wilson, a young soldier from Franklin, Tennessee, who joins Forrest after being wounded at Antietam and follows him through the Battle of Franklin, where Wilson is wounded again. Wilson and his family are portrayed, as is Forrest, as progressives on the slavery question, and the story features a loyal, freed slave named Jacob, who loves Forrest. The responsibility for the Fort Pillow massacre is placed largely on "intoxicated black troops" who refused to surrender. In another Armistead novel, *Warrior Forrest*, the general is put in charge of an army composed of units taken from the Army of Northern Virginia and other forces. He relieves Vicksburg, kills Sherman, captures Grant and Grant's entire army, returns to Richmond as a conquering hero, and then negotiates the surrender of the city of Washington with Abraham Lincoln. This novel is really the ultimate realization of the Forrest Myth—the notion that if Richmond had simply put Forrest in charge in the West, the South would have won the war.[50]

The God of War: When I Rode with N. B. Forrest, the Letters of Henry Wylie by Robert E. Chambers purports to be sixty-five letters that one of Forrest's cavalry officers wrote to his wife. Henry Wylie, a pressman at the *Memphis Daily Appeal*, joins Forrest as the war commences and fights with him to the end. After the war, Wylie becomes "one of the outstanding journalists of his age" and eventually goes down with the *Titanic* while on assignment to cover the ship's maiden voyage for the *Saturday Evening Post*. Chambers offers a fairly straightforward account of Forrest's campaigns with conventional insights into the general's character. Of interest, however, is the evolution of Forrest as a myth created by reporters, as titanic as the famous ship in terms of news value and doomed grandeur.[51]

In *The Cavalryman*, Clayton Williams turns to the true story of Lieutenant Joseph Hedges, a Federal cavalryman who tangles with Forrest's forces in Tennessee. Hedges and Forrest encounter each other throughout the war. Some of Hedges's actual letters to his family are included to move the story along. Williams, who commanded a U.S. military detachment in Iraq prior to the first Gulf War, claims that "Army folklore and military doctrine have been influenced [by Forrest] to this day. The tactics of 'Desert Storm' . . . were classic Forrest."

Gene Ladnier's *Fame's Eternal Camping Ground* is a tragic love story involving a Confederate soldier and a young girl in the unlikely setting of the Battle of Brice's Cross Roads. Two black soldiers figure in the plot as Forrest outwits Grierson and Sturgis. The focus is on how individuals are swept up in the events of the unfolding battle.[52]

Wave the Bloody Shirt: The Life and Times of General Nathan Bedford Forrest, CSA, by Robert Sigafoos, mixes biography and fiction to give a credible portrait of the general. Sigafoos harvests important biographical details to round out the characters of Forrest and some of the leading figures in the war. Journalist Lafcadio Hearn is a minor character in the novel, used as a literary device that allows the inquisitive reporter to seek out answers to questions about the paradoxical Forrest.[53]

All these novels work, up to a point, but they illustrate that it is as difficult to capture Forrest in fiction as it was to capture him during the war. Only the most competent novelists, such as Faulkner, Foote, and Lentz, come close to depicting the mythic and daring Forrest who can live on in literature.

RIVERBOATS AND RELIGION

One of Forrest's soldiers appears as a besotted insurance investigator and sleuth-for-hire who gets involved in discovering the cause of a Mississippi riverboat's sinking in James D. Brewer's *No Bottom* (1994), the first in a series of thrillers involving Masey Baldridge and Luke Williamson. Wounded near Selma a few days before Forrest disbands his command, Baldridge later finds a job with an insurance company run by one of the general's staff officers. He foils a plot to blow up Union ships with leftover weapons developed by the Confederate Torpedo Bureau and saves a riverboat piloted by Williamson, a former Union officer, from destruction. Forrest is building railroads in the novel and has no interest in perpetuating the war. In *No Virtue* (1995), a prostitute is murdered on Williamson's riverboat, and his first mate is framed for the crime. Baldridge investigates the murder and clears the mate but endures regular flashbacks to his fighting days with Forrest. The investigation also reveals a counterfeiting conspiracy involving Confederate gold coins stolen by a former Union officer who worked with the Freedman's Bureau and is mounting a campaign to run for governor of Tennessee. Baldridge is helped by an old friend, a black man who hates Yankees and thinks other blacks are being manipulated by the Freedman's Bureau and the Republicans. Forrest again is in the background, the stalwart soldier who is unable to save the South from the Reconstruction-era greed and rapacity that ultimately affects conqueror and conquered alike. In *No Remorse* (1997), conflicts between riverboat owners and railroad men form the backdrop to a tale of family intrigue and murder. Baldridge, who had joined Forrest in raiding railroads, realizes that the war proved the advantage of rail over riverboats. In a clash of technologies the riverboat gives way to the iron horse as the South yields to the power of Northern industrialism, and the officer corps in both armies —including Forrest—are the driving force behind the railroads.[54]

Christian inspiration would seem to be an unlikely genre for a Forrest story, but he strides through the pages of *Toward the Sunrising*, the fourth volume in the Cheney Duvall, M.D., series written by Gilbert and Lynn Morris, a father-daughter writing team. Dr. Duvall is a young New York physician in the romance novel tradition, modified to fit the market for inspirational literature. She and her "nurse," a tough veteran of Forrest's cavalry named Shiloh Irons, arrive in Charleston, South Carolina, just after the end of the Civil War to settle some family matters. They meet Shadrach Forrest Luxton, a Citadel cadet and Bedford Forrest's younger half-brother. Luxton, who is a member of a Klan-like order, gets framed for a murder by some corrupt Federal agents. Forrest, attired in a canvas duster and a broad-brimmed hat shading raptor eyes, rides into town on King Phillip like a Western gunfighter, beats up a provost marshal, threatens a judge, and gets his brother released pending trial. Duvall eventually flushes out the real killers, who get slapped around by Forrest before he leaves town to resume his railroad-building endeavors. There's a lot of praying and proselytizing, and in a curious note at the end of the novel, the authors tell the story of Forrest's conversion to Christianity, ending with their belief "that he and King Phillip ride still, though now as simple soldiers in the presence of the Great King." This is not exactly the same river that runs through Lytle's *Bedford Forrest and His Critter Company*, with its mythic Christian knight holding back the barbarians at the gates in the service of Western civilization, but the story bubbles up from the same spring. To bring home the homage to the Confederacy, the authors dedicate the book to "all of us who have seen, in the deep secret woods and the sudden glades, glimpses of the Gray Riders, and because we, in our dreams, sometimes hear King Phillip's sudden hoofbeats, and hear his [Forrest's] boys' wild cries borne on the hot South wind." Lest some reader note that those Gray Riders later wore white bedsheets, the authors append a nuanced history of the Ku Klux Klan and Forrest's role in disbanding it. The Forrest of *Toward the Sunrising* is an incarnate myth whose fame freezes the Northern soldiers who occupy Charleston as much as it does the unrepentant Rebels who treat him as a Confederate deity. When Duvall tells him she has sympathy for anyone who has gained such fame, Forrest replies: "You're a smart woman. But bein' famous ain't the problem. Bein' IN-famous is."[55]

FANTASY, FORREST, AND COUNTERFACTUALS

Alternative history is a genre that attracts the attention of talented historians, popular novelists, and science fiction writers as well as some of the most egregious hacks in the literary trade. Successful and interesting alternative Civil War history novels include MacKinlay Kantor's centennial-era standard, *If the South Had Won the Civil War*; Robert Skimin's *Gray Victory*; David C. Poyer's *The Shiloh Project*; and Harry Turtledove's *Guns of the South*. For Turtledove, alternative history about the Civil War isn't far removed from much of the history that has been written by self-aggrandizing generals. Alternative historians, however, either introduce some plausible but counterfactual event that changes history in an interesting way, or they rely on a far-fetched device such as time travel to speculate on what might have been or might yet be. The underlying premise has to pique the reader's curiosity without compromising common sense. Critical readers will seize upon small inaccuracies that seem to discredit the alternative consequences that follow even a plausible turn of events. Ultimately, the "what if" has to be worth the reader's time and attention. Writers are free to invent alternative scenarios but not to change human nature, for historical figures, like actors in a well-known play, have to stay in character when someone improvises the script.[56]

Lawrence Wells did quite a bit of improvising in *Rommel and the Rebel*, drawing on the old rumor that the Desert Fox had been sent to the United States by Hitler to study Forrest's tactics.[57] Such fantastic stories always get around after a war, and they tell us something about how myths are constructed. It shouldn't be surprising that military strategists study warfare, and if the appeal is to national pride and our fascination with snoops and conspiracies, who better than Forrest to instruct Erwin Rommel and the Wehrmacht?

Wells, who is married to Faulkner's niece, got the idea for his story when he found an article from a Mississippi newspaper dated July 9, 1937. Reproduced in the novel, it is an account of a reception honoring unnamed German military officials in Jackson, Mississippi. According to the article, the Germans were in the United States to tour Civil War battlefields, including Brice's Cross Roads. Although Wells later learned from Rommel's son that the field marshal had never been in America, he had the elements of a good story: the basic thesis is that if you study the tactics of both soldiers, you find similarities, so it seems possible that Rommel knew something about Forrest. Indeed, that Rommel had written a military manual in 1937 thickens the plot.[58]

The story starts with Rommel and his companions traveling under assumed names to visit New York, the Gettysburg battlefield, and then Mississippi in 1937. Lieutenant Maxwell Speigner, a German-speaking U.S. intelligence officer, is ordered to Mississippi to serve as a translator and liaison officer for the visiting Germans. "Germans? In Mississippi? What for?" Speigner asks Major Shoemaker, his Forrest-obsessed former commanding officer in the University of Mississippi's ROTC program. "Nathan B. Forrest, of course," says the major. "What else has Mis'ippi got?" Speigner recalls Major Shoemaker's lectures on Forrest, who he claimed "had a Ph.D. in horsemanship and local terrain. . . . His mind was uncluttered by the baggage of an education." Introduced in Jackson to "Colonel Rilke," Speigner quickly figures out that the visitor is Rommel, who relishes the chance "to wear the cavalry boots of Bedford Forrest" by studying his battles in Mississippi.[59]

In Oxford, Mississippi, Rommel inevitably meets Faulkner, who is asked by Speigner to assess the colonel's strengths and weaknesses for the benefit of military intelligence. Faulkner baits Rommel with comparisons between the Klan and Hitler's Brown Shirts, but Rommel claims he is apolitical and interested only in military affairs. A drunken Faulkner then accompanies Rommel and Speigner on a midnight tour of the Shiloh battlefield. Wells projects Forrest's thoughts and actions into the narrative in italics in a Faulknerian literary technique. The next morning, Faulkner tells Speigner that Rommel will make a deadly enemy and predicts that the United States will soon be at war with Germany.

The story then rolls forward to the predicted war. Speigner is summoned to Africa by British intelligence officers who have read his reports on Rommel, which conclude that the field marshal is a cavalryman in the tradition of Forrest. Speigner anticipate Rommel's tactics by invoking Forrest's battlefield maneuvers. Rommel captures Speigner late in 1941 after America enters the war, but Speigner escapes and forces the Desert Fox to drive him through the desert toward the British lines. Speigner, insisting that Rommel cannot remain apolitical in the face of Nazi atrocities, asserts that Hitler is using him as much for propaganda as for military purposes. The Afrika Korps rescues Rommel, and Speigner is forced to witness his capture of Benghazi in January 1942 with a plan that replicates Forrest's movements at Brice's Cross Roads.

Farfetched though the story is, it shows the mythic affinities between the two commanders. Like Forrest, Rommel is a good soldier fighting for a sullied cause. Beneath its grandeur and gallantry, the Afrika Korps fights in the service of evil. Forrest's ghost, in this sense, becomes a kind of hayseed Aryan knight enlisted in the cause of National Socialism via Rommel. As for the culpability of both men, in the terrain of myth such questions may be moot. In a biography of Rommel, David Fraser suggests that Rommel and Forrest project the classic warrior image: "It is the sheer energy of these men which leaps across the years, and which made them in their own day centres of myth. . . . Their broader judgement of politics and events, inevitably affected by the circumstances and sentiments around them, may have been limited or distorted; and in studying any of them it is necessary to be wary of verdicts deriving from wholly different eras, places, cultures. . . . We may think of our admiration as immature crudity, but it will not go away."[60]

Howard Means's *C.S.A.—Confederate States of America* sets up some bizarre historical twists while imaginatively addressing the crucial issue of the war—race. The South is on the brink of losing until Davis's martyrdom rallies the troops. Forrest raids a button factory at Chambersburg, Pennsylvania, enabling Confederate soldiers to regain some dignity: "It was so much easier to charge a gun emplacement when you knew your pants wouldn't fall down on the way." Lee turns into a Confederate Genghis Khan, torching Trenton, driving Federal troops in Philadelphia into the Delaware River, sacking New York City and hanging the generals who try to defend it, scouring New England, and dragging Lincoln in chains from the White House. Forrest becomes president of the Confederate States of America, but being "baptized in blood," he is "unfit for the letting of much of anything else. Policy languished while he fumed at this adviser or that and railed at the foolishness of politicians. His leadership, so brilliant in war, proved almost nonexistent in peace." Finally, pressured by England, the Confederacy sets up a rigidly segregated-but-equal society with blacks in control of the House of Representatives and whites in control of the Senate. In the year 2000 the Confederacy is headed by a white descendant of both Lee and Davis and a black vice president. Washington is a neglected, rat-infested necropolis. The Northern states are now territories, a toxic industrial zone crowded with sweatshops and exploited, cheap immigrant labor, while a revolutionary group plots against Confederate leaders. The mythologies that sustain the C.S.A. are tested, and the principal characters, at least some of them, in this far-out tale, begin to question the past and its hold on the present.[61]

Means parodies the genre while addressing some important contemporary issues. History, he reminds his readers, is written by the winners, and the "what ifs" challenge the history the winners have created. He inverts historical events—turning the North rather than the South into a protracted postbellum wasteland—and invents a kind of benign-but-sinister racism and an American imperialism worse than anything today's antiglobalism protesters could imagine. Forrest becomes a rough counterpart to the historical Grant as the stereotypical general-as-failed-president, and it is the failure of Forrest's Old South–style administration that makes possible the "reformed" racism of the novel's premise.

Racism is also the central theme in Turtledove's *The Guns of the South.* Facing the imminent defeat of the Confederacy in 1864, Lee receives a visit from mysterious strangers offering the Rebels a new kind of weapon—the AK-47. As the repeating rifle turns the tide of war, Lee learns that the strangers, whose cause is called "America

Will Break," have come by time machine from 150 years in the future. Their support for the Confederacy is based only on their desire to help perpetuate white supremacy. Lee, however, takes a more moderate approach toward the continuation of slavery in the Confederacy and is opposed by America Will Break. Forrest, boasting of his victory at Fort Pillow, keeps his troops in the field after the Union surrender and fights black partisans who resist being returned to slavery. Backed by America Will Break, Forrest confronts Lee when he learns of the general's support for gradual emancipation and runs against him in the 1867 Confederate presidential election as the candidate of the Patriot Party, his campaign for white supremacy supported by gray-hooded proto-Klansmen. The election turns on some last-minute votes from East Tennessee. Lee emerges as the victor and survives an assassination attempt, and a new civil war breaks out with Forrest in command of Confederate troops. America Will Break is revealed for what it is—the neo-Nazi *Afrikaner Weerstandsbeweging*, the Afrikaner Resistance Movement, with its three-spiked insignia—and defeated. Forrest does not renounce racism but chooses constitutional nationalism as Lee looks forward to a more enlightened future for the Confederacy.

Turtledove's Forrest is a patchwork of clichés drawn from the Forrest Myth. Although he can be "a polished simulacrum" of a gentleman, he is at the core the crude frontiersman, in contrast to the courtly, aristocratic Lee. He is less soldier than avenging dark angel of death. Lee is a polite racist within whose breast liberal tendencies begin to stir; Forrest is a frothing, unreconstructed racist practicing what a later generation would call "ethnic cleansing." "Bedford Forrest," says Lee, "is a very devil," a sentiment shared in a different context by Sherman. And yet Forrest can rise to principle, defending Lee and the Confederacy against the interlopers from the future. Perhaps the underlying suggestion is that the Confederacy has to make a deal with the devil to survive: for every Lee there is a Forrest; for every enlightened impulse there is a gravitational pull to the heart of darkness. Forrest is little more than a domestic fascist, but he sees something in Lee that transcends the kind of terrorist state represented by the *Afrikaner Weerstandsbeweging*.[62]

Turtledove used Forrest again in *Sentry Peak*, blending alternative Civil War history and fantasy by transporting the battles of Chickamauga and Chattanooga to a mythical time filled with magic carpets and unicorns, bowmen, crystal balls and catapults, and recognizable historical figures with preposterous names. The Kingdom of Detina (United States of America) has been sundered by a quarrel between Grand Duke Geoffrey, who rules a subtropical North with estates worked by blond serfs, and his cousin King Avram, who rules a proto-industrial South from the Black Palace in George-town and intends to free the serfs when he reunites the kingdom.

A test of wills arises between Count Thraxton the Braggart (Braxton Bragg), the "northern" commander of the Army of Franklin (Army of Tennessee) and also a powerful magus, and the drunken General Guildenstern (William Rosecrans), who heads the "southron" army as they maneuver around Sentry Peak (Lookout Mountain). General Guildenstern is pushing Count Thraxton's army out of the Province of Franklin (Tennessee) and into Peachtree Prov-ince (Georgia). Other familiar generals appear on the scene, but it is Ned of the Forest, commander of the northern unicorn-riders, who seems most at home in this fantasy universe. Turtledove's publisher provides some eye-popping cover art depicting Ned of the Forest astride a white unicorn and impaling a gigantic serpent as a Confederate battle flag flies in the background.

Before the war, the uncouth Ned, a "backwoods ruffian," was "a gambler and a serfcatcher, and highly successful at both trades." His troopers were "as much ruffians as he was, not proper knights at all—on unicornback." Count Thraxton, a cantankerous, ineffec-tual sorcerer and military poltroon, abhors Ned, "a boor, a bump-kin, a lout" sprung from "the wild northeast," and hopes he will be killed in battle. Ned's eyes are "hard and black and unyielding as polished jet. A killer's eyes, Thraxton thought. A lot of men were killers, of course. The world was a hard, cruel place. But most men pretended otherwise. Ned of the Forest didn't bother." Ned prides himself on the number of unicorns shot out from under him in com-bat, boasting that "generals who were known for their mounts—Duke Edward of Arlington, for instance—didn't take their beasts into battle." Ned fights with unremitting ferocity at the River of Death, harvesting southrons for the "Soulstealer," a kind of devil spirit, and then confronts Count Thraxton for his timidity after General Guildenstern's army escapes from the battlefield and re-turns to Rising Rock. Count Thraxton strips Ned of his command and sends him east on grounds that he is "ignorant, and does not know anything of cooperation. He is nothing more than a good raider." Ned, however, is admired as a true fighter by all combat-ants, one of whom says: "Ned's a *man*, by the gods. He doesn't need any blue blood to make him a man, either. He just is."[63]

Forrest seems at home in the pseudo-mythical Middle Ages because, perhaps more than any other Civil War general, he came to represent the individual knight-errant—though less the noble warrior of Sir Walter Scott romances and more the primitive horseman of the steppes; more Tamerlane and Genghis Khan than Ivanhoe. No matter what others make of him, *he just is*, a man who lives to kill. Other officers can't measure up. Says one soldier of a pretender to Ned's audacity, "He'd probably give his left ballock to be Ned of the Forest." Says another, noting that most generals have won their stars by noble lineage, "Ned got his command on account of he's a son of a bitch." His very blood is toxic, says Ned himself; "any snake bites me, *it* dies." All the sorcery and magic conjured up by Count Thraxton and his wizards isn't as powerful as the primitive Ned and his unicorns.

Turtledove is insightful in demonstrating the clash between the primitive and the proto-technologies of modernity. Before modern weapons of mass destruction came the alchemists and magicians of our own Middle Ages. In every cannon, rocket, and bomb is a memory of a blunderbuss, a catapult, and a cannonball. In our own Civil War, for every modern warrior like Grant and Sherman there was a Stuart or Forrest. We remember the daring men on horseback, but artillery, railroads, and massed infantry won the war. The horsemen prevailed for a season. But when the snake of modernity bit the Confederacy, Forrest survived, but the South died.[64]

The premise of Dennis P. McIntire's more realistic but still "what if" book, *Lee at Chattanooga*, is that Jefferson Davis persuades the commander of the Army of Northern Virginia to come to the aid of the Army of Tennessee after the Confederate victory at Chickamauga. Lee doesn't replace Bragg as commander but serves rather as an unwelcome adviser. Lee summons Forrest, recently detached from Bragg's army, to a conference to try to engender his support. The meeting begins badly, with the rustic Forrest arrogantly mocking the civilities proffered by the aristocratic Lee. Their exchange symbolizes one of the problems of the Confederate army—how to reconcile the westerner's roughneck tactics, temperament, and temerity with the Tidewater aristocracy directing the war. Forrest rails against Bragg and warns Lee that whatever "you have a notion to try here ain't gonna amount to a bucket of horse dung so long as that man's left in charge." Lee nevertheless enlists Forrest in a plan to attack the Union forces in Chattanooga by pulling Longstreet's army back from Knoxville before Grant can be reinforced by

Sherman. Bragg's obstinacy, however, ruins the plan; Lee loses a leg in the battle, and the South is lost.[65]

John Duke Merriam's *Meade's Reprise* not only gives General George Meade the victory at Gettysburg but has him counterattacking after Pickett's Charge, rolling up the Confederate flank and capturing Robert E. Lee. Forrest takes to the mountains and fights on after Lee's defeat, thus prolonging the war, then leads some secret societies in a resistance movement that gains strength after the trial and hanging of former general John Gordon. With Forrest in control, it is "like the beginning of the war all over again." His followers don bedsheets and hold "campfires" to stir up the population and terrify former slaves. Meade is eventually killed by John Wilkes Booth while defending Lincoln, who serves out his second term and is succeeded as president by Grant. Forrest's role in the Klan is more open in this fictional speculation than it was in history.[66]

"ACHILLES WITH PINWORMS AND SLAVES"

Talented authors continue to bring Forrest to the attention of the general book-reading public. Howard Bahr, the former curator of Faulkner's homestead in Oxford, Mississippi, was much inspired by Faulkner in writing *The Black Flower*, which was nominated for several literary prizes. Padgett Powell, also a National Book Award nominee, made Forrest a central character in *Mrs. Hollingsworth's Men*. The eleventh novel by Peter Abrahams, *Last of the Dixie Heroes*, brings Forrest into a contemporary suspense story involving a family crisis and Civil War reenactors. Legal thriller author John Grisham wrote about a Forrest-obsessed judge in *The Summons*. And James Lee Burke, best known for his highly regarded crime fiction, gave Forrest an important cameo role in a work of historical fiction, *White Doves at Morning*.

The Black Flower is an ethereal meditation about the Battle of Franklin. During the fighting a frightened young woman visiting relatives in Franklin has an encounter with Forrest. When she looks in Forrest's eyes, she sees "the shadow of a weariness that she knew he would never lose, and a dark wisdom she had no desire to own." He tells her there is no shame in being afraid, and that what she saw of the Army of Tennessee "was the last of a great army. You will forget about being afraid one day, but you will never forget that. Not ever." He gives her the black ostrich plume from his hat as a remembrance. On the day after the battle she prays for a mortally wounded soldier and tries to imagine God listening to her prayer: "She searched for an image of Him, found instead the face of General Nathan Bedford Forrest, looking just as he had on the stairs during the battle." Forrest, in a priestly role, offers her the assurance of God's grace and forgiveness. Years later the plume evokes his memory and sanctifies the dead, whose presence becomes real to her as she lingers over their graves. This image for her is in contrast to the hollow Lost Cause memorials that rise up all over the South. In time, she accepts Forrest's "dark wisdom," which chooses courage and commitment over fear, the constructive power of repentance, and acceptance of God's will.[67]

Powell's Mrs. Hollingsworth—a fey, middle-aged Southern woman out of sorts with her "indistinct husband" the judge, her trendy daughters, and an America that seems to have lost its mettle—sits down to write a grocery list at her kitchen table. The list gradually becomes a rant filled with surreal images that emerge from what she suspects is the fog of her demented mind. Although virtually ignorant of the Civil War yet haunted by it, she finds that Forrest is "in her head like the hook of a pop-radio tune." The local high school bears his name, and the "idea had formed in her mind that he had been indomitable; he had been the War's Achilles. Achilles with pinworms and slaves besmirching his heroic profile."[68]

She invents a character who has "a strange waking dream of a man on a horse larger and louder than Hollywood, whom he knew to be representing Nathan Bedford Forrest." Some see him, some do not, as he rides through a town square, "horse and hair aflame, salt and leather and sweat and steel penetrating the trailing air, and a malaise of sadness and loss consuming all who witness to him, leaving us diffident and afraid and idle in his wake." Forrest, the dreamer recognizes, is a symbol of something, perhaps a kind of Jesus figure. "I will not fail Forrest. Forrest was made so that a man, even a confused one, a little afraid, or a lot, might not fail him, and thereby might not fail himself," he says. Forrest, ostensibly a projection of Mrs. Hollingworth's discontent, expresses her suspicion that as a result of the Civil War, "woman is gone pay for this for the rest of her everliving life. She gone put up with shanks and heroes what wasn't there and the luckiest of heroes what was."

Forrest then becomes a gigantic hologram created by a media mogul seeking a New Southerner who will make himself known by recognizing Forrest for what he is, a Lost Cause icon in opposition to all that's wrong with postmodern America or, at least, all that's wrong with Mrs. Hollingsworth. The New Southerner will then be "eugenically engineered to found a line of men in the New South who will perforce raise up the Old by eliminating the genetic dearth effected by the War."[69]

In this book, however, Forrest seems to have a mind of his own, hologram or no. "They is no telling what will become of him," says the character who is projecting the hologram with something like a ray gun. "He is indestructible, though. I know that. No matter *what* you push, you get something." And that, perhaps, is the essence of Forrest—a doomed hero, a hologram representing a continuing, ill-fated war against the zeitgeist, a resistance fighter against the maladies of the spirit, an icon of all lost causes, however demented or noble. Invoke Forrest and you get, at least, *something* back for your troubles. Forrest becomes a hologram of history, as familiar as a town square monument and as spectral as an imagined reality. History and narrative are personal and subjective experiences. Thus, Forrest is both story and myth, received history and present problem, that won't go away, like a horseman on a plinth who animates himself whenever things become too settled.[70]

In Abrahams's *Last of the Dixie Heroes*, Roy Hill, the great-great-grandson of Roy Singleton Hill of Tennessee, who fought with Forrest, is a commodities trader for the Atlanta office of a giant corporation. After his wife leaves him and he is fired from his job, he takes up with a group of Confederate reenactors who find living in a perpetual 1863 preferable to living in the spiritually dead, Yankee-"occupied" South. Hill, who learns from the Forrest Homepage that the general called his ancestor "the Angel of Death," gradually assumes the old soldier's identity. He finds his great-great-grandfather's uniform, carbine, and diary and discovers that the ancestor fought at Fort Pillow. The diary says:

Twelve April 1864, Fort Pillow. Best day
of this conflict so far. Forrest asks for
unconditional surrender but they refuse.
And thems tauntin' us from over the walls.
So's we charge down from the east. . . .
Now theys thinkin' twicet bout not
surrenderin' but we has our orders from
Forrest and they was to . . .

At that point the diary ends because the next page has been ripped out.

Visiting his ancestor's homestead in Tennessee, Hill meets Ezekiel Hill, who claims to be a descendant of the Confederate soldier and one of his slaves. Roy Hill finds the last page of the diary in a coffin that Ezekiel believes contains the ashes of their mutual ancestor. The entry continues: ". . . kill the last God damn one of em. Was What Forrest says." The diary details the Fort Pillow massacre with the added fact that "the Angel of Death" also killed his own slave, Zeke. Roy burns the last page of the diary as he contemplates "where the line between the white Hills and the black Hills was drawn." The novel ends with Roy Hill and his companions shooting it out with live ammo with some Union reenactors who kidnap Hill's son. Roy Hill finds dignity by assuming the mantle of resistance to his untenable circumstances, even as he accepts the ambiguity of war and his ancestor's role in it. Forrest is exposed, in this fiction at least, as the culprit in the Fort Pillow massacre. As a killer and a man of his times, Forrest leaves the South with a legacy. The violence of the war continues, and if there is meaning in the mayhem, it is that while the sins of the fathers are visited on the next generations, fighting back is worth the struggle. Roy Hill, like the South, "unconquered, unoccupied, waiting," carries the "gene" of his famous ancestor, and it cannot be repressed.[71]

In *The Summons*, Grisham introduces Ray Atlee, a University of Virginia law professor, who has a black-sheep younger brother named after the famous general. Their father, Judge Atlee, sitting beneath a portrait of Forrest, under whom his grandfather fought at Shiloh, summons both brothers home to Clanton, Mississippi, to discuss his estate. The judge was known to his sons as a man who would never stop fighting the Civil War. But his father is dead when Ray arrives. He finds several million dollars in the judge's home; a mystery ensues, and Ray has to solve it beneath the portrait of Forrest, who looms over the story as a ghostly presence.[72]

Burke has written twenty novels, the most popular featuring a burned-out Louisiana police officer named Dave Robicheaux. *White Doves at Morning* tells a story based on the experiences of two of the author's ancestors, his great-grandfather Robert Perry and his great-great-uncle Willie Burke, as they fight in the Civil War and endure the early Reconstruction period in Louisiana. Willie Burke encounters Forrest at Shiloh. Separated from his regiment, the Eighteenth Louisiana, after it is all but wiped out by Union artillery while charging up a hill near Owl Creek, Willie reaches the bluffs over-looking the Tennessee River and sees the Union army being rein-forced. He tells Forrest what he has seen but not before condemning the "thumb-sucking incompetent sods" who ordered the charge without proper support. "I don't doubt you're a brave man and killed the enemy behind his own lines today," Forrest says. "Wars get won by such as yourself. But don't ever address me profanely or disrespectfully again. I won't have you shot. I'll do it myself."

The historical Forrest did indeed acquire information from scouts about Union reinforcements, but that it was Willie Burke who initially alerted him to the troop movements may be a bit of Burke family apocrypha. Willie later ponders the possibility that he may have earned a footnote in history by scouting for Forrest at Shiloh; he *knows* he has acquired a reputation as one of the few living men who ever sassed the famous cavalryman. Willie, how-ever, is unimpressed: "If someone were to ask him of his impres-sions about the colonel, he would reply he recalled little about him, other than the fact he was a coarse-skinned, profane man who bathed in horse tanks and put enough string tobacco in his mouth to clog a cannon, and if Willie saw him amid a gathering of grocery clerks, he would probably not recognize him nor wish to do so."[73]

AN AMERICAN MYTH

Across the span of a century, then, several dozen authors have ap-propriated Forrest for tales ranging from historical romance to al-ternative history and crime fiction. The Forrest Myth is now practically a literary genre unto itself. Although typically one-dimensional in fiction, Forrest appears in many guises: a cornpone philosopher, an agent of evil, a personification of impersonal na-ture, a holy fool, a Christian convert, and a specter. Whether por-trayed as a knight in a golden age before the South succumbed to Yankee lucre and morality, as a military genius, raptor-eyed homi-cidal maniac, tutor to Nazis, frontier fascist, Lost Cause icon, dream, resistance fighter against modernity, unicorn-riding faux-medieval knight-errant, hologram, avenger, Southern savior, or rip-roaring racist, Forrest emerges with smoking breath, slashing sword, and smoldering testosterone as one of the most protean characters in all of literature. No mere mortal, often more epic hero or monster than man, Forrest is a fiction, a legend, and, ultimately, an Ameri-can myth.

NOTES

1. Richard M. Weaver, *The Southern Essays of Richard M. Weaver*, ed. George M. Curtis III and James J. Thompson Jr. (Indianapolis, IN: Liberty Press, 1987), 68–69.

2. Eileen Gregory, preface to Caroline Gordon, *None Shall Look Back* (Nashville: J. S. Sanders and Company, 1992), viii–ix.

3. Andrew Lytle, *The Hero with the Private Parts* (Baton Rouge: Louisiana State University Press, 1966), 6–7.

4. "Buried Alive," *Harper's Weekly*, May 7, 1864, in *To Live and Die: Collected Stories of the Civil War, 1861–1876*, ed. Kathleen Diffley (Durham, NC: Duke University Press, 2002), 284–88; Kathleen Diffley, *Where My Heart Is Turning Ever: Civil War Stories and Constitutional Reform, 1861–1876* (Athens: University of Georgia Press, 1992), xxvi–xxvii.

5. *Memphis Press-Scimitar*, February 9, 1908, 7, quoted in Hurst, *Nathan Bedford Forrest*, 387; Thomas Dixon, *The Leopard's Spots: A Romance of the White Man's Burden, 1865–1900* (New York: Doubleday, Page and Company, 1903); Thomas Dixon, *The Clansman: An Historical Romance of the Ku Klux Klan* (New York: Doubleday, Page and Company, 1905); Thomas Dixon, *The Traitor: A Story of the Fall of the Invisible Empire* (New York: Doubleday, Page and Company, 1907); Thomas Dixon, *The Clansman: Four Acts*, 1905, typescript in the Library of Congress; Raymond A. Cook, *Fire from the Flint: The Amazing Careers of Thomas Dixon* (Winston-Salem, NC: John F. Blair, 1968); Raymond A. Cook, *Thomas Dixon* (New York: Twayne Publishers, 1974); Davenport, *The Myth of Southern History*, 25, 28; Everett Carter, "Cultural History Written with Lightning: The Significance of *The Birth of a Nation*," *American Quarterly* 12 (Fall 1960): 347–57.

6. Paul M. Cousins, *Joel Chandler Harris* (Baton Rouge: Louisiana State University Press, 1968), 191; Blight, *Race and Reunion*, 228–29.

7. *New York Times*, May 7, 1904; Joel Chandler Harris, *A Little Union Scout* (New York: McClure, Phillips and Company, 1904), 120.

8. Harris, *A Little Union Scout*, 48.

9. Ibid., 176–77.

10. Joel Chandler Harris, *The Shadow between His Shoulder-Blades* (Boston: Small, Maynard and Company, 1909), 45; Hurst, *Nathan Bedford Forrest*, 210; Cousins, *Joel Chandler Harris*, 216; Henry, *"First with the Most" Forrest*, 329.

11. Harris, *The Shadow between His Shoulder-Blades*, 62–63, 66, 127, 132.

12. Anita Lawson, *Irvin S. Cobb* (Bowling Green, OH: Bowling Green State University Popular Press, 1984); Irvin S. Cobb, preface to his *Back Home* (New York: Grosset and Dunlap, 1912), x.

13. Wayne Chatterton, *Irvin S. Cobb* (Boston: Twayne Publishers, 1986), 101; Irvin S. Cobb, "The Sun Shines Bright," in *Down Yonder with Judge Priest and Irvin S. Cobb* (New York: R. Long and R. R. Smith, 1932); Irvin S. Cobb, "Forrest's Last Charge," in *Old Judge Priest* (New York: Review of Reviews Corp., 1916), 280–323.

14. William R. Taylor, *Cavalier and Yankee: The Old South and American National Character* (1961; reprint ed., New York: Oxford University Press, 1993), 341; Carol Reardon, *Pickett's Charge in History and Memory* (Chapel Hill: University of North Carolina Press, 1997), 204.

15. Hurst, *Nathan Bedford Forrest*, 213–14; Thomas E. Dasher, *William Faulkner's Characters: An Index to the Published and Unpublished Fiction* (New York: Garland Publishing, 1981), 412–13; Joel Williamson, *William Faulkner and Southern History* (New York: Oxford University Press, 1993), 41–44, 64–71; Cleanth Brooks, *William Faulkner: Toward Yoknapatawpha and Beyond* (New Haven, CT: Yale University Press, 1978), 375; Howard W. Odum, "On Southern Literature and Southern Culture," in *Southern Renascence: The Literature of the Modern South*, ed. Louis D. Rubin Jr. and Robert D. Jacobs (Baltimore, MD: Johns Hopkins University Press, 1953), 97.

16. Dasher, *William Faulkner's Characters*; William Faulkner, "My Grandmother Millard and Bedford Forrest at the Battle of Harrykin Creek," in *Story* (March–April 1943), reprinted in *Collected Stories of William Faulkner* (New York: Random House, 1950), 667–99.

17. Elmo Howell, "William Faulkner's General Forrest and the Uses of History," *Tennessee Historical Quarterly* 29 (Fall 1970): 287–94.

18. William Faulkner, "Shall Not Perish," *Story* (July–August 1943), reprinted in *Collected Stories of William Faulkner*, 101–15.

19. Singal, *The War Within*, 154, 170.

20. Wills, *A Battle from the Start*, 2; William Faulkner, *Go Down, Moses* (New York: Modern Library, 1955), 263–64, cited in Wills.

21. Edmond L. Volpe, *A Reader's Guide to William Faulkner* (New York: Farrar, Straus and Giroux, 1964), 76–86.

22. Jim Cullen, *The Civil War in Popular Culture: A Reusable Past* (Washington, DC: Smithsonian Institution Press, 1995), 65–107.

23. Ann Waldron, *Close Connections: Caroline Gordon and the Southern Renaissance* (Knoxville: University of Tennessee Press, 1989), 143; Caroline Gordon to Robert Penn Warren, Beinecke Library, Yale University, n.d.; Caroline Gordon to Maxwell Perkins, December 13, 1934, Scribner Deposit, Princeton University; Caroline Gordon to Brainard Lon Cheney, Jean and Alexander Heard Library, Vanderbilt University, n.d., all three letters quoted in Waldron, *Close Connections*, 143, 168.

24. Waldron, *Close Connections*, 160, 164, 169, 173; Caroline Gordon to Maxwell Perkins, Scribner Deposit, Princeton University, 1936, quoted in Waldron, *Close Connections*, 173; Cullen, *The Civil War in Popular Culture*, 74, 80; Walter Allen, *The Modern Novel in Britain and the United States* (New York: Dutton, 1964), 113, 114; Louise Cowan, "Nature and Grace in Caroline Gordon," *Critique* 1 (Winter 1956): 11–27; Jane Gibson Brown, "The Early Novels of Caroline Gordon: Myth and History as a Fictional Technique," *Southern Review* 13 (1977): 289–98.

25. Caroline Gordon, *None Shall Look Back* (New York: Charles Scribner's Sons, 1937), 27–28.

26. Ibid., 241, 340, 375.

27. Ashley Brown, "None Shall Look Back: The Novel as History," *Southern Review* 7 (1971): 483, 493; Nahum 2:8.

28. Gordon, *None Shall Look Back*, 373; Eileen Gregory, preface to Gordon, *None Shall Look Back*, xii, xiii, xix, xv, xx.

29. Alfred Leland Crabb, *A Mockingbird Sang at Chickamauga* (Indianapolis, IN: Bobbs-Merrill, 1949), 227.

30. Faulkner quoted in Malcolm Franklin, *Bitterweeds: Life with William Faulkner at Rowan Oak* (Irving, TX: Society for the Study of Traditional

Culture, 1977), 59; Robert L. Phillips Jr., *Shelby Foote, Novelist and Historian* (Jackson: University of Mississippi Press, 1992), 3–18.

31. Toplin, *Ken Burns's "The Civil War": Historians Respond*, xv, 33; Shelby Foote, *Shiloh* (New York: Dial Press, 1952), 145–46, 150.

32. Foote, *Shiloh*, 158, 200, 212–14, 218.

33. Helen White and Redding S. Sugg Jr., *Shelby Foote* (Boston: Twayne Publishers, 1982), 74, 79.

34. Edward C. Reilly, "Shelby Foote," in *Critical Survey of Long Fiction* 3, rev. ed., ed. Frank N. Magill (Pasadena, CA: Salem Press, 1991), 1151–64; Thomas H. Landess, "Southern History and Manhood: Major Themes in the Works of Shelby Foote," *Mississippi Quarterly* 24 (Fall 1971): 321–47. See also Allen Shepherd, "Technique and Theme in Shelby Foote's *Shiloh*," *Notes on Mississippi Writers* 5 (Spring 1972): 3–10.

35. Elmore Leonard, *Last Stand at Saber River* (1959; reprint ed., New York: Bantam, 1980), 58.

36. Elmore Leonard, *Tishomingo Blues* (New York: HarperCollins, 2002), 178 .

37. Perry Lentz, *The Falling Hills* (New York: Charles Scribner's Sons, 1967; Columbia: University of South Carolina Press, 1994), preface to the 1994 edition, n.p.; Henry, *"First with the Most" Forrest*, after p. 256.

38. Lentz, *The Falling Hills*, 208, 216, 233.

39. Ibid., 234, 419, 437, 440.

40. Frank Yerby, *The Foxes of Harrow* (New York: Dial Press, 1946), 397; James Sherburne, *The Way to Fort Pillow* (Boston: Houghton Mifflin, 1972), 246; Allen B. Ballard, *Where I'm Bound* (New York: Simon and Schuster, 2000).

41. Jesse Hill Ford, *The Raider* (Boston: Little, Brown and Company, 1975), 212, 396, 405, 410, 419, 464; "The Making of Fables: Jesse Hill Ford," an interview by James Seay, in *Kite-Flying and Other Irrational Acts: Conversations with Twelve Southern Writers*, ed. John Carr (Baton Rouge: Louisiana State University Press, 1972), 199–215; John Alvis, "Jesse Hill Ford," in *American Novelists since World War II*, 2d ser., 5, ed. James E. Kibler Jr., Dictionary of Literary Biography 6 (Detroit: Gail Research Company, 1980), 100–104.

42. Robert Penn Warren, "When the Light Gets Green," *Southern Review* 1 (Spring 1936): 799–806; idem, "When the Light Gets Green," in *The Circus in the Attic and Other Stories* (New York: Harcourt, Brace and Company, 1947), 88–95; Peter Taylor, "In the Miro District," *The New Yorker*, May 14, 1977, 34–48, collected in *In the Miro District and Other Stories* (New York: Alfred A. Knopf, 1977), 157–204.

43. Taylor, *In the Miro District*, 165.

44. Ibid., 173, 180

45. Ibid., 164, 185–86, 203; Peter Taylor, interview by James Curry Robison, September 9, 1987, in Robison, *Peter Taylor: A Study of the Short Fiction* (Boston: Twayne Publishers, 1988), 144–45; Catherine Clark Graham, *Southern Accents: The Fiction of Peter Taylor* (New York: Peter Lang, 1994).

46. Peter Taylor to Robert Penn Warren, August 30, 1974, Warren Papers, Yale Collection of American Literature, Beinecke Rare Book and Manuscript Library, Yale University, New Haven, Connecticut, quoted in Beck, *The Fugitive Legacy*, 228.

47. Winston Groom, *Forrest Gump* (1986; reprint ed., New York: Pocket Books, 1994), 1–3.

48. Sam Hodges, *B-Four* (New York: St. Martin's Press, 1992), 191.

49. Charles Gordon Yeager, *Fightin' with Forrest* (Gretna, LA: Pelican Publishing Company, 1987).

50. Bob Armistead, *Never to Quit* (Nashville: Eggman Publishing, 1993), 119; Bob Armistead, *Warrior Forrest* (Nashville: Southern Historical Showcase, 1997).

51. Robert S. Chambers, *The God of War: When I Rode with N. B. Forrest, the Letters of Henry Wylie* (Cumberland, OH: King Phillip Publishing, 1996), 2.

52. Clayton Williams, *The Cavalryman* (New York: Vantage Press, 1997), xiv; Gene Ladnier, *Fame's Eternal Camping Ground* (Philadelphia: Ex Libris, 1999).

53. Robert A. Sigafoos, *Wave the Bloody Shirt: The Life and Times of General Nathan Bedford Forrest, CSA* (Cane Hill, AR: ARC Press of Cane Hill, 2000).

54. James D. Brewer, *No Bottom* (New York: Walker and Company, 1994); James D. Brewer, *No Virtue* (New York: Walker and Company, 1995); James D. Brewer, *No Remorse* (New York: Walker and Company, 1997).

55. Gilbert Morris and Lynn Morris, *Toward the Sunrising* (Minneapolis, MN: Bethany House Publishers, 1996), 291, 368.

56. See MacKinlay Kantor, *If the South Had Won the Civil War* (New York: Bantam Books, 1961); Robert Skimin, *Gray Victory* (New York: St. Martin's Press, 1988); Harry Turtledove, *Guns of the South* (New York: Del Rey, 1992); Harry Turtledove, introduction to *The Best Alternative History Stories of the 20th Century*, ed. Harry Turtledove with Martin H. Greenberg (New York: Ballantine, 2001), ix; Poyer, *The Shiloh Project*; and Noah Andre Trudeau, "What Might Have Been," *Civil War Times Illustrated* 33 (September/October 1994): 56–59.

57. Lawrence Wells, *Rommel and the Rebel* (1986, 1987; reprint ed., Oxford, MS: Yoknapatawpha Press, 1992).

58. Untitled newspaper article, *Capitol Herald* (Jackson, MS), July 9, 1937, quoted in Wells, *Rommel and the Rebel*, n.p.; "Lawrence Wells," *The Mississippi Writers Page*, www.olemiss.edu/mwp/dir/wells_lawrence; Erwin Rommel, *Infanterie greift an* (1937; reprint ed., Vienna, VA: Athena Press, 1979).

59. Wells, *Rommel and the Rebel*, 4, 29, 54.

60. Ibid., 176; David Fraser, *Knight's Cross: A Life of Field Marshal Erwin Rommel* (New York: HarperCollins, 1993), 1, 4.

61. Howard Means, *C.S.A.—Confederate States of America* (New York: William Morrow and Company, 1998), 4, 5, 70, 74, 139, 240.

62. Turtledove, *The Guns of the South*, 348, 377, 378.

63. Harry Turtledove, *Sentry Peak* (Riverdale, NY: Baen Books, 2000), 13, 14, 18, 39, 41, 82, 269, 275.

64. Ibid., 14, 194, 276.

65. Dennis P. McIntire, *Lee at Chattanooga* (Nashville, TN: Cumberland House, 2002), 143.

66. John Duke Merriman, *Meade's Reprise: A Novel of Gettysburg, War, and Intrigue* (Chevy Chase, MD: Posterity Press, 2002), 290.

67. Howard Bahr, *The Black Flower* (New York: Henry Holt and Company, 1998), 128–29, 260.

68. Padgett Powell, *Mrs. Hollingsworth's Men* (New York: Houghton Mifflin, 2000), 4–5, 13.

69. Ibid., 13, 16, 56, 66.

70. Ibid., 93, 133–34.

71. Peter Abrahams, *Last of the Dixie Heroes* (New York: Ballantine Books, 2001), 149, 230–31, 273–74.

72. John Grisham, *The Summons* (New York: Doubleday, 2002).

73. James Lee Burke, *White Doves at Morning* (New York: Simon and Schuster, 2002), 82–83, 116.

PART THREE

NO PEACE IN TENNESSEE

The war was done, but the peace was reluctant. . . . Just as the war itself had been slow in coming, so it was that the return of peace to the district was gradual and like a river that will not be hurried but takes its own way and its own time.
—Jesse Hill Ford, *The Raider* (1975)

So whatever else ole General Forrest done, startin up that Klan thing was not a good idea—any idiot could tell you that.
—Winston Groom, *Forrest Gump* (1986)

Do the dead still ride by night in Memphis? Some might think so, judging from the controversy that still swirls around Forrest's statue and grave site in the heart of the city. Photograph by Chloe White. *Courtesy of Chloe White*

CHAPTER SEVEN

ONLY THE DEAD CAN RIDE

ANDREW LYTLE ENDED a new edition of his biography of Forrest with a story about "an old negress" who was taken to see the equestrian statue of the general in Memphis in the mid-1950s. The woman "grunted" to her "mistress" that King Phillip, the general's horse, was looking spent. Told that a bronze horse cannot wither, the woman said, "Well'm, I see 'em when dey put him up dar, and I see him now—and he show is poe." Asked how that could happen, she remarked, "I don't know'm. I regon de Gin'ral must ride him of a night." Lytle told this story to Donald Davidson, who used it as the inspiration for a poem, "The Last Rider," with these lines:

> . . . we know too much of Forrest
> Not to believe it true,
> And we know what call has a rider
> To come between dark and dawn
> To the bluegrass that sired him
> And the roads he fought on;
> And do not doubt that Forrest can come
> From Mississippi side
> Back where the living do not fight
> And only the dead can ride.

Mark Royden Winchell calls Davidson's homage to the ghostly general a hymn of resistance to a complacent modern South "where the living do not fight," and perhaps that is what Lytle also intended. Davidson seems to have had a fascination for statues of Forrest and what they might symbolically represent. One Sunday in 1933, while passing through Rome, Georgia—the city Forrest had entered in triumph after his great victory over Colonel Abel Streight seventy years earlier—Davidson paused to study a statue of Forrest in Myrtle Hill Cemetery, where many Confederate soldiers were buried. He noted the inscription on another monument towering over the graves: "the testimony of the present to the future that these were they who kept the faith as it was given them by the fathers." Perhaps inspired by that testimony to the future, he wrote a long poem titled "The Running of Streight (A Fragment of the Forrest Saga)," which reads in part:

> . . . And then rode on to Rome where hills and trees
> Pierce the sweet mountain air by Coosa River.
> They saw the pretty girls crying and laughing all
> Together, and children waving flags, the South
> Swept into victory on Forrest's shoulders.
> Forrest they followed all in that great riding
> And had their time of glory under the sun.[1]

A medallion depicting Forrest on horseback now stands near the city hall in Chapel Hill, Tennessee. The medallion was once located on the campus of Middle Tennessee State University. Photograph by Jennifer Allen. *Courtesy of Jennifer Allen*

Forrest's statue in Rome, Georgia, inspired poet Donald Davidson to medi-
tate on the "time of glory under the sun." Photograph by Marcie Hinton.
Courtesy of Marcie Hinton

Forrest is just one of many Confederate heroes honored in
bronze and stone all over the South, but monuments to the Wizard
of the Saddle are especially prolific. Tennessee alone has erected
thirty-two statues to the general, even more than Illinois has dedicated to Abraham Lincoln or Virginia to George Washington. His bust

has a place of honor in Tennessee's Capitol. Middle Tennessee State University in Murfreesboro once used his image in its logo and as its unofficial mascot, and huge papier mâché likenesses of the general were paraded through the campus on homecoming floats. Schools and parks as well as monuments also honor Forrest in Georgia, Alabama, Mississippi, Florida, and Texas. A city in Arkansas and a county in Mississippi bear his name. As the Forrest Myth has shifted with changing political and cultural currents, his name has sometimes caused embarrassment and always generated passionate partisanship.[2]

Some of the most passionate of those debates have erupted in Forrest's hometown. Long before the Memphis statue was unveiled in Forrest Park in 1905 and the general's and his wife's remains were interred beneath its marble plinth, Forrest's ghost had been riding through the South and bringing controversy wherever it went. The statue, however, became a particular rallying point for those who would either praise him or bury him for good. Memphis newspapers in 1905 found the monument a point of civic and historic pride. The *News-Scimitar* devoted an entire section to it, including a front-page photograph of veterans and citizens congregated at the unveiling ceremony. According to the story, a Rebel yell from as many as 20,000 people went up as "the parting flags revealed the heroic figure, the wizard of the saddle."

The *Commercial Appeal* echoed the idea that the "South's great hero" was a historic figure for the ages: "A little later and these survivors will become shadows themselves, but the great bronze statue of Gen. Forrest will stand for all times to come a vindication of a nation's hero; a tribute to a great man's greater achievements; a figure of supreme interest; a record of an epoch in the experience of a generation, during a period of awful stress and vicissitude; an illustration that the memory of daring deeds well done can never die."[3] It was as though the war had just ended: "His career will always adorn one of the most romantic pages of history. There need be no apology for erecting this striking monument to commemorate his splendid deeds. Memphis can at last point with genuine pride to this enduring recognition of the achievements of one of her greatest citizens."[4]

The *News-Scimitar* was only slightly less effusive. At that time, when the Klan affiliation was not an issue but a point of pride, the writer said the veil covering the statue reminded him of Forrest's

Klan robe, especially in the light of the moon, and he found it an inspiring sight. The article cast Forrest as something of a founding father of modern Memphis, praising him for the glorious past of the city, which would bode well for its present and future. Nearly twenty years later, even small details about the statue could provoke debate—such as the direction the statue faced, which was south. Some objected that it symbolized retreat from Union troops; it was also noted that the statue faced Union Avenue, just outside the park. And so it went in the early part of the century, with the Tennessee legislature in 1921 declaring July 13 a legal holiday to commemorate Forrest's birthday and getting press accolades for doing so.[5]

Even in midcentury, the *Commercial Appeal*, shortly after World War II and in his defense, explained that Forrest's Klan had been a very different and justifiable entity following the Civil War. In fact, it blamed the North for the creation of the Klan:

> When the South lay torn and bleeding, prey to the jackals who swept down on her prostrate form, [Forrest] rallied the forces of decency behind the cross of the Ku Klux Klan. Since then the Klan has come to have a far different meaning, and its good name was seized upon by latter-day exponents of bigotry and hate to perpetrate their program of intolerance. Forrest it was who ordered the Klan disbanded after it had served its purpose of restoring a semblance of law and order to this unhappy land, for he could perceive the sinister results that the unscrupulous might achieve through it.[6]

The same story complained in a downright impetuous tone that the city had planned no adequate ceremony to honor Forrest's birthday beyond closing the banks because of the state holiday. In fact, the "fiery commander's" birthday became something of a cause for the *Commercial Appeal*, which returned to the subject a few years later, noting the lack of ceremonies in Forrest Park to mark the occasion. It was even worse the next year, 1950: not only were there no ceremonies, but now even the banks were staying open on the holiday. The headline captured the sentiment well: "A Bronze Hero Is Lonely Today as the Dixie He Loved Forgets." Yet some sort of celebration must have taken place, if not one of sufficient caliber for the *Commercial Appeal*, because in 1958 the *Press-Scimitar* noted that Forrest's birthday was passing without public notice for the first time since the Civil War. It was also just two years after the

U.S. Supreme Court's *Brown v. Board of Education* decision, and the times had changed. It was a monument to different ideals, depending on who viewed it.[7]

Throughout the 1960s and 1970s the civil rights movement increased racial tensions throughout the South, and the monument became increasingly controversial. In 1979 a black civil rights activist climbed onto its base and called for its removal: "Why should we stand for black tax dollars going to support and maintain Forrest's image when he organized the Klan? . . . If somebody proposed putting up a statue of Adolph Hitler the Jewish citizens would rise up."[8]

In 1985 the *Tri-State Defender* looked to the statue when it editorialized that the city needed to acknowledge Forrest's dark side if race relations were to improve and if Memphis were to be a progressive city with a progressive image. Referring to Fort Pillow, the paper asked, "Can we continue to ignore the truth and blindly hope that others outside of our area will never become aware that we honor murderers in Memphis?" The shifting sentiment was all too evident in the news that park employees were sandblasting the statue in order to remove KKK slogans. The *Commercial Appeal*, in 1986, reported that experts frowned on the sandblasting, fearing permanent damage: "It's far from a normal way to treat a bronze statue." The resulting erosion was altering the surface image, not only cleaning it of crudely, hastily applied graffitti but simultaneously pitting the bronze that had been cast for the ages.[9]

In 1987 the University of Tennessee's downtown Memphis campus offered to clean up and maintain nearby Forrest Park and its monument, which had often been covered with graffitti. When the university announced it would honor its retiring president in a ceremony at the park, the local NAACP chapter objected and urged that the park be renamed and the statue and the bodies of Forrest and his wife be removed. The university canceled the festivities and declared that its offer to care for the park implied no endorsement of its namesake. When author Shelby Foote tried to defend Forrest, the affair soon degenerated into a shouting match between an African American newspaper and another local journal. On another occasion, Foote told a reporter that Forrest was "a fine man. My black friends abhor him. They want to take his statue down, dig up his and his wife's bones, and throw them to the wind."[10]

The debate about Forrest monuments was not confined to Memphis. A similar controversy erupted in Nashville in 1997, when plans

Forrest straddles a fiberglass horse in a Confederate flag park visible from an interstate highway in Nashville. The mount appears ready to leap over the barbed-wire fence and carry its rider into another controversy. Photograph by Andrew Plant. *Courtesy of Andrew Plant*

were revealed for a new Forrest statue. The next year, Jack Kershaw —grandson of one of the general's cavalrymen as well as an attorney who briefly represented James Earl Ray, the convicted assassin of Martin Luther King, and a segregationist and states' rights advocate associated with Donald Davidson—unveiled a garish fiberglass statue of a sword-and-pistol-wielding Forrest astride a rearing horse. Rising about thirty feet above the landscape of a private Confederate flag park just visible from Interstate 65 in Brentwood, the statue, which many residents thought an embarrassing eyesore, was protected by a chain-link fence topped by barbed wire. A letter to the editor of the *Tennessean* condemned the statue not for its subject but for its lack of aesthetic substance: "What I saw, and could not get past, was the ugliest piece of overblown yard art imaginable. The fake appearance of the garish silver paint color combined with the poorly crafted features places this cheap-looking 'statue' on the same aesthetic level as pink elephants in front of liquor stores and cows atop farm house roofs." That Forrest had become "yard art" may be the strongest testament yet to his legend's secured place in American mythology.[11]

In January 1998, black school board members in Gadsden, Alabama, campaigned to change the name of the General Forrest Middle School, which they said offended the 125 black children who attended the school. One member claimed that she lost her seat on the board because of her part in the campaign. In Atlanta in 2001 a neighborhood association succeeded in persuading the city to change the names of Bedford Place and Bedford Pine Park once they had proved that the sites were named for Forrest. Twenty years earlier, Forrest Avenue, a major thoroughfare, had been changed to Ralph McGill Boulevard, named for the civil rights advocate and editor of the *Atlanta Constitution*.[12]

A HARDENING IDEOLOGICAL EDGE

Tony Horwitz, a Pulitzer Prize–winning journalist, probed the modern manifestations of the Forrest Myth and discussed his findings in a best-selling book, *Confederates in the Attic: Dispatches from the Unfinished Civil War* (1998). He concluded that Forrest continues to have a strong appeal for working-class Southerners, for whom he is the antithesis of Lee's Southern gentleman, a genteel symbol of reconciliation. Forrest, by contrast, represents the same spirit of resistance that Winchell noted in Davidson's poem, a hard-

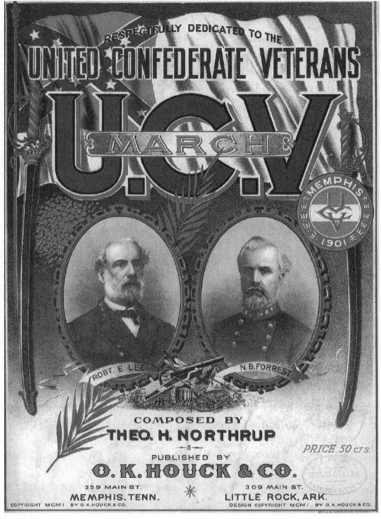

Forrest received equal billing with Robert E. Lee when O. K. Houck & Co. published the sheet music to a United Confederate Veterans march in 1901. From Historic American Sheet Music, "U.C.V. March," Music B-284, Duke University Rare Book, Manuscript, and Special Collections Library.

charging contrariness, a refusal to submit to the deracination of Confederate heritage, and perhaps a swelling racial pride. A Confederate memorabilia salesman in Georgia showed Horwitz a Forrest T-shirt he was hawking and told him, "Lee, of course, used to be our best seller. But Forrest has eclipsed Lee fivefold in the last few years." This fact reinforced a trend Horwitz had noted across the South, "a hardening ideological edge to Confederate remembrance."

When Horwitz visited Selma, Alabama, the city Forrest had tried to defend in the last days of the war, he found a petition drive under way to change the name of the Nathan B. Forrest Homes, a housing project in an all-black neighborhood. The director of the Voting Rights Museum and organizer of the drive asked him if he could imagine "Jews living in some subdivision named for Himmler." But she said she was disappointed in her efforts: "Most folks don't know their history enough to be insulted. They've never heard of Forrest, unless it's *Forrest Gump*, so they take it. The whites make heroes of killers like Forrest and because of our own ignorance or internalized oppression, we let it happen."

In September 2000 a bronze bust to the general was unveiled on city property. The bust might have been less controversial had it not been dedicated soon after the election of the city's first black mayor, or had the site not been a black neighborhood in a city whose population is 60 percent black, or had Selma not been associated in the national memory with violence during civil rights marches in 1965. Although the bust was later relocated, the *Wall Street Journal*, noting Forrest's "baggage" as a slave trader and Klansman, linked the issue to the Confederate flag controversies of the time and commented that "without the spirit of compromise and prudence so essential to civic peace, those insisting on ever more public affirmations of a Confederate 'heritage' may find themselves inadvertently helping to demonize what they legitimately hope to preserve." A National Public Radio commentator, Diane Roberts, argued that the Forrest statue dispute was significant because "Selma is a metaphor for the South, a living paradox." Regardless of where the statue winds up, she said, "the first imperial wizard of the Ku Klux Klan won't leave Selma. He'll just decamp to private land where those who wish to may still worship at the cold altar of the Confederacy."[13]

Confederate heritage groups often try to show that Forrest was not the racist he is usually portrayed to be. One contentious issue in the battle over Confederate memory is the role that blacks played in the Confederate army. In Knoxville, Tennessee, a retired African American teacher who claims that his grandfather served with Forrest's Seventh Tennessee Cavalry at Shiloh and Brice's Cross Roads, told a Sons of Confederate Veterans audience that his grandfather was buried in his uniform. He said his grandfather had told him that Forrest was a great general who had received "bad press. He had seven Negro guards and he must not have been all that bad if he could lay down to sleep at night guarded by seven Negroes. . . . The war wasn't about slavery, that's an outright lie. The issue was state's rights and tariffs."[14]

The burden of Confederate heritage, of course, is a problem for the South in general and Southern politicians in particular. In 1978, a few months after the bust of Forrest was installed in the Tennessee Capitol, the Republican governor (and later U.S. senator) Lamar Alexander was confronted by a group called Black Tennesseans for Action, who protested alleged racism in the governor's administration. The statue was damaged during the protests. And in the course of the 2000 presidential campaign, reporters pointed out that Al Gore, who had tried to wound George W. Bush and the Republicans on the Confederate flag controversy in South Carolina, had nothing to say about Tennessee's monuments to Forrest and, by implication, Forrest's association with the Ku Klux Klan. After Gore spoke out against Senate majority leader Trent Lott, who was under fire in 2002 for saying the country would have been better off if Senator Strom Thurmond had been elected president in 1948, syndicated columnist John McCaslin claimed in the *Washington Times* that Gore had dedicated Nathan Bedford Forrest State Park and should speak out against Forrest monuments in Tennessee before criticizing Lott. McCaslin backed off a bit in a subsequent column after reportedly hearing from numerous Tennesseans who defended both Forrest and Gore, but he included a comment from a letter writer who said, "Every time I hear Al 'Forrest' Gore speak, I picture Tom Hanks as Forrest Gump saying, 'Stupid is as stupid does.' " The damage was done.[15]

David Ignatius, writing in the *International Herald Tribune* a few months after the start of George W. Bush's presidency, offered a different spin on the relationship between Forrest and contemporary politics. Having read Jay Winik's *April 1865*, Ignatius argued that Forrest had risen above partisan politics immediately after the war, and that "America was supremely lucky in April 1865 to have men like this who could look beyond themselves and the bitter battles that had divided the country. They were big men. They had the largeness of spirit that historians call 'vision' or 'stature,' or simply 'leadership.' " Bush, on the other hand, he said, seemed small-minded and partisan. In other words, Bush was no Nathan Bedford Forrest.

Just how Forrest might have led the nation after the September 11 attacks might be a good topic for another column, a novel of alternative history, or a chapter in a book on applied, or implied, leadership. Randall Bedwell considered Forrest's leadership style in a 1997 collection of the general's homespun aphorisms. *May I Quote You, General Forrest?* includes not only remarks attributed to Forrest but also things said about him by others. Bedwell, interestingly, dedicated his book to Andrew Lytle, Forrest's great literary apostle and biographer. An introductory chapter presents Forrest as a military genius. His association with the Klan is called "a short-lived resort to clandestine activities" during a harsh military occupation, and his postwar public statements show that he "unequivocally favored reconciliation and the rule of law." Bedwell contended that Forrest was a self-effacing commander but that "no general officer left a more impressive paper trail" documenting his activities. He describes Forrest as having the leadership style of a contemporary micromanager, owing to his background in business, but claimed that he avoided the micromanager's frequent inability to distinguish between the necessary and the trivial.

Forrest's value to contemporary managers has also received a plug in a British business newspaper. Writing in the *Financial Times*, Morgan Witzel interpreted Forrest's famously mangled and misquoted "git thar fustest with the mostest" strategy as foreshadowing the modern business concept called the first-mover advantage: gaining an advantage over competitors by being the first to enter a new market.[16]

FORREST IN FILM, TELEVISION, AND POPULAR CULTURE

Forrest may have tried to disband the Ku Klux Klan in 1869, but getting rid of it permanently would prove more difficult than just snatching a white hood off the head of a night rider. D. W. Griffith's controversial film *The Birth of a Nation* had its premiere in Woodrow Wilson's White House on February 18, 1915. Adapted from the several novels of Thomas Dixon, it presented a romantic defense of Forrest's Klan. Although Forrest never appears as a character in the film, which takes place primarily in the Carolinas, he is part of its strange history. Like all historical films, *The Birth of a Nation* says more about its own time than about the past from which it draws inspiration. David W. Blight claimed that the minority report including Forrest's testimony at the congressional Klan hearings, published in 1872, "could have served as an initial script" for the film. He said that the "alienation of the emancipationist vision, and of the basic substance of black memory, from mainstream popular remembrance of the Civil War era received no greater long-term stimulus" than when the film premiered across the country. By February 1916 alone, it had been seen in greater New York by an estimated 3,000,000 people. In 1949 the show business journal *Variety* estimated its total revenue at almost $45 million, or close to $1 billion in end-of-the century currency.

The Birth of a Nation, according to the journalist and film historian Bruce Chadwick, is a film "shredded by intellectuals, picketed by thousands of African Americans and torn apart for generations by film scholars as an ugly racist epic that denigrated all blacks as thugs and rapists and glorified the terrorists of the Ku Klux Klan. It was at once the best and worst silent movie of all time, a film that would, indeed, live forever—in ignominy." It has been linked to race riots, outbreaks of lynchings, the resurgence of the Klan, imperialism, and the rise of fascism. Following the resurrection of the Klan in Atlanta after its release, Forrest's grandson Nathan Bedford Forrest II served as Grand Dragon in Georgia and as secretary of the national organization, which claimed 3,000,000 members in the early 1920s. Based on white supremacy, the Klan promoted a kind of nationalist civil religion mixing "Americanism," spurious morality, and mythic ritual. By the time of Dixon's death in 1946, he and Griffith had been thoroughly pilloried. One obituary writer wrote that Dixon's and Griffith's "white-robed klansmen fired a nation's imagination to such an extent that the Latter Day K.K.K. found it a pushover sucker list when it started organizing on a grand scale. The Klan died down in America but Hitler picked up the threads of intolerance in Germany."

As a work of cinematic art, however, *The Birth of a Nation* has had notable champions. In a now-famous essay published in *The Nation* in 1948, James Agee, arguably America's greatest film critic, judged the film as a tragic epic "equal with Brady's photographs, Lincoln's speeches, Whitman's war poems; for all its imperfections and absurdities it is equal, in fact, to the best work that has been done in this country." Agee saw Griffith creating nothing less than a national consciousness and mythology. If some of the raw source material for that consciousness was mined from the Forrest Myth, either for good or evil, the general would be held accountable.[17]

Another great director, John Ford, also made use of Forrest, but more benignly, when he brought Irvin Cobb's "Judge Priest" stories to the screen in 1934. Will Rogers plays the small-town Kentucky judge who fought with Forrest and rides a horse named after the general as he goes about dispensing commonsense wisdom. The judge and his cronies attend Confederate reunions, sip mint juleps, and swap tales about Forrest while a background chorus moans spirituals and Stephen Foster ballads. Even though the judge tries to fight intolerance and prejudice, the film is loaded with the racial stereotypes of the era. Black character actor Stepin Fetchit fawns and fumbles in minstrel-show fashion as the judge indulges him. Ford remade *Judge Priest* as *The Sun Shines Bright* in 1953, with Fetchit again in the cast. Ford's *The Horse Soldiers*, based on Colonel Benjamin Grierson's 1863 raid through Mississippi and adapted from Harold Sinclair's novel about the raid, appeared in 1959; it starred John Wayne as Colonel John Marlow, a surrogate for Grierson. Marlow's cavalrymen are chased by Confederate raiders, but late in the film they all merge into a mythic "Forrest" who seems to be everywhere—though during Grierson's actual raid, Forrest was off chasing Streight in Alabama. In the final scene the raiders escape across a bridge just as the Confederates arrive. A figure who looks very much like Forrest, at the head of the pursuing column, gallantly stops to offer his assistance to wounded soldiers.

The film to some degree reverses the role more often played by Forrest in the actual war. Marlow and Forrest are doppelgängers on horseback in a war where enemies are brothers; pursued and pursuer become one. *The Horse Soldiers* shows the possibility of a "morally usable past," according to Neil Longley York, demonstrating that honor and reconciliation are possible even in war. Deborah L. Madsen also noted that the cavalry is always an agent of Manifest Destiny in Ford's films, heroically working for the expansion of the United States toward its rightful place under the sun. *The Horse Soldiers* is part of that tradition: Marlow seeks to return the South to the Union; Forrest opposes Marlow but not a Manifest Destiny that might be realized under a Confederate flag. Although divided by war, both the Union and Confederate cavalries are ultimately American.[18]

Forrest's reputation got a significant boost in 1990 when Shelby Foote appeared as a commentator on Ken Burns's 11-hour PBS series *The Civil War*, some portion of which was seen by an estimated 40,000,000 American viewers and millions more in other nations.

The series was rebroadcast in 2002 and has had significant home video exposure. Foote, who looked as if he could have stepped right out of a Matthew Brady photograph, related that one of Forrest's relatives had permitted him to swing the general's sword around her living room. The series made Foote a national celebrity and Forrest one of the most vividly imagined figures of the war. As the historian Gary W. Gallagher commented,

> On the Confederate side, viewers might infer that cavalryman Nathan Bedford Forrest ranked as the most important officer in the West. Shelby Foote relates a number of colorful anecdotes about the roughhewn general and, incredibly, places him alongside Abraham Lincoln as one of the war's "two authentic geniuses." Although Forrest never commanded more than a few thousand men, his appearances in the series outnumbered those of Braxton Bragg, Albert Sidney Johnston, Joseph E. Johnston, P. G. T. Beauregard, and others who led southern armies during major campaigns. This treatment grossly inflates Forrest's prominence.[19]

The hugely popular *Forrest Gump*, released in 1994, also put the general's name before a global audience and told it that he founded the Klan and had some strange branches in his family tree. Gump says his mother told him he was named after his relative "to remind me that sometimes we all do things that, well, just don't make sense." In one 30-second segment, Gump is transformed into Nathan Bedford Forrest and rides off with the Klan in a scene from *The Birth of a Nation*. Thus, memory is shaped by myth rather than by history itself. Actor Tom Hanks plays both Forrest Gump and the general, making his ancestry explicit. The guileless Gump, like Forrest, is present symbolically at all the important events of his time, especially those suggesting racial conflict. The film has something to say about collective memory, history, and consciousness in an age saturated with media images. Like his namesake, Forrest Gump is not elaborately disguised emotionally and says what he understands, even if he does not always understand what he's saying.

Elmore Leonard's novel *Last Stand at Saber River* was brought to the screen in a 1997 film starring Tom Selleck and Keith Carradine. The film takes liberties with the novel: Selleck's Paul Cable, a wounded soldier who once rode with Forrest, out-Forrests his old boss as he tries to claim his property in Arizona. Cable, who was at Fort Pillow, now sees Forrest as "a butcher in a black coat." When Union sympathizers tell him they know he "rode with that murderous son of a bitch Nathan Bedford Forrest" and promise to see the general hanged after the war, Cable says, "You're gonna need a long rope." *Last Stand at Saber River* preaches that violence—especially Forrest's kind—begets more violence but that some things are still worth fighting for.

Forrest also appeared obliquely in an NBC and PBS television series in the early 1990s, *I'll Fly Away*, set in rural Georgia in the 1950s. Forrest Bedford, played by Sam Waterston, is the district attorney in the town, which struggles with racism and prejudice. Bedford and his children are prosperous whites whose lives intersect with those of their poor black housekeeper and her family. The Civil War and its legacy are discussed in the popular series, which garnered more than a dozen Emmy nominations.

COMIC BOOKS AND CATHOLICS

Comic book art has often made use of history to fashion stories of heroes and superheroes. Forrest appeared as a character in the comic book series *It Really Happened*, published in 1946 by William H. Wise and Company. The series featured "picture stories of popular heroes," including Lou Gehrig, Amelia Earhart, and General Israel Putnam. Forrest leads the daring "Forrest Rangers" in a six-page episode that tells the story of his early life and later military success. His style of fighting, at least in the comic pages, was not much different from the cowboys-and-Indians fare typical of the genre. He is depicted as defending black slaves, shooting and slashing Union soldiers in close combat, dissolving the Klan, and devoting his final years "to peace—to true democracy!" Forrest, although he fought on the losing side, was thus made into an ideal hero for a country that had just finished a war and was likewise thinking about peace and democracy. He also appears in a single-page episode of *Real Heroes* in 1946, which tells the story of Emma Sansom showing Forrest the ford across the Black Warrior River during his pursuit of Colonel Abel Streight.

He is not always made the hero; sometimes his villainy is at least equally exaggerated. An anti-Catholic cartoon tract series drawn by Jack Chick in 2001 cited Forrest as a secret agent of the Vatican along with John Wilkes Booth, Adolph Hitler, Fidel Castro, Jimmy Carter, and Mohammed. These tracts claim that the Klan was founded by Roman Catholic Confederate officers after the war and directed by Jesuits.[20]

Forrest was a comic book hero in 1946 in this episode from the *It Really Happened* series, published by William H. Wise and Company. *Courtesy of the Michigan State University Libraries Special Collections Division, Comic Art Collection*

In the 1940s comic book publishers looked for historical heroes to inspire young readers. This issue of *Real Heroes* told the story of Emma Sansom leading Forrest across the Black Warrior River. *Courtesy of the Michigan State University Libraries Special Collections Division, Comic Art Collection*

CONCLUSION

In "The Contested Image of Nathan Bedford Forrest," Court Carney shows how Forrest's legend and memory became bifurcated over the years. The Northern and Southern views of the general were very different in the years immediately following the war—the "butcher of Fort Pillow" versus the courageous Southern warrior—and the images continued to diverge as Forrest became a symbol of the emergent cult of the Lost Cause in the early decades of the twentieth century. Carney identifies the revitalization of the Forrest Myth with the Confederate Lost Cause mythos. In 1905 the unveiling of the Forrest statue in Memphis revealed a new set of bifurcated values: "The Forrest statue symbolized different themes, primarily because Forrest represented different ideals." Those focused on the Old South, and its heroism saw in the statue a symbol of martial virtues. Another group, however, looked to it as a monument to civic virtues, the symbol of someone dedicated to community building; they were, essentially, boosters.[21]

Carney argues correctly for the contested image of Forrest in turn-of-the-century Memphis; his argument about bifurcation is built largely around events and sources there, where feelings about Forrest are strongest and his historical presence is the most immediate. The general's image across larger time and space is far more complex, with nearly unlimited variations and applications. The polarization exemplified by the debate between Foote and Memphis's *Tri-State Defender* in the 1980s tends not to be so acute elsewhere. Still, Forrest can and does evoke a strong response in other parts of the South, and the nation. He requires a more nuanced study of the Forrest Myth. Its meaning is up to individual interpretations of the evidence in the same way as in the debate that has raged in recent years over the meaning of the Confederate flag, a symbol of both unrepentant racism and justifiable regional pride. Like the flag, the Forrest Myth is a case of "useful history," the kind that Michael Kammen is talking about when he comments that cultures "reconstruct their pasts rather than faithfully record them."[22] The Forrest Myth exemplifies a past, reconstructed time and again, not to discover history but to invent it for the sake of the present. The Memphis statue shows an attempt to repossess the heroic South that Forrest symbolized. The protests against the statue are an attempt to dispossess that same South of its heroism, equating it with the night riders in white robes.

Forrest is an issue anew at the height of cultural value shifts, the debate growing sharper and louder as emerging views are defined and defended, as was the case with the Lost Cause in the early twentieth century and again in the 1950s and 1960s with civil rights activism and expansion. In the 1990s the myth debate erupted once more with Ken Burns's *The Civil War* and Foote's praise of Forrest. The series brought new attention to the war, and the political climate's fresh challenge to institutions generally defended by African Americans set the stage for a good public fight over Forrest yet again.

No consensus has ever been reached in any of the episodic outbursts fueled by the Forrest Myth, in part because the debate has never been over discovering what "really" happened at Fort Pillow, or Forrest's real role in the Klan, or the historical facts of any other part of his life. At its heart, the debate is over contemporary culture, institutions, and attitudes, and how well history supports one side or the other.

Not only does the myth change and multiply in form, but it also moves seamlessly from the individual to the culture. In the conduct of war, Forrest understood its essence and acted upon it. That essence was killing, and he was very good at killing, both personally and as a leader. This is an important part of his myth for several reasons. First, no matter which Forrest one adopts or assails, the warrior is central to the figure—whether it is the heroic Southern cavalryman or the racist killer who allegedly headed the Klan. Second, it is important because his myth cuts to the essence of Southern mythology. He, like the South, is a former slaver who eventually repents of the institution but clings to the vestiges of planter aspirations and trappings, attempting to recreate antebellum plantation life and its wealth without slaves. It is what the Agrarians attempted, intellectually, a half-century later. It is the myth of both a man and a culture of violence and redemption, with the pretense of nobility and a noble heritage. As for the rest of the country, Forrest and the institution of slavery are part of its own heritage, a reminder that its own hands are still bloody from segregation, racism, and greed.

Two elements of the myth, in particular, are most provocative—Forrest's military genius and his popular legacy as the founder of the Klan. They are not antithetical, but each is malleable to the extent that either one can subsume the other, and in a positive or negative way. The "racist legacy" proponents can point to the warrior legend, especially Fort Pillow, to support their view. The "warrior legacy" proponents can point to Fort Pillow and the Klan as continued battles for Southern, even American, values and culture. The latter cite conflicting and inconclusive evidence, changes in perceptions, but undeniable bravery and allegiance to a cause.

It is ironic that an individual whose success is attributed to a great extent to his realism—"the ability to see things as they are and to do what needs to be done"—is also someone whose historical reality is subject to so much argument. Albert Castel said that the ultimate explanation of Forrest's success was his realism: "Despite all the rhetoric from the South's politicians and editors about 'States Rights' and 'Southern Nationalism,' he had no illusions about its true purpose: 'If we ain't fightin' to keep slavery, then what the hell are we fightin' for?' " Following the failure to turn the hard-won victory at Chickamauga into a decisive one, he concluded that both the Confederacy and slavery were doomed, and accordingly he later freed the forty-five slaves who were serving him as teamsters. But the fight over his legacy is based as much on ideals as it is on historical reality, or what little we know of it. If something cannot be defended rationally, then it is abandoned or defended irrationally. Such was the case for slavery in the South. Forrest was and is suited to its defense because he represents both primitivism and passion, a symbol of dedication without intellectualization. Only later, with the Agrarians of the 1920s and 1930s, is a philosophical foundation added to the legend. Ideals as much as historical realism are at the core of the contemporary debates.[23]

Sherman once predicted that there would never be peace in Tennessee until Forrest was dead. The continuing legacy of the Civil War, the Scopes trial, the Nashville Agrarians, the civil rights movement, and the ferment over monuments and memory all suggest that Sherman's prophecy has come to pass. Tennessee, and the nation, may never be at peace until Forrest is truly dead. Like that of the Scopes trial, his shadow over Tennessee's history is long and dark. Both are relatively inconsequential in that the trial left no legal legacy and Forrest had little impact on the outcome of the war. The enduring attention to each is a matter of obsession with images, whether it is over the trial's tainting of the South as an intellectual backwater or Forrest's legacy of racism. The promoters in each case are often little more than local boosters. Both were fights against the North, and those who cling to special interpretations of the event and the man are in many instances still fighting the incursion of industrialism into an idealized South. In the 1920s and early 1930s the Scopes trial and Lytle's Forrest were chapters of the same manifesto—that the Old South not only lived but also thrived. Fundamentalism no more died in Dayton with William Jennings Bryan than the Old South died with Forrest in 1877.

No matter how much Forrest's image is reviled or revered, the general himself just might prefer to be tarnished by time rather than burnished for posterity. When Shelby Foote showed Tony Horwitz the frequently vandalized Forrest statue in Memphis, Foote said, "They ruined it when they cleaned it up. It used to be a dark green bronze. Now it looks like it's made out of Hershey bars."[24]

NOTES

1. Lytle, *Bedford Forrest and His Critter Company*, 390; Donald Davidson, *Lee in the Mountains and Other Poems* (Boston: Houghton Mifflin, 1938), 23–35, 44–45; Mark Royden Winchell, *Where No Flag Flies: Donald Davidson and the Southern Resistance* (Columbia: University of Missouri Press, 2000), 157, 173–74, 290–98.

2. Walter Edgar, "Monuments," in *Encyclopedia of Southern Culture*, ed. Charles Reagan Wilson and William Ferris (Chapel Hill: University of North Carolina Press, 1989), 644–46; James W. Loewen, *Lies across America: What Our Historic Sites Get Wrong* (New York: Simon and Schuster, 1999), 16, 258; Hugh Walker, "Notes on N. B. Forrest," *Tennessean*, February 2, 1975.

3. *Memphis Commercial Appeal*, May 17, 1905.

4. Ibid.

5. *Memphis News-Scimitar*, April 30, 1905, May 17, 1905, November 7, 1931; *Memphis Commercial Appeal*, July 13, 1921.

6. *Memphis Commercial Appeal*, July 13, 1947.

7. Ibid., July 13, 1949, July 13, 1950; *Memphis Press-Scimitar*, July 14, 1958.

8. Lee Seago, "Forrest, Hitler Linked; Statue Move Demanded," *Tennessean*, November 9, 1979.

9. *Tri-State Defender*, August 10, 1985; *Memphis Commercial Appeal*, March 11 and 20, 1986.

10. David Dawson, "Another Skirmish for N. B. Forrest," *Southern Magazine* 16 (August 1988): 16; Carney, "The Contested Image of Nathan Bedford Forrest," 626–28; Shelby Foote, quoted in Tony Horwitz, *Confederates in the Attic: Dispatches from the Unfinished Civil War* (1998; reprint ed., New York: Vintage Books, 1999), 153.

11. David Ribar, "Monumental Failure," *Nashville Scene*, July 16, 1998; Winchell, *Where No Flag Flies*, 290–99; Jay Hamburg, "Artist Hopes Statue of Confederate General Will Spark 'Civilized Discussion,' " *Tennessean*, August, 30, 1997; *Tennessean*, July 14, 1998.

12. "Black Begins Bid to Change School's Name," *New York Times*, January 14, 1998; Larry Copeland, "Civil War Breeds Cultural Conflict," *USA*

Today, May 13, 2002; Stacy Shelton, "Erasing a Relic to War: Bedford Street, Park Quietly Renamed," *Atlanta Constitution*, February 3, 2001.

13. "Forrest Fires," *Wall Street Journal*, March 2, 2001; *Washington Post*, February 14, 2001; National Public Radio, *Weekend Edition Sunday*, February 4, 2001.

14. "Ancestor Proud to Fight for Flag," *Civil War Courier* 17 (March 2001): 1, 14. On black Confederates, see also Horwitz, *Confederates in the Attic*, 251; Trudeau, *Like Men of War*, 8–9; and Richard Rollins, ed., *Black Southerners in Gray* (Murfreesboro, TN: Southern Heritage Press, 1994).

15. Hugh Walker, "A Cavalry Commander Who Became a Symbol," *Tennessean*, February 25, 1979; Alicia Montgomery, "Gore's KKK conundrum: The Democrat Bashed Conservatives for Confederate Symbols, but Kept Quiet about Those in Tennessee," *Salon*, July 28, 2000, archive.salon. com/politics/trail/2000/07/28/trail mix/; John McCaslin, "Inside the Beltway," *Washington Times*, December 11 and 12, 2002.

16. David Ignatius, "It's a Good Time for Bush to Brush Up on History," *International Herald Tribune*, April 5, 2001; Bedwell, *May I Quote You, General Forrest?* xii, 23–24; Morgan Witzel, "Prelude to a Larger and Longer Plan A–Z of Management First-Mover Advantage," *Financial Times*, August 12, 2002.

17. Bruce Chadwick, *The Reel Civil War: Mythmaking in American Film* (New York: Alfred A. Knopf, 2001), 96–150; Robert Lang, ed., *The Birth of a Nation: D. W. Griffith, Director* (New Brunswick, NJ: Rutgers University Press, 1994); Blight, *Race and Reunion*, 122, 394; *Variety*, February 9, 1949; David M. Chalmers, *Hooded Americanism: The First Century of the Ku Klux Klan, 1865–1965* (Garden City, NY: Doubleday and Company, 1965), 73; Hurst, *Nathan Bedford Forrest*, 386–87; Loewen, *Lies across America*, 261–66; "Thomas Dixon," *Fayetteville (North Carolina) Observer*, April 4, 1946, quoted in Cook, *Thomas Dixon*, 133; Charles Reagan Wilson, *Baptized in Blood: The Religion of the Lost Cause, 1865–1920* (Athens: University of Georgia Press, 1980), 110–18; James Agee, *Agee on Film* (Boston: Beacon Press, 1964), 314.

18. Neil Longley York, *Fiction as Fact: The Horse Soldiers and Popular Memory* (Kent, OH: Kent State University Press, 2001), 142; John M. Cassidy, *Civil War Cinema: A Pictorial History of Hollywood and the War between the States* (Missoula, MT: Pictorial Histories Publishing Company, 1986), 114–24; Deborah L. Madsen, *American Exceptionalism* (Jackson: University Press of Mississippi, 1998), 137–38.

19. Gary Gallagher, "How Familiarity Bred Success: Military Campaigns and Leaders in Ken Burns's *The Civil War*," in Toplin, *Ken Burns's "The Civil War*," 55.

20. "Nathan B. Forrest: Leader of the Daring Forrest Rangers," *It Really Happened* 5 (1946); and "Confederate Patriot," *Real Heroes* 13 (March/April 1946), both in Comic Art Collection, Special Collections Division, Michigan State University Libraries; Søren Filipski, "To Hang, Burn, Waste, Boil, Flay, Strangle, and Bury Alive: Jack Chick's Cartoon Jihad and the Catholic Response," *Los Angeles Lay Catholic Mission*, December 2001, www.losangelesmission.com/ed.articles/2001; Chick Publications, Ontario, California, www.chick.com/reading/comics.

21. Carney, "The Contested Image of Nathan Bedford Forrest."

22. Michael Kammen, *Mystic Chords of Memory: The Transformation of Tradition in American Culture* (New York: Vintage Books, 1993), 30–31.

23. Albert Castel, *Articles of War: Winners, Losers, and Some Who Were Both during the Civil War* (Mechanicsburg, PA: Stackpole Books, 2001), 85.

24. Quoted in Horwitz, *Confederates in the Attic*, 155.

Bibliography

Aaron, Daniel. *The Unwritten War: American Writers and the Civil War.* Madison: University of Wisconsin Press, 1987.

Abrahams, Peter. *Last of the Dixie Heroes.* New York: Ballantine Books, 2001.

Agar, Herbert, and Allan Tate, eds. *Who Owns America? A New Declaration of Independence.* Boston: Houghton Mifflin, 1936.

Agee, James. *Agee on Film.* Boston: Beacon Press, 1964.

_____, and Walker Evans. *Let Us Now Praise Famous Men.* Boston: Houghton Mifflin, 1941.

Alexander, Benjamin B. "Nathan Bedford Forrest and Southern Folkways." *Southern Partisan* 7 (Summer 1987): 27–32.

Allen, Walter. *The Modern Novel in Britain and the United States.* New York: Dutton, 1964.

Alvis, John. "Jesse Hill Ford." In *American Novelists since World War II,* 2d ser. ed. James E. Kibler Jr., 100–104. Dictionary of Literary Biography 6. Detroit: Gail Research Company, 1980.

Anderson, Paul Christopher. *Blood Image: Turner Ashby in the Civil War and the Southern Mind.* Baton Rouge: Louisiana State University Press, 2002.

Angle, Paul M., and Earl Schneck Meir. *Tragic Years, 1860–1865: A Documentary History of the American Civil War,* 2 vols. New York: Simon and Schuster, 1960.

Armistead, Bob. *Never to Quit.* Nashville, TN: Eggman Publishing, 1993.

_____. *Warrior Forrest.* Nashville, TN: Southern Historical Showcase, 1997.

Ashdown, Paul. "The Battle of Johnsonville." In *Tennessee Encyclopedia of History and Culture,* 489–90. Murfreesboro, TN: Tennessee Historical Society, 1988.

_____. "Prophet from Highland Avenue: Agee's Visionary Journalism." In *James Agee: Reconsiderations,* ed. Michael A. Lofaro. Knoxville: University of Tennessee Press, 1992.

_____, ed. *James Agee: Selected Journalism.* Knoxville: University of Tennessee Press, 1985, 2004.

Bahr, Howard. *The Black Flower.* New York: Henry Holt and Company, 1998.

Ballard, Allen B. *Where I'm Bound.* New York: Simon and Schuster, 2000.

Ballard, Michael B. "Tension at Tupelo." *America's Civil War* 15 (May 2002): 52–74.

Beck, Charlotte H. *The Fugitive Legacy: A Critical History*. Baton Rouge: Louisiana State University Press, 2001.

Bedwell, Randall. *May I Quote You, General Forrest?* Nashville, TN: Cumberland House, 1997.

Bishop, John Peale. *The Collected Essays of John Peale Bishop*. Ed. Edmund Wilson. New York: Charles Scribner's Sons, 1948.

Blight, David W. *Race and Reunion*. Cambridge, MA: Harvard University Press, 2001.

Bolté, Philip L. "Dismount and Prepare to Fight Gunboats!" *Civil War* 65 (December 1997): 22–31.

Bond, Brian. "Colonial Wars and Punitive Expeditions, 1856–99." In *History of the British Army*, ed. Peter Young and J. P. Lawford, 172–89. New York: G. P. Putnam's Sons, 1970.

Bowers, John. *Chickamauga and Chattanooga: The Battles That Doomed the Confederacy*. 1994; Reprint ed., New York: Avon Books, 1995.

Brewer, James D. *No Bottom*. New York: Walker and Company, 1994.

_____. *No Escape*. New York: Walker and Company, 1998.

_____. *No Justice*. New York: Walker and Company, 1996.

_____. *No Remorse*. New York: Walker and Company, 1997.

_____. *No Virtue*. New York: Walker and Company, 1995.

Brookeman, Christopher. *American Culture and Society since the 1930s*. New York: Schocken Books, 1984.

Browder, George Richard. *The Heavens Are Weeping: The Diaries of George Richard Browder, 1852–1886*, ed. Richard L. Troutman. Grand Rapids, MI: Zondervan Publishing House, 1987.

Brown, Ashley. "None Shall Look Back: The Novel as History." *Southern Review* 7 (1971): 480–94.

Brown, Jane Gibson. "The Early Novels of Caroline Gordon: Myth and History as a Fictional Technique." *Southern Review* 13 (1977): 289–98.

Burke, James Lee. *White Doves at Morning*. New York: Simon and Schuster, 2002.

Caldwell, Erskine, and Margaret Bourke-White. *You Have Seen Their Faces*. New York: Modern Age Books, 1937.

Carney, Court. "The Contested Image of Nathan Bedford Forrest." *Journal of Southern History* 67 (August 2001): 601–30.

Carter, Dan T. *When the War Was Over*. Baton Rouge: Louisiana State University Press, 1985.

Carter, Everett. "Cultural History Written with Lightning: The Significance of *The Birth of a Nation*." *American Quarterly* 12 (Fall 1960): 347–57.

Cash, Wilbur J. *The Mind of the South*. New York: Alfred A. Knopf, 1941.

Cassidy, John M. *Civil War Cinema: A Pictorial History of Hollywood and the War between the States*. Missoula, MT: Pictorial Histories Publishing Company, 1986.

Castel, Albert E. *Winning and Losing in the Civil War: Essays and Stories*. Columbia: University of South Carolina Press, 1996.

_____. *Articles of War: Winners, Losers, and Some Who Were Both during the Civil War*. Mechanicsburg, PA: Stackpole Books, 2001.

Caudill, Edward. *Darwinism in the Press: The Evolution of an Idea*. Hillsdale, NJ: Lawrence Erlbaum, 1989.

Chadwick, Bruce. *The Reel Civil War: Mythmaking in American Film*. New York: Alfred A. Knopf, 2001.

Chalmers, David. *Hooded Americanism: The First Century of the Ku Klux Klan, 1865–1965*. Garden City, NY: Doubleday and Company, 1965.

Chambers, Robert S. *The God of War: When I Rode with N. B. Forrest, the Letters of Henry Wylie*. Cumberland, OH: King Phillip Publishing, 1996.

Chatterton, Wayne. *Irvin S. Cobb*. Boston: Twayne Publishers, 1986.

Cimprich, John, and Robert C. Mainfort Jr. "The Fort Pillow Massacre: A Statistical Note." *Journal of American History* 76 (December 1989): 835–37.

Cobb, Irvin S. *Back Home*. New York: Grosset and Dunlap, 1912.

_____. *Down Yonder with Judge Priest and Irvin S. Cobb*. New York: R. Long and R. R. Smith, 1932.

_____. *Old Judge Priest*. New York: Review of Reviews Corporation, 1916.

Commager, Henry Steele. "The Terror of the Damnyankees." *New Republic* (July 22, 1931): 266–67.

Conkin, Paul K. *The Southern Agrarians*. Knoxville: University of Tennessee Press, 1988.

Connelly, Thomas L., and Barbara L. Bellows. *God and General Longstreet*. Baton Rouge: Louisiana State University Press, 1982.

Cook, Raymond A. *Fire from the Flint: The Amazing Careers of Thomas Dixon*. Winston Salem, NC: J. F. Blair, 1968.

_____. *Thomas Dixon*. New York: Twayne Publishers, 1974.

Cousins, Paul M. *Joel Chandler Harris*. Baton Rouge: Louisiana State University Press, 1968.

Cowan, Louise. "Nature and Grace in Caroline Gordon." *Critique* 1 (Winter 1956): 11–27.

Crabb, Alfred Leland. *A Mockingbird Sang at Chickamauga*. Indianapolis, IN: Bobbs-Merrill, 1949.

Cullen, Jim. *The Civil War in Popular Culture: A Reusable Past*. Washington, DC: Smithsonian Institution Press, 1995.

Cutrer, Thomas W. "Nathan Bedford Forrest." In *Encyclopedia of Southern Culture*, ed. Charles Reagan Wilson and William Ferris. Chapel Hill: University of North Carolina Press, 1989.

Dabney, Virginius. *The Last Review: The Confederate Reunion, Richmond, 1932*. Chapel Hill, NC: Algonquin Books, 1984.

Dasher, Thomas E. *William Faulkner's Characters: An Index to the Published and Unpublished Fiction*. New York: Garland Publishing, 1981.

Daughtrey, Larry. "Moral Flaw Diminishes VU's Glory." *Nashville Tennesseean*, May 23, 1997.

Davenport, F. Gavin, Jr. *The Myth of Southern History: Historical Consciousness in Twentieth-Century Southern Literature*. Nashville, TN: Vanderbilt University Press, 1970.

Davidson, Donald. *Attack on Leviathan: Regionalism and Nationalism in the United States*. Chapel Hill: University of North Carolina Press, 1938.

———. *Lee in the Mountains and Other Poems*. Boston: Houghton Mifflin, 1938.

———. *Poems, 1922–1961*. Minneapolis: University of Minnesota Press, 1966.

———. *Southern Writers in the Modern World*. Athens: University of Georgia Press, 1958.

Davis, William C., Brian C. Pohanka, and Don Troiani. *Civil War Journal: The Leaders*. Nashville, TN: Rutledge Hill Press, 1997.

Davison, Eddy W., and Daniel Foxx. "A Journey to the Most Controversial Battlefield in America." *Confederate Veteran* 6 (2001): 33.

Dawson, David. "Another Skirmish for N. B. Forrest: Will the General Rise Again?" *Southern Magazine* (August 1988): 16.

Denny, Norman R. "The Devil's Navy." *Civil War Times* (August 1996): 24–30.

Dicken-Garcia, Hazel. *Journalistic Standards in Nineteenth-Century America*. Madison: University of Wisconsin Press, 1989.

Diffley, Kathleen. *Where My Heart Is Turning Ever: Civil War Stories and Constitutional Reform, 1861–1876*. Athens: University of Georgia Press, 1992.

———, ed. *To Live and Die: Collected Stories of the Civil War, 1861–1876*. Durham, NC: Duke University Press, 2002.

Dinkins, James. *Personal Recollections and Experiences in the Confederate Army, 1861–1865*. Cincinnati: Robert Clarke Company, 1897.

Dixon, Thomas. *The Clansman: An Historical Romance of the Ku Klux Klan*. New York: Doubleday, Page and Company, 1905.

———. *The Clansman: Four Acts*. 1905. Typescript in the Library of Congress.

———. *The Leopard's Spots: A Romance of the White Man's Burden, 1865–1900*. New York: Doubleday, Page and Company, 1902.

———. *The Traitor: A Story of the Fall of the Invisible Empire*. New York: Doubleday, Page and Company, 1907.

Eckenrode, H. J. *Life of Nathan B. Forrest*. Richmond, VA: B. F. Johnson Publishing Company, 1918.

Egerton, John. *Speak Now against the Day: The Generation before the Civil Rights Movement in the South*. New York: Alfred A. Knopf, 1994.

Ellis, Barbara G. *The Moving Appeal: Mr. McClanahan, Mrs. Dill and the Civil War's Great Newspaper Run*. Macon, GA: Mercer University Press, 2003.

Faulkner, William. *Collected Stories of William Faulkner*. New York: Random House, 1950.

_____. "My Grandmother Millard and Bedford Forrest at the Battle of Harrykin Creek," *Story*, March–April 1943.

_____. "Shall Not Perish." *Story*, July–August 1943.

Foote, Shelby. *Shiloh*. New York: Dial Press, 1952.

Ford, Jesse Hill. *The Raider*. Boston: Little, Brown and Company, 1975.

"Forrest Fires." *Wall Street Journal*, March 2, 2001.

Franklin, Malcolm. *Bitterweeds: Life with William Faulkner at Rowan Oak*. Irving, TX: Society for the Study of Traditional Culture, 1977.

Fuchs, Richard L. *An Unerring Fire: The Massacre at Fort Pillow*. Rutherford, NJ: Fairleigh Dickinson University Press, 1994.

Gallagher, Gary W. "How Familiarity Bred Success: Military Campaigns and Leaders in Ken Burns's *The Civil War*." In *Ken Burns's "The Civil War": Historians Respond*, ed. Robert Brent Toplin, 37–59. New York: Oxford University Press, 1996.

Genovese, Eugene D. *The Southern Tradition: The Achievement and Limitations of an American Conservatism*. Cambridge, MA: Harvard University Press, 1994.

Gordon, Caroline. *None Shall Look Back*. New York: Charles Scribner's Sons, 1937.

Gordon, Martin. "Surrender Temporary for Many in South." *Washington Times*, November 17, 2001.

Graham, Catherine Clark. *Southern Accents: The Fiction of Peter Taylor*. New York: Peter Lang, 1994.

Grant, Ulysses S. *Personal Memoirs of U. S. Grant*, 2 vols. New York: Charles L. Webster and Company, 1886.

Gregory, Eileen. Preface to Caroline Gordon, *None Shall Look Back*. Nashville, TN: J. S. Sanders and Company, 1992.

Grisham, John. *The Summons*. New York: Doubleday, 2002.

Groom, Winston. *Forrest Gump*. 1986. New York: Pocket Books, 1994.

_____. *Gump and Co.* New York: Pocket Books, 1996.

_____. *Shrouds of Glory: Atlanta to Nashville, the Last Great Campaign of the Civil War*. New York: Atlantic Monthly Press, 1995.

Harris, Joel Chandler. *A Little Union Scout*. New York: McClure, Phillips and Company, 1904.

_____. *The Shadow between His Shoulder-Blades*. Boston: Small, Maynard and Company, 1909.

Hearn, Lafcadio. *Occidental Gleanings*. New York: Dodd, Mead and Company, 1925.

Henry, Robert Selph. *"First With the Most" Forrest*. Indianapolis, IN: Bobbs-Merrill, 1944.

_____, ed. *As They Saw Forrest*. Jackson, TN: McCowat-Mercer Press, 1956.

Hobson, Fred. *Serpent in Eden: H. L. Mencken and the South*. Chapel Hill: University of North Carolina Press, 1974.

Horwitz, Tony. *Confederates in the Attic: Dispatches from the Unfinished Civil War*. 1998; reprint ed., New York: Vintage Books, 1999.

Howell, Elmo. "William Faulkner's General Forrest and the Uses of History." *Tennessee Historical Quarterly* 29 (Fall 1970): 287–94.

Hurst, Jack. *Nathan Bedford Forrest*. New York: Alfred A. Knopf, 1994.

Johnson, Ben F., III. *Fierce Solitude: A Life of John Gould Fletcher*. Fayetteville: University of Arkansas Press, 1994.

Jones, James Pickett. *Yankee Blitzkrieg: Wilson's Raid through Alabama and Georgia*. Athens: University of Georgia Press, 1976.

Jordan, John L. "Was There a Massacre at Fort Pillow?" *Tennessee Historical Quarterly* 6 (June 1947): 99–133.

Jordan, Thomas, and J. P. Pryor. *The Campaigns of General Nathan Bedford Forrest and of Forrest's Cavalry*. 1868; reprint ed., New York: Da Capo Press, 1996.

Kammen, Michael. *Mystic Chords of Memory: The Transformation of Tradition in American Culture*. New York: Vintage Books, 1993.

Kantor, MacKinlay. *If the South Had Won the Civil War*. New York: Bantam Books, 1961.

Karanikas, Alexander. *Tillers of a Myth: Southern Agrarians as Social Critics*. Madison: University of Wisconsin Press, 1966.

King, Richard H. *A Southern Renaissance: The Cultural Awakening of the American South, 1930–1955*. New York: Oxford University Press, 1980.

Ladnier, Gene. *Fame's Eternal Camping Ground*. Philadelphia: Ex Libris, 1999.

Landess, Thomas H. "Southern History and Manhood: Major Themes in the Works of Shelby Foote." *Mississippi Quarterly* 24 (Fall 1971): 321–47.

Lang, Robert, ed. *The Birth of a Nation: D. W. Griffith, Director*. New Brunswick, NJ: Rutgers University Press, 1994.

Larson, Edward J. *Summer for the Gods: The Scopes Trial and America's Continuing Debate over Science and Religion*. New York: Basic Books, 1997.

Lawson, Anita. *Irvin S. Cobb*. Bowling Green, OH: Bowling Green State University Popular Press, 1984.

Lemann, Nicholas. "The Talk of the Town." *The New Yorker* 78 (April 22 and 29, 2002): 55–56.

Lentz, Perry. *The Falling Hills*. New York: Charles Scribner's Sons, 1967; Columbia: University of South Carolina Press, 1994.

Leonard, Elmore. *Last Stand at Saber River*. New York: Dell, 1959; New York: Bantam, 1980.

_____. *Tishomingo Blues*. New York: HarperCollins, 2002.

Leowen, James W. *Lies across America: What Our Historic Sites Get Wrong*. New York: Simon and Schuster, 1999.

Lockett, James D. "The Lynching Massacre of Black and White Soldiers at Fort Pillow, Tennessee, April 12, 1864." *Western Journal of Black Studies* 22 (Summer 1998): 84–93.

Lucas, Mark. *The Southern Vision of Andrew Lytle*. Baton Rouge: Louisiana State University Press, 1986.

Luraghi, Raimondo. *The Rise and Fall of the Plantation South*. New York: Franklin Watts, 1978.

Lytle, Andrew. *Bedford Forrest and His Critter Company*. 1931; Reprint ed., Nashville, TN: J. P. Sanders and Company, 1992.

———. *The Hero with the Private Parts*. Baton Rouge: Louisiana State University Press, 1966.

McDonough, James Lee, and Thomas L. Connelly. *Five Tragic Hours: The Battle of Franklin*. Knoxville: University of Tennessee Press, 1983.

McGill, Ralph. *The South and the Southerner*. Boston: Little, Brown and Company, 1964.

McIntire, Dennis. *Lee at Chattanooga*. Nashville, TN: Cumberland House, 2002.

McLuhan, Marshall. *The Gutenberg Galaxy: The Making of Typographic Man*. Toronto: University of Toronto Press, 1962.

———. *The Mechanical Bride: Folklore of Industrial Man*. New York: Vanguard, 1951.

———. "The Southern Quality." *Sewanee Review* 55 (July 1947): 357–83.

———. *Understanding Media: The Extensions of Man*. New York: McGraw Hill, 1964.

Madsen, Deborah L. *American Exceptionalism*. Jackson: University Press of Mississippi, 1998.

Malvasi, Mark G. *The Unregenerate South: The Agrarian Thought of John Crowe Ransom, Allen Tate, and Donald Davidson*. Baton Rouge: Louisiana State University Press, 1997.

Marchard, Phillip. *Marshall McLuhan: The Medium and the Messenger*. New York: Ticknor and Fields, 1989.

Mathes, J. Harvey. *General Forrest*. New York: D. Appleton and Company, 1902.

Means, Howard. *C.S.A.—Confederate States of America*. New York: William Morrow and Company, 1998.

Mencken, H. L. *Prejudices: Fifth Series*. New York: Alfred A. Knopf, 1926.

Merriman, John Duke. *Meade's Reprise: A Novel of Gettysburg, War, and Intrigue*. Chevy Chase, MD: Posterity Press, 2002.

Miller, Jonathan. *Marshall McLuhan*. New York: Viking, 1971.

Moore, Ward. *Bring the Jubilee*. New York: Farrar, Straus and Young, 1952.

Morris, Lynn, and Gilbert Morris. *Toward the Sunrising*. Minneapolis, MN: Bethany House Publishers, 1996.

Morton, John. *The Artillery of Nathan Bedford Forrest's Cavalry*. Nashville, TN: Publishing House of the M.E. Church, South, 1909.

Murphy, Paul V. *The Rebuke of History: The Southern Agrarians and American Conservative Thought*. Chapel Hill: University of North Carolina Press, 2001.

Parks, Aileen Wells. *Bedford Forrest: Boy on Horseback*. Indianapolis, IN: Bobbs-Merrill Company, 1952.

Phillips, Robert L., Jr. *Shelby Foote, Novelist and Historian*. Jackson: University of Mississippi Press, 1992.

Powell, Barry B. *Classical Myth*. 2d ed. Upper Saddle River, NJ: Prentice-Hall, 1998.

Poyer, David C. *The Shiloh Project*. New York: Avon, 1981.

Purdy, R. R., ed. *The Fugitives' Reunion: Conversations at Vanderbilt*. Nashville, TN: Vanderbilt University Press, 1959.

Ransom, John Crowe. *God without Thunder: An Unorthodox Defense of Orthodoxy*. 1930; reprint ed., Hamden, CT: Archon Books, 1965.

Ratner, Lorman A., and Dwight L. Teeter Jr. *Fanatics and Fire-eaters: Newspapers and the Coming of the Civil War*. Urbana: University of Illinois Press, 2003.

Rawley, James A. Introduction to Field Marshal Joseph Viscount Wolseley, *The American Civil War: An English View*, ix–xxxvii. Charlottesville: University Press of Virginia, 1964.

Reardon, Carol. *Pickett's Charge in History and Memory*. Chapel Hill: University of North Carolina Press, 1997.

Reilly, Edward C. "Shelby Foote." In *Critical Survey of Long Fiction* 3, rev. ed., ed. Frank N. Magill, 1151–64. Pasadena, CA: Salem Press, 1991.

Robison, James Curry. *Peter Taylor: A Study of the Short Fiction*. Boston: Twayne Publishers, 1988.

Rollins, Richard, ed. *Black Southerners in Gray*. Murfreesboro, TN: Southern Heritage Press, 1994.

Royster, Charles. "Slaver, General, Klansman." *Atlantic Monthly* (May 1993): 125.

Seay, James. "The Making of Fables: Jesse Hill Ford." Interview. In *Kite-Flying and Other Irrational Acts: Conversations with Twelve Southern Writers*, ed. John Carr, 199–215. Baton Rouge: Louisiana State University Press, 1972.

Seymour, Digby Gordon. *Divided Loyalties: Fort Sanders and the Civil War in East Tennessee*, 3d ed. Knoxville: East Tennessee Historical Society, 2002.

Shepherd, Allen. "Technique and Theme in Shelby Foote's *Shiloh*." *Notes on Mississippi Writers* 5 (Spring 1972): 3–10.

Sheppard, Eric William. *Bedford Forrest: The Confederacy's Greatest Cavalryman*. New York: Dial Press, 1930.

Sherman, William T. *Memoirs of General William T. Sherman*, 2 vols. 1875; reprint ed., Bloomington: Indiana University Press, 1957.

Sigafoos, Robert A. *Wave the Bloody Shirt: The Life and Times of General Nathan Bedford Forrest, CSA.* Cane Hill, AR: ARC Press of Cane Hill, 2000.

Simpson, Lewis P. "Garden Myth." In *Encyclopedia of Southern Culture,* ed. Charles Reagan Wilson and William Ferris. Chapel Hill: University of North Carolina Press, 1989.

Singal, Daniel Joseph. *The War Within: From Victorian to Modernist Thought in the South, 1919–1945.* Chapel Hill: University of North Carolina Press, 1982.

Skimin, Robert. *Gray Victory.* New York: St. Martin's Press, 1988.

Slotkin, Richard. *Gunfighter Nation: The Myth of the Frontier in Twentieth-Century America.* New York: Atheneum, 1992.

Smith, Henry Nash. *Virgin Land: The American West as Symbol and Myth.* 1950; reprint ed., Cambridge, MA: Harvard University Press, 1979.

Smith, Jonathan K. T. *Benton County.* Memphis, TN: Memphis State University Press, 1979.

Stone, Albert E., Jr. "Seward Collins and the *American Review*: Experiment in Pro-Fascism, 1933–37." *American Quarterly* 12 (Spring 1960): 3–19.

Strode, Hudson. *Jefferson Davis, Tragic Hero: The Last Twenty-Five Years, 1864–1889.* New York: Harcourt, Brace, 1964.

Tap, Bruce. " 'These Devils Are Not Fit to Live on God's Earth': War Crimes and the Committee on the Conduct of the War, 1864–1865." *Civil War History* 17 (1966): 116–32.

Tate, Allen. *The Fathers.* New York: G. P. Putnam's Sons, 1938.

_____. *Jefferson Davis, His Rise and Fall.* New York: Minton, Balch and Company, 1929.

_____. *Stonewall Jackson, The Good Soldier.* New York: Minton, Balch and Company, 1928.

Tate, J. O. "On Bedford Forrest (and the Death of Heroes)." *Southern Partisan* 4 (Summer 1984): 42–45.

Taylor, Peter. "In the Miro District." *The New Yorker* (May 14, 1977): 34–48.

_____. "In the Miro District." In *In the Miro District and Other Stories,* 157–204. New York: Alfred A. Knopf, 1977.

Taylor, Richard. *Destruction and Reconstruction: Personal Experiences of the Late War.* 1879; reprint ed., New York: Longman's, Green and Company, 1955.

Taylor, William R. *Cavalier and Yankee: The Old South and American National Character.* New York: Braziller, 1961; reprint ed., New York: Oxford University Press, 1993.

Tindall, George Brown. *The Emergence of the New South, 1913–1945.* Baton Rouge: Louisiana State University Press, 1967.

Toplin, Robert Brent, ed. *Ken Burns's "The Civil War": Historians Respond.* New York: Oxford University Press, 1996.

Trudeau, Noah Andre. "What Might Have Been." *Civil War Times Illustrated* 33 (September/October 1994): 56–59.

_____. *Like Men of War: Black Troops in the Civil War, 1862–1865.* Boston: Little, Brown and Company, 1998.

Turtledove, Harry. *Guns of the South.* New York: Del Rey, 1992.

_____. Introduction to *The Best Alternative History Stories of the 20th Century.* Ed. Harry Turtledove with Martin H. Greenberg. New York: Ballantine, 2001.

_____. *Sentry Peak.* Riverdale, NY: Baen Books, 2000.

Twelve Southerners. *I'll Take My Stand: The South and the Agrarian Tradition.* New York: Harper and Brothers, 1930.

U.S. Senate. *Ku Klux Klan Conspiracy: Report of the Joint Select Committee to Inquire into the Condition of Affairs in the Late Insurrectionary States.* 13 vols. February 19, 1872. 42d Cong., 2d sess. S.R. 41, vol. 13.

Veysey, Laurence R. "Myth and Reality in Approaching American Regionalism." *American Quarterly* 12 (Spring 1960): 31–43.

Vinh, Alphonse. "Southern Agrarian Warrior Hero." *Southern Partisan* 14 (4th Quarter 1994): 42–45.

Volpe, Edmond L. *A Reader's Guide to William Faulkner.* New York: Farrar, Straus and Giroux, 1964.

Waldron, Ann. *Close Connections: Caroline Gordon and the Southern Renaissance.* Knoxville: University of Tennessee Press, 1989.

Wall, Joseph Frazier. *Henry Watterson: Reconstructed Rebel.* New York: Oxford University Press, 1956.

Ward, Geoffrey C., with Ken Burns and Ric Burns. *The Civil War: An Illustrated History.* New York: Alfred A. Knopf, 1990.

War of the Rebellion: A Compilation of the Official Records of the Union and Confederate Armies. 70 vols. Washington, DC: Government Printing Office, 1890–91.

Warren, Robert Penn. "When the Light Gets Green." *Southern Review* 1 (Spring 1936): 799–806.

_____. "When the Light Gets Green." In *The Circus in the Attic and Other Stories,* 88–95. New York: Harcourt, Brace and Company, 1947.

Weaver, Richard M. "The South and the Revolution of Nihilism." *South Atlantic Quarterly* 43 (April 1944): 194–98.

_____. *The Southern Essays of Richard M. Weaver.* Ed. George M. Curtis III and James J. Thompson Jr. Indianapolis, IN: Liberty Press, 1987.

Wells, Lawrence. *Rommel and the Rebel.* Garden City, NY: Doubleday, 1986; reprint ed., Oxford, MS: Yoknapatawpha Press, 1992.

White, Helen, and Redding S. Sugg Jr. *Shelby Foote.* Boston: Twayne Publishers, 1982.

Wilkinson, Rupert. *American Tough: The Tough-Guy Tradition and American Character.* New York: Harper and Row, 1986.

Williams, Clayton. *The Cavalryman*. New York: Vantage, 1997.

Williamson, Joel. *The Crucible of Race*. New York: Oxford University Press, 1984.

Wills, Brian Steel. *A Battle from the Start: The Life of Nathan Bedford Forrest*. New York: HarperCollins, 1992.

Wilson, Charles Reagan. *Baptized in Blood: The Religion of the Lost Cause, 1865–1920*. Athens: University of Georgia Press, 1980.

Wilson, Edmund. *Patriotic Gore*. New York: Oxford University Press, 1962.

Winchell, Mark Royden. *Where No Flag Flies: Donald Davidson and the Southern Resistance*. Columbia: University of Missouri Press, 2000.

Winick, Jay. *April 1865: The Month That Saved America*. New York: HarperCollins, 2001.

Wolseley, Joseph Viscount. *The American Civil War: An English View*. Ed. James A. Rawley. Charlottesville: University Press of Virginia, 1964.

_____. "General Viscount Wolseley on Forrest." 1892. In *As They Saw Forrest*, ed. Robert Selph Henry, 17–53. Jackson, TN: McCowat-Mercer Press, 1956.

Womack, Bob. *Call Forth the Mighty Men*. Bessemer, AL: Colonial Press, 1987

Woodworth, Steven E. *Jefferson Davis and His Generals: The Failure of Confederate Command in the West*. Lawrence: University Press of Kansas, 1990.

Wyeth, John Allan. *That Devil Forrest: Life of General Nathan Bedford Forrest*. New York: Harper and Brothers, 1899 (originally titled *Life of General Nathan Bedford Forrest*); New York: Harper, 1959; Reprint, Baton Rouge: Louisiana State University Press, 1989.

Yeager, Charles Gordon. *Fightin' with Forrest*. Gretna, LA: Pelican Publishing Company, 1987.

York, Neil Longley. *Fiction as Fact: The Horse Soldiers and Popular Memory*. Kent, OH: Kent State University Press, 2001.

Young, Thomas Daniel. *Tennessee Writers*. Knoxville: University of Tennessee Press, 1981.

_____, and M. Thomas Inge. *Donald Davidson*. New York: Twayne, 1971.

INDEX